Going smoke-free

The medical case for clean air in the home, at work and in public places

A report on passive smoking by the Tobacco Advisory Group of the Royal College of Physicians, July 2005

Royal College of Physicians
Setting higher medical standards

Acknowledgements

The members of the Tobacco Advisory Group acknowledge with thanks Diana Beaven, Hannah Thompson and Suzanne Fuzzey of the RCP Publications Department for the editing and production of this book. Thanks are also due to Rachel Lea for administrative support throughout the development of the report.

Royal College of Physicians of London
11 St Andrew's Place, London NW1 4LE
www.rcplondon.ac.uk
Registered Charity No 210508

ISBN 1 86016 246 0

Cover
photograph: Getty Images
design: Chris Hewitt MCSD

Typeset by Dan-Set Graphics, Telford, Shropshire
Printed in Great Britain by The Lavenham Press Ltd, Suffolk

Contents

Contributors

Shane Allwright *Senior Lecturer in Epidemiology, University of Dublin*

Deborah Arnott *Director, Action on Smoking and Health, London*

Richard Ashcroft *Reader in Biomedical Ethics, Imperial College London*

John Britton *Professor of Epidemiology, University of Nottingham*

Richard Edwards *Senior Lecturer in Public Health, University of Manchester*

Christine Godfrey *Professor of Health Economics, University of York*

Allan Hackshaw *Deputy Director, Cancer Research UK & UCL Cancer Trials Centre, University College London*

John Hall *Solicitor, Thompsons Solicitors*

Fenton Howell *Dean, Faculty of Public Health Medicine of the Royal College of Physicians of Ireland, Dublin*

Konrad Jamrozik *Professor of Evidence-based Health Care, University of Queensland*

Martin J Jarvis *Professor Emeritus of Health Psychology, University College London*

Sinéad Jones *Head of Tobacco Control, International Union Against Cancer*

Ann McNeill *Honorary Senior Research Fellow, University College London*

David Strachan *Professor of Epidemiology, St George's, University of London*

Judith Watt *Tobacco Control Consultant, Sydney*

Stephen Woodward *Government and Public Affairs Consultant, Sydney*

Members of the Tobacco Advisory Group of the Royal College of Physicians

John Britton (Chair)

Deborah Arnott

Simon Capewell

Tim Coleman

Linda Cuthbertson

Richard Edwards

Christine Godfrey

Konrad Jamrozik

Martin Jarvis

Lawrence McAlpine

Ann McNeill

Dawn Milner

Jennifer Percival

Douglas Seaton

Ashley Woodcock

Preface

Tobacco smoke kills more people in the UK than any other avoidable cause. Therefore, effective tobacco control policies have a major part in improving public health. Since publishing the White Paper *Smoking kills* in 1998, the Government has made progress in many areas, particularly in developing smoking cessation services and banning the advertising and marketing of tobacco products. But much more can be done.

One important area is the harm caused by passive smoking. The 1998 White Paper recognised this and contained proposals for a voluntary code of practice to prevent passive smoke exposure in most workplaces, and a Public Places Charter to reduce exposure to smoke in pubs, restaurants and other hospitality industry venues. Although the voluntary code of practice was drafted it was not implemented, and the Public Places Charter has failed.

This report sets out in detail the impact of passive smoking in the UK. It reviews the effectiveness, and the ethical and economic implications of legislating to prevent exposure, and concludes that the only viable solution is legislation to make all workplaces and public places smoke-free. The Scottish Parliament has already decided on this approach.

The primary reason for smoke-free workplaces and public places is to protect individuals against involuntary exposure to passive smoking and the associated health risks. However, comprehensive smoke-free policies offer more than simple protection against passive smoke. Smoke-free policies help smokers to give up smoking, and discourage young people from starting to smoke in the first place. They also protect children at home by helping parents to quit, or at least by encouraging them to make their homes smoke-free. The particular benefit to children and other vulnerable or disadvantaged people in our society are important additional justifications for smoke-free legislation.

This report demonstrates how smoke-free legislation will save lives, reduce health inequalities, and improve public health. Smoke-free policies are popular and they are highly effective. Introducing comprehensive smoke-free legislation should be a public health priority for the UK.

July 2005

Professor Dame Carol Black
President, Royal College of Physicians

Frequently used abbreviations and acronyms

ASH Action on Smoking and Health
BAT British American Tobacco
CI confidence interval
COPD chronic obstructive pulmonary disease
ETS environmental tobacco smoke
FCTC Framework Convention on Tobacco Control
HSE Health Survey for England
HSE Health and Safety Executive
IARC International Agency for Research on Cancer
IHD ischaemic heart disease
LVA Licensed Vintners Association
NRT nicotine replacement therapy
ONS Office for National Statistics
OTC Office of Tobacco Control (Ireland)
PPAH particulate polycyclic aromatic hydrocarbons
RSP respiratory suspended particles
TMA Tobacco Manufacturers Association (previously known as the Tobacco Advisory Council)
VFI Vintners' Federation of Ireland
VPN vapour phase nicotine
WHO World Health Organization

KEY POINTS

Passive smoking: what it is and why it is harmful

- Passive smoking is exposure to environmental tobacco smoke (ETS) arising from other people smoking tobacco.
- ETS contains the same substances as the smoke inhaled by active smokers, including poisons such as carbon monoxide, ammonia, arsenic, mercury and formaldehyde, and a range of established carcinogens.
- Non-smokers exposed to ETS have raised levels of tobacco breakdown products and tobacco-related poisons and carcinogens such as carbon monoxide and nitrosamines in their bodies.
- ETS is, therefore, likely to be harmful and to cause the same disorders as active smoking.
- Passive smokers are typically exposed to about 1% of the tobacco smoke exposure sustained by a smoker.
- Maternal ETS exposure results in fetal exposure to ETS products.

Health effects of environmental tobacco smoke

- ETS has been shown to cause lung cancer and ischaemic heart disease, and probably to cause COPD, asthma and stroke in adults.
- ETS is harmful to children, causing sudden infant death, pneumonia and bronchitis, asthma, respiratory symptoms and middle ear disease.
- Maternal exposure to ETS may also adversely affect the unborn child, causing low birth weight, fetal death and preterm delivery.
- For most of these effects the level of individual risk is low relative to active smoking, but the fact that large numbers of people are exposed results in a substantial burden of disease.

- Since non-smokers exposed to ETS inhale the same chemicals as active smokers, they probably also have an increased incidence of most other disorders linked to active smoking, though at a lower level of risk.
- The risk of ischaemic heart disease from passive smoking is disproportionately high, equivalent to approximately half that of an active smoker.

Exposure to passive smoking

- Most non-smokers are exposed to ETS.
- Exposure is especially high in children and the relatively disadvantaged, and tends to be higher in men than in women.
- The strongest determinants of exposure in children are parents who smoke and low socio-economic status.
- In adults, the strongest determinants of exposure are living with a smoker and low socio-economic status.
- There has been a consistent trend towards lower levels of exposure in all groups over time.
- People who live in smoke-free homes have much lower levels of exposure.
- The proportion of smoking households that are smoke-free has increased from 22% in 1996 to 37% in 2003, and this is contributing to lowered exposures.
- While it is clear that the home is now the major source of exposure for most adults, occupational groups such as bar workers remain at risk for exceptionally high exposure.
- This suggests that lower levels of smoking in the general population, increased restrictions on smoking in public, and household smoking bans have all helped to reduce exposure.

Deaths from exposure to environmental tobacco smoke in the UK

- ETS exposure caused approximately 12,200 deaths in the UK in 2003. This estimate is likely to be conservative.
- The great majority of these deaths (over 95%) occurred as a result of exposure to ETS at home.

- Preventing exposure to ETS at home would have significant benefit to public health.
- A minimum of approximately 500 deaths were caused by exposure to ETS at work, including 50 deaths among employees in the hospitality industry.
- Deaths from exposure to ETS at work would be prevented by making all workplaces smoke-free.

Control of environmental tobacco smoke exposure in the workplace

- Partial restrictions on smoking and/or ventilation can reduce the nuisance effects of ETS, but do not reduce levels sufficiently to protect the health of staff.
- Even if these measures were more effective, a safe level for ETS in the environment has not been defined. The precautionary principle of removing the source of the pollutant should apply.
- Smoke-free policies improve air quality dramatically, minimise ETS exposure, and have significant health benefits.
- There is, therefore, a strong scientific and moral case that smoke-free policies in the workplace are the only method that can currently be recommended to protect staff.

Control measures in the home – effects on exposure

- ETS exposure in the home is particularly harmful for young children.
- Awareness of the health risks of ETS exposure in children is relatively low.
- The most effective control measure is for parents and carers to quit smoking entirely.
- Alternatively, making homes completely smoke-free reduces ETS exposure significantly.
- Attempts to reduce ETS exposure by limiting smoking to parts of the home away from children have not proved successful.
- Measures targeted at individuals or households and intended to reduce smoking in the home while stopping short of making the

home smoke-free are unlikely to have a major impact on ETS exposure at home.

- Smoke-free public places reduce the exposure of children to tobacco smoke outside the home.
- There is no evidence that smoke-free workplaces and enclosed public places increase the exposure of children to ETS at home.
- Smoke-free workplaces and enclosed public places lead to reductions in smoking prevalence and also to reduced smoking and, therefore, reduced ETS exposure at home, particularly if backed up by comprehensive health education programmes.
- Population and individual-level interventions to encourage smoking cessation, including smoke-free public places, are, therefore, the most effective means of reducing ETS exposure at home.

The impact of partial and complete smoke-free policies on the prevalence of smoking and consumption of tobacco

- Comprehensive smoke-free policies can be implemented successfully in a wide variety of settings, in private as well as public venues, are generally well accepted, and achieve high levels of compliance.
- Making workplaces and other public places smoke-free is the best way to prevent the harmful effects of exposure to ETS.
- Smoke-free policies reduce the prevalence and uptake of smoking, and hence indirectly reduce smoking-related harm. Smoke-free policies also reduce consumption of cigarettes in those who continue to smoke. These effects are likely to be realised wherever smoke-free policies are applied, including workplaces, schools and private homes.
- The precise magnitude of the effects of smoke-free policies on health is difficult to quantify, but the evidence suggests that the impact is important at both individual and population levels.
- Smoke-free policies are, therefore, an important component of public health policy.

The legal perspective on work and leisure exposure to environmental tobacco smoke

- Employers have a general duty to safeguard their workforce.
- ETS exposure is known to be harmful but is not subject currently to specific workplace legislation.
- Employers who continue to allow employees to be exposed to ETS are at increasing risk of being found liable for personal injuries sustained by employees.
- Employers who do nothing to protect their workforce are those most at risk from legal action in the future.

Public attitudes to smoke-free policy

- There is majority support in the UK for all public places and workplaces to go smoke-free.
- Support for smoke-free legislation is higher in England, and smoking prevalence is lower, than it was in Ireland before the introduction of successful smoke-free legislation.
- The trends show that support for smoke-free legislation in the UK is increasing.
- Evidence from Ireland and New York shows that support for the legislation grows in the period after the announcement of the intention to implement smoke-free legislation, and increases further after implementation.
- A combination of political leadership and commitment to introducing smoke-free legislation, together with provision of public information and encouragement of public debate, will ensure that smoke-free legislation can be implemented successfully with public support throughout the UK.

Legislating to prevent exposure to environmental tobacco smoke in public places and workplaces: ethical and civil liberties arguments

- The ethical justification for smoke-free public places and workplaces rests primarily on the harm caused by second-hand smoke to third parties.

- Other arguments, such as that smoke-free policies protect ex-smokers from relapse, protect children and other vulnerable groups from starting to smoke, reduce smoking prevalence in the population, and protect against the nuisance of ETS exposure, give secondary support to the main ethical justification.
- Smoke-free public places do not represent an unfair imposition on smokers.
- Appeals to smokers' rights and to the values of sociability and tolerance systematically mislead as to the true nature of rights, sociability and tolerance.
- Smoke-free public places protect the most vulnerable in society from harms caused wittingly or unwittingly by smokers.
- Making all public places smoke-free is, therefore, ethically justified.

Economics of smoke-free policies

- The most cost-effective and quickest means of reducing ETS exposure is to legislate to make all public places smoke-free.
- Making all workplaces in the UK smoke-free would realise substantial economic benefits, of approximately:
  - at least £832 million from prevention of death and disease
  - £181 million from prevention of fires and reduced cleaning costs
  - £2,854 million from improved productivity.
- The likely total economic benefit to society of implementing comprehensive smoke-free policies would be, therefore, of the order of £4,000 million per annum at current prices.

Economics of smoke-free policies and the hospitality industry

- Evidence from high quality studies carried out around the world suggests that implementing comprehensive smoke-free policies in the hospitality industry is likely to have a small positive impact on overall revenues from the sector.
- There is little evidence to predict the impact of more partial regulations.
- The evidence from Ireland suggests that alcohol sales in public houses declined minimally immediately after the introduction of smoke-free workplaces by approximately 0.2%.

- In the longer term, smoke-free policies improve the health of workers, so costs to employers are likely to fall. Therefore, profits are likely to increase in the hospitality sector as well as other sectors of the economy.

Tobacco industry responses and approaches to smoke-free policy

- The tobacco industry has recognised for many years the significance of the passive smoking issue and the enormous threat it poses to its short-term profits and long-term viability.
- Internal documents demonstrate that the industry's strategy on the passive smoking issue is sophisticated and subversive, with the overall goal to maintain sales and profits by preventing the introduction of smoke-free legislation.
- The key strands of the industry strategy are to dispute the science, advance courtesy as a social solution, portray opponents as extremists, champion ventilation as a technical solution, warn of dire economic consequences of restrictions and argue that enforcement will be difficult.
- The industry engages in these tactics directly but also covertly through the funding of third party 'arms length' organisations that appear independent of the tobacco industry.
- The industry has been successful in influencing scientists and policy makers and subverting normal decision-making processes.
- The industry is seeking to market products which reduce the impact of tobacco smoke on non-smokers.
- Any and all of the above tactics and strategies are likely to be in use now, or used in the future, to counter the introduction of smoke-free policies.

Special cases: smoke-free policies in long-stay institutions

- Very high levels of smoking are observed in some categories of long-stay institutions such as psychiatric institutions and prisons.
- Smoking is often condoned by staff, and is the accepted norm in such settings. Exposure to ETS can be very high.
- Experience shows that comprehensive smoke-free policies can be implemented successfully in these settings, but they should be

flexible and pragmatic, and supported by greatly increased accessibility to advice and support in stopping smoking.

- No blanket exemptions should be made to exclude long-stay institutions from implementing smoke-free policies. Whilst exceptions can be made on a case-by-case basis, these should be reviewed regularly and every effort must be made to minimise exposure of non-smokers to tobacco smoke.

Smoke-free public places in Ireland: how was it achieved and what has been learnt?

- Smoke-free legislation in Ireland has proved to be highly popular, and has encountered no major compliance problems.
- Public support for smoke-free policies has increased substantially since legislation.
- Smoke-free policies have proved to be an effective means of protecting workers against ETS effects.
- Although not the primary objective of the Irish legislation, it is likely that smoking prevalence and consumption will now fall in Ireland, contributing to a major public health gain.

Key conclusions and recommendations

- There is an unanswerable moral case to protect all people from passive smoking at work. All employees have a right to work in a safe environment, and all employers have a duty to ensure that they do.
- Comprehensive smoke-free legislation, making all public places and workplaces completely smoke-free, without exception, is the only effective means of achieving this.
- Comprehensive smoke-free policies also improve public health by helping existing smokers to quit, and discouraging young people from starting to smoke.
- Preventing passive smoking at home, particularly for children, is a public health priority. Home exposure is prevented only by helping parents and carers to quit smoking completely, and/or by making homes completely smoke-free.

- Population and individual-level interventions to encourage smoking cessation and smoke-free households, including comprehensive smoke-free legislation and sustained health promotion campaigns, are the most effective means of reducing ETS exposure at home.
- We recommend that the UK Government enact comprehensive legislation to make all workplaces and other enclosed public places smoke-free at the earliest possible opportunity.

1 Passive smoking: what it is and why it is harmful

1.1 Passive smoking

Passive smoking is secondary exposure of individuals to tobacco smoke as a result of other people smoking tobacco. Passive smoking occurs typically by the inhalation of tobacco smoke in the ambient air, sometimes referred to as second-hand smoke, tobacco smoke pollution or, as in this report, environmental tobacco smoke or ETS. Unborn children are exposed to passive smoking as a direct result of maternal smoking, and indirectly from maternal exposure to ETS. This report addresses the effects of passive smoking arising from direct and indirect ETS exposure.

1.2 Environmental tobacco smoke (ETS)

ETS is the smoke released into the general atmosphere by cigarettes, pipes, cigars or other smoked tobacco product. In practice, the great majority of ETS arises from cigarette smoking, and most of the available evidence on ETS effects and control relates to cigarette smoke.

Cigarettes generate smoke in two ways. *Sidestream* smoke arises from the lit end of the cigarette, predominantly between puffs or after smoking has finished. It is generated by relatively slow burning and passes directly into the atmosphere. *Mainstream* smoke is the smoke produced by the smoker drawing air through a cigarette in the act of smoking. Mainstream smoke is generated more quickly and at higher temperatures than sidestream smoke. It usually passes through a cigarette filter before being inhaled, and is held for a short time in the lungs before being exhaled into the atmosphere (at which point it is also referred to as second-hand smoke). Typically, about 85% of ETS originates as sidestream smoke, and most of the remainder is exhaled mainstream smoke.[1]

Active smoking is probably the most well proven environmental cause of ill health and premature death, with strong causal associations demonstrated for many diseases. Since the range of toxins in mainstream smoke and ETS is broadly similar, it is almost inevitable that ETS exposure will result in a similar range of adverse effects on health as active smoking. The main issue is not, therefore, whether ETS causes ill health or not, but rather to what extent, given the lower intake of toxins from ETS compared to that from active smoking.

1.3 Content of ETS

The range of chemicals contained in mainstream and sidestream smoke is broadly similar, and comprises about 4,000 different substances including several known poisons such as carbon monoxide, ammonia, arsenic, mercury and formaldehyde. However, because of the differences in the way that sidestream and exhaled mainstream smoke are generated, the relative quantities of these chemicals, and their distribution in particles and vapour in the smoke, can be different. For example, nicotine inhaled by the smoker (and subsequently exhaled) is in particle form, whereas in sidestream smoke it is mainly in gaseous form. The relative concentrations of a range of known carcinogens of sidestream to mainstream cigarette smoke are listed in Table 1.1. Most are greater than one, indicating the higher concentration in sidestream smoke.

1.4 Measuring intake of ETS

The extent to which individuals are exposed to ETS can be assessed objectively by measuring levels of substances derived from cigarette smoke in blood or other biological samples from non-smokers. Nicotine and its metabolite, cotinine, are commonly used biomarkers of ETS exposure because they are, for practical purposes, specific to tobacco smoke, and because the measures are sensitive to low levels of exposure. Inhaled nicotine is absorbed directly into the bloodstream but is broken down relatively quickly; the half-life in blood being about two hours. Nicotine levels, therefore, tend to reflect very recent exposure. Cotinine is one of the main products of nicotine metabolism and has a half-life of about

Table 1.1. The ratio of the concentration of known carcinogens* in sidestream smoke compared to mainstream smoke.

Carcinogen	Sidestream/mainstream smoke
Acetaldehyde	1.31
Acrylonitrile	1.27
4-Aminobiphenyl	5.41
2-Aminonapththalene	8.83
Arsenic	1.51
Benzene	1.07
Benzo[a]pyrene	3.22
1,3-Butadiene	1.30
Cadmium	1.47
Catechol	0.85
Formaldehyde	14.78
Isoprene	1.33
Lead	0.09
NNK	0.40
NNN	0.47
Styrene	2.60

*Classified as carcinogens by IARC. (Data adapted from Ref 1.)
NNK: 4-(methylnitrosamino)-1-(3-pyridyl)-1-butanone
NNN: N'-Nitrosonornicotine

20 hours. It is detectable in the blood for three to four days after exposure and is therefore a better marker of ETS exposure in recent days.[2] Nicotine and cotinine can also be measured in urine and saliva.

1.5 How much ETS exposure does a non-smoker sustain?

Table 1.2 summarises data from several studies of average cotinine levels in the blood and urine of non-smokers who do and do not report that they are exposed to ETS, and in active smokers. Together, this evidence demonstrates clearly that non-smokers who say they are exposed to ETS have levels of cotinine around two to three times higher than non-smokers who say they are not exposed. The data also show that passive smokers typically have cotinine levels of about 1% of those seen in active smokers, indicating that their exposure to cigarette smoke from ETS is equivalent to about 1% of that associated with active smoking.

Table 1.2. Nicotine and cotinine concentrations in non-smokers who do or do not report exposure to ETS, and in active smokers.

Study	Country	Mean or median concentration (number of individuals)			Ratio of exposed to unexposed non-smokers	Concentration in exposed non-smokers expressed as a percentage of the level in active smokers
		Unexposed non-smokers	Exposed non-smokers	Active smokers		
(%)						
Cotinine in urine (ng/ml)						
Jarvis *et al* 1984[3]	UK	1.6 (46)	7.6 (54)	1,391 (94)	4.8	0.5
Matsukura *et al* 1984[4]	Japan	0.5 (200)	0.8 (272)	8.6 (392)	1.6	9.3
Wald *et al* 1984[5]	UK	3.0 (22)	14.1 (199)	2,005.6 (131)	4.7	0.7
Wall *et al* 1988[6]	USA	6.0 (28)	9.2 (20)	1,017 (49)	1.5	0.9
Coultas *et al* 1989[7]	USA	2.5 (30)	11.3 (46)	–	4.5	–
Haley *et al* 1989[8]	USA	5.3 (16)	7.2 (246)	–	1.4	–
Cummings *et al* 1990[9]	USA	6.2 (162)	9.7 (501)	1,254 (130)	1.6	0.8
Thompson *et al* 1990[10]	UK	11.0 (158)	28.0 (26)	1,691 (49)	2.5	1.7
Riboli *et al* 1990[11]	Europe	2.7 (629)	7.9 (693)	–	2.9	–
Willers *et al* 1992[12]	Sweden	2.3 (42)	6.2 (14)	2,554 (39)	2.7	0.2
O'Connor *et al* 1995[13]	USA	2.0 (141)	2.3 (141)	–	1.2	
Foundas *et al* 1997[14]	Australia	9.5 (39)	14.8 (22)	2,455 (40)	1.6	0.6
Forastiere *et al* 2000[15]	Italy	6.5 (460)	9.4 (781)	–	1.4	–
Scherer *et al* 2000[16]	Germany	2.3 (23)	12.3 (19)	2,060 (27)	5.3	0.6
Kuo *et al* 2002[17]	Taiwan	16.2 (28)	27.9 (39)	2,784.6 (27)	1.7	1.0
Kim *et al* 2004[18]	Korea	7.5 (31)	10.0 (26)	–	1.3	–

Cotinine in serum or plasma (ng/ml)						
Jarvis *et al* 1984[3]	UK	0.82 (46)	2.05 (54)	275 (94)	2.5	0.7
Haddow *et al* 1988[19]	USA	0.28 (376)	1.35 (855)	–	4.8	–
Tunstall-Pedoe *et al* 1991[20]	UK	0.01 (319)	1.04 (1245)	250 (1940)	>100	0.4
		0.01 (493)	0.54 (1326)	243 (1386)	54	0.2
Kemmeren *et al* 1993[21]	Holland	0.6 (55)	1.6 (50)	327 (148)	2.7	0.5
Crawford *et al* 1994[22]	USA	0.96 (24)	1.64 (32)	170 (31)	1.7	1.0
Pirkle *et al* 1996[23]	USA	0.13 (1332)	0.51 (1340)	251 (3712)	3.9	0.2
Peacock *et al* 1998[24]	UK	0.5 (429)	0.7 (283)	62.6 (328)	1.4	1.1
Steenland *et al* 1998[25]	USA	0.12 (2126)	0.48 (1212)	–	4	–
Scherer *et al* 2000[16]	Germany	0.71 (23)	1.32 (19)	298 (27)	1.8	0.4
Jarvis *et al* 2001[26]	UK	0.31 (6760)	1.02 (1410)	162 (6025)	3.3	0.6
Chen *et al* 2002[27]	UK	0.98 (100)	1.25 (952)	–	1.3	–
		1.20 (91)	2.04 (459)	–	1.7	–
DeLorenze *et al* 2002[28]	USA	0.05 (490)	0.18 (190)	–	3.6	–
Dietrich *et al* 2003[29]	USA	0.57 (36)	3.5 (40)	1,469 (83)	6.1	0.2
Secareccia *et al* 2003[30]	Italy	2.8 (1520)	4.4 (882)	277 (977)	1.6	1.6

There is also a clear exposure-response relation between the amount of exposure and cotinine level (Fig 1.1), such that the greater the exposure to ETS, the higher the concentration of cotinine in the body. The expectation is, therefore, that any risk of disease arising from ETS will increase with increasing exposure. This is confirmed in, for example, studies of lung cancer and ETS exposure from a spouse, which show that the risk of lung cancer increases with the number of cigarettes smoked by the spouse, and with the number of years spent living with a smoker (see Chapter 2).

The observation that non-smokers who report exposure to ETS have noticeably raised levels of cotinine in their body fluids, and that the levels increase significantly with increasing exposure, confirms that tobacco smoke is taken into the lungs of non-smokers and subsequently metabolised in the body in a similar way to active smokers. The fact that cotinine is detectable in non-smokers who report no ETS exposure (Table 1.2) suggests that people in the latter group are still exposed to ETS, but either not at a noticeable level or at a level they do not consider worth reporting. In short, most of us will breathe in tobacco smoke at some point, but some are exposed much more than others.

1.6 Toxicological studies

Rather than using cotinine or nicotine as a marker of exposure to toxins in ETS, some studies have measured levels of known carcinogens, including polycyclic

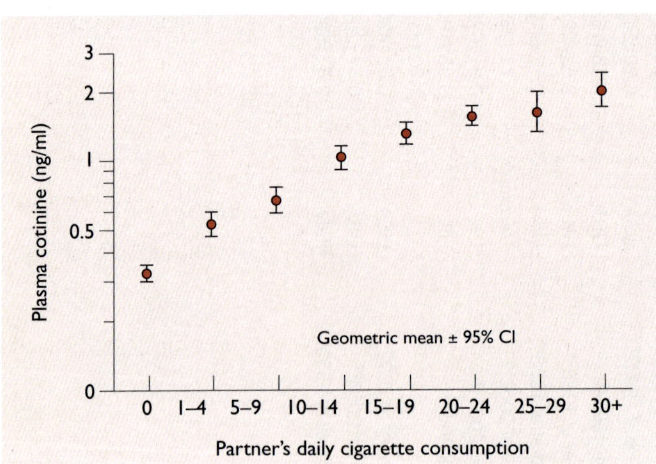

Fig 1.1 Mean plasma cotinine in 8,170 married or cohabiting non-smokers according to the cigarette consumption of their partner. Health Survey for England 1994 and 1996.[26]

aromatic hydrocarbons, aromatic amines and nitrososamines. Once breathed into the lungs, these carcinogens pass into the bloodstream and chemically bond with, for example, haemoglobin or DNA to form adducts. It is possible to measure these adducts in blood or urine. Table 1.3 shows average concentrations in non-smokers who do and do not report exposure to ETS. The levels are almost always higher in passive smokers. Experimental studies, in which non-smokers are exposed purposely to cigarette smoke, confirm the uptake and metabolism of carcinogens.[37]

1.7 Markers of tobacco smoke in indoor air

Many of the chemical substances found in tobacco smoke, including nicotine, can be measured in ambient air. Several studies have used these measures to attempt to quantify tobacco smoke in the indoor environment.[38-40] The concentrations of specific substances vary considerably and depend on factors such as ventilation,

Table 1.3. Studies that have reported the average level of carcinogens or carcinogen adducts in the blood or urine of non-smokers who report exposure to ETS.

Study	Carcinogen or carcinogen adduct	Mean or median concentration (number of individuals): Unexposed non-smokers	Mean or median concentration (number of individuals): Exposed non-smokers	Ratio of exposed to unexposed non-smokers
Maclure *et al* 1989[31]	4-ABP (pg/g Hb) (1)	40 (29)	43 (28)	1.1
	3-ABP (pg/g Hb)(1)	1.0 (29)	1.4 (28)	1.4
Bartsch *et al* 1990[32]	4-ABP (pg/g Hb)(1)	16.0 (35)	34.4 (15)	2.2
Hammond *et al* 1993[33]	4-ABP (pg/g Hb)(1)	15 (7)	20 (29)	1.3
Crawford *et al* 1994[34]	PAH-albumin (fmol/mg)(2)	0.31 (24)	0.49 (32)	1.6
Scherer *et al* 2000[35]	BaP-Hb (fmol/mg)(1)	0.083 (23)	0.049 (19)	0.6
	BaP-albumin (fmol/mg)(1)	0.019	0.021	1.1
Anderson *et al* 2001[36]	NNAL+NNAL-Gluc (pmol/mg)(3)	0.007 (22)	0.045 (23)	6.4

(1) In blood
(2) In plasma
(3) In urine

PAH: polycyclic aromatic hydrocarbon; BaP: Benzo[a]pyrene; ABP: aminobiphenyl;
NNAL: 4-(methylnitrosamino)-L-(3-pyridyl)-L-butanol,; Gluc: glucuronide

the number of smokers in the room and the size of the room, but these studies confirm that in the presence of smoking levels can be substantially increased (for example, see Figure 1.2).[41]

1.8 Fetal ETS exposure in pregnancy

ETS components in maternal blood can cross the placenta and so affect the fetus. The two substances in tobacco smoke thought to have the most effect are carbon monoxide and nicotine.[42,43] Carbon monoxide binds to haemoglobin resulting in a deficiency of oxygen in fetal tissue (hypoxia). Nicotine has vasoconstrictive properties and can affect the utero-placental blood flow. Both substances, therefore, have potential adverse effects on fetal growth and development (see Chapter 2).

1.9 Summary

- Passive smoking is exposure to environmental tobacco smoke (ETS) arising from other people smoking tobacco.
- ETS contains the same substances as the smoke inhaled by active smokers, including poisons such as carbon monoxide, ammonia, arsenic, mercury and formaldehyde, and a range of established carcinogens.

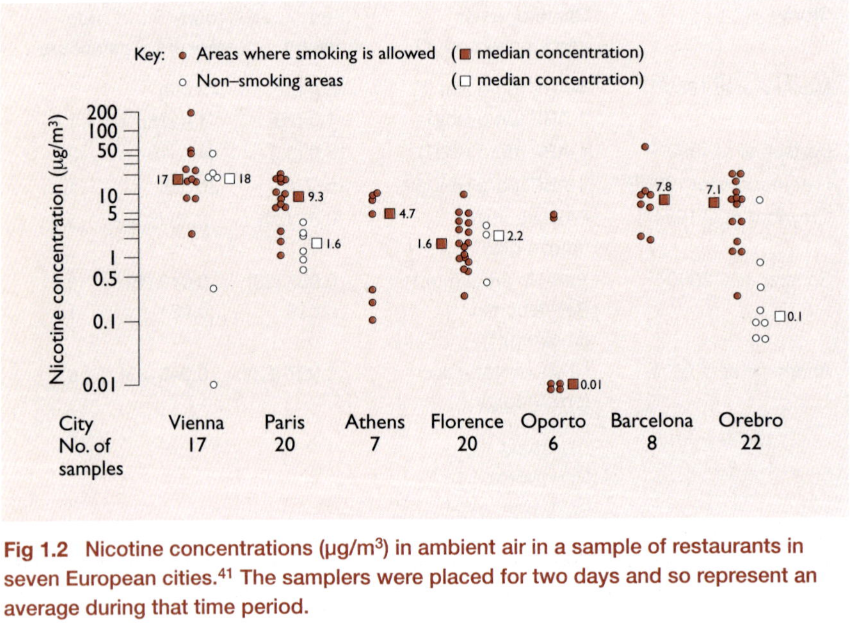

Fig 1.2 Nicotine concentrations (µg/m³) in ambient air in a sample of restaurants in seven European cities.[41] The samplers were placed for two days and so represent an average during that time period.

- Non-smokers exposed to ETS have raised levels of tobacco breakdown products and tobacco-related poisons and carcinogens such as carbon monoxide and nitrosamines in their bodies.
- ETS is, therefore, likely to be harmful and to cause the same disorders as active smoking.
- Passive smokers are typically exposed to about 1% of the tobacco smoke exposure sustained by a smoker.
- Maternal ETS exposure results in fetal exposure to ETS products.

References

1 International Agency for Research on Cancer. *IARC Monographs Vol 83: Tobacco smoke and involuntary smoking.* Lyon, France: WHO/IARC, 2004.

2 Benowitz N. Biomarkers of environmental tobacco smoke exposure. *Environ Health Perspect* 1999;**107**(suppl 2):349–355.

3 Jarvis M, Tunstall-Pedoe H, Feyerabend C, Vesey C, Salloojee Y. Biochemical markers of smoke absorption and self reported exposure to passive smoking. *J Epidemiol and Comm Health* 1984;**38**:335–339.

4 Matsukura S, Tomohiko T, Kitano N, Seino Y *et al.* Effects of environmental tobacco smoke on urinary cotinine excretion in non-smokers. *New Eng J Med* 1984;**311**:828–832.

5 Wald N, Boreham J, Bailey A, Ritchie C. Urinary cotinine as marker of breathing other people's tobacco smoke. *Lancet* 1984;**1**:230–231.

6 Wall MA, Johnson J, Jacob P, Benowitz NL. Cotinine in the serum, saliva and urine of non-smokers, passive smokers and active smokers. *AJPH* 1988;**78**:699–701.

7 Coultas DB, Peake GT, Samet JM. Questionnaire assessment of lifetime and recent exposure to environmental tobacco smoke. *Am J Epidemiol* 1989;**130**:338–346.

8 Haley NJ, Colosimo SG, Axelrad CM, Harris R, Sepkovic DW. Biochemical validation of self-reported exposure to environmental tobacco smoke. *Envir Research* 1989;**49**:127–135.

9 Cummings KM, Markello SJ, Mahoney M, Bhargava AK, McElroy PD, Marshall JR. Measurement of current exposure to environmental tobacco smoke. *Arch Environ Health* 1990;**45**:74–79.

10 Thompson SG, Stone R, Nanchahal K, Wald NJ. Relation of urinary cotinine concentrations to cigarette smoking and to exposure to other people's smoke. *Thorax* 1990;**45**:356–361.

11 Riboli E, Preston-Martin S, Saracci R, Haley NJ *et al.* Exposure of non-smoking women to environmental tobacco smoke: a 10-country collaborative study. *Cancer causes control* 1990;**1**:243–252.

12 Willers S, Attewell R, Bensryd I, Schutz A *et al.* Exposure to environmental tobacco smoke in the household and urinary cotinine excretion, heavy metals retention, and lung function. *Arch Environ Health* 1992;**47**:357–363.

13 O'Connor TZ, Holford TR, Leaderer BP, Hammond SK, Bracken MB. Measurement of exposure to environmental tobacco smoke in pregnant women. *Am J Epidemiology* 1995;**142**:1315–1321.

14 Foundas M, Hawkrigg NC, Smith SMS, Devadason SG, Le Souef PN. Urinary cotinine levels in early pregnancy. *Aust NZ J Obstet Gynaecol* 1997;**37**:383–386.

15 Forastiere F, Mallone S, Presti EL, Baldacci S *et al.* Characteristics of non-smoking women exposed to spouses who smoke: epidemiologic study on environment and health in women from four Italian Areas. *Environ Health Perspec* 2000;**108**:1171–1177.

16 Scherer G, Frank S, Reidel K, Meger-Kossien I, Renner T. Biomonitoring of exposure to Polycyclic Aromatic Hydrocarbons of Nonoccupationally exposed persons. *Cancer Epidemiol Biomarkers Prev* 2000;**9**:373–380.

17 Kuo HW, Yang JS, Chui MC. Determination of urinary and salivary cotinine using gas and liquid chromatography and enzyme-linked immunosorbent assay. *J Chromatogr B Analyt Technol Biomed Life Sci* 2002;**768**:297–303.

18 Kim H, Lim Y, Lee S, Park S *et al.* Relationship between environmental tobacco smoke and urinary cotinine levels in passive smokers at their residence. *J Expo Anal Environ Epidemiol* 2004;**14**:S65–S70.

19 Haddow JE, Knight GJ, Palomaki GE, McCarthy JE. Second-trimester serum cotinine levels in non-smokers on relation to birth weight. *Am J Obstet gynaecol* 1988;**159**:481–484.

20 Tunstall-Pedoe H, Woodward M, Brown CA. Tea drinking, passive smoking, smoking deception and serum cotinine in the Scottish heart health study. *J Clin Epidemiol* 1991;**44**:1411–1414.

21 Kemmeren JM, Van Poppel G, Verhoef P, Jarvist MJ. Plasma cotinine: stability in smokers and validation of self-reported smoke exposure in non-smokers. *Environ research* 1994;**66**:235–243.

22 Crawford FG, Mayer J, Santella RM, Cooper TB *et al.* Biomarkers of environmental tobacco smoke in preschool children and their mothers. *JNCI* 1994;**86**:1398–1402.

23 Pirkle JL, Flegal KM, Bernett JT, Brody DJ *et al.* Exposure of the US population to environmental tobacco smoke. *JAMA* 1996;**275**:1233–1240.

24 Peacock JL, Cook DG, Carey IM, Jarvis MJ *et al.* Maternal cotinine level during pregnancy and birth weight for gestational age. *Int J Epidemiol* 1998;**27**:647–656.

25 Steenland K, Sieber K, Etzel RA, Pechacek T, Maurer K. Exposure to environmental tobacco smoke and risk factors for heart disease among never smokers in the third national health and nutrition examination survey. *Am J Epidemiol* 1998;**147**:932–939.

26 Jarvis MJ, Feyerabend C, Bryant A, Hedges B, Primatesta P. Passive smoking in the home: plasma cotinine concentrations in non-smokers with smoking partners. *Tob Control* 2001;**10**:368–374.

27 Chen R, Tavendale R, Tunstall-Pedoe H. Measurement of passive smoking in adults: self-reported questionnaire or serum cotinine? *J Cancer Epidemiol Prev* 2002;**7**:85–95.

28 DeLorenze GN, Kharrazi M, Kaufman FL, Eskenazi B, Bernert JT. Exposure to environmental tobacco smoke in pregnant women: the association between self-report and serum cotinine. *Environ Res* 2002;**90**:21–32.

29 Dietrich M, Block G, Norkus EP, Hudes M *et al.* Smoking and exposure to environmental tobacco smoke decrease some plasma antioxidants and increase y-tocopherol in vivo after adjustment for dietary antioxidants intakes. *Am J Clin Nutr* 2003;**77**:160–166.

30 Seccareccia F, Zuccaro P, Pacifici R, Meli P *et al.* Serum cotinine as a marker of environmental tobacco smoke exposure in epidemiological studies: the experience of the Matiss project. *Eur J Epidemiol* 2003;**18**:487–92.

31 Maclure M, Katz RB, Bryant MS, Skipper PL, Tannenbaum SR. Elevated blood levels of carcinogens in passive smokers. *Am J Public Health* 1989;**79**:1381–4.

32 Bartsch H, Caporaso N, Coda M *et al.* Carcinogen hemoglobin adducts, urinary mutagencity and metabolic phenotype in active and passive smokers. *JNCI* 1990;**82**: 1826–31.

33 Hammond SK, Coghlin J, Gann PH, Paul M *et al.* Relationship between environmental tobacco smoke exposure and carcinogen-hemoglobin adduct levels in non-smokers. *JNCI* 1993;**85**:474–8.

34 Crawford FG, Mayer J, Santella RM, Cooper TB *et al.* Biomarkers of environmental tobacco smoke in preschool children and their mothers. *JNCI* 1994;**86**:1398–1402.

35 Scherer G, Frank S, Riedel K, Meger-Kossien I, Renner T. Biomonitoring of exposure to polycyclic aromatic hydrocarbons of nonoccupationally exposed persons. *Cancer Epidemiol Biomarkers Prev* 2000;**9**:373–80.

36 Anderson KE, Carmella SG, Ye M, Bliss RL *et al.* Metabolites of a tobacco-specific lung carcinogen in non-smoking women exposed to environmental tobacco smoke. *JNCI* 2001;**93**:378–81.

37 Hecht SS, Carmella SG, Murphy SE, Akerkar S, Brunnemann KD. A tobacco-specific lung carcinogen in the urine of men exposed to cigarette smoke. *N Eng J Med* 1993;**329**: 1543–46.

38 US Environmental Protection Agency. *Respiratory health effects of passive smoking: lung cancer and other disorders.* Washington DC: US EPA, 1992.

39 Guerin MR, Jenkins RA, Tomkins BA (eds); Center for Indoor Air Research. *The chemistry of environmental tobacco smoke: composition and measurement.* Chelsea, MI: Lewis Publishers, 1992.

40 Hammond SK. Exposure of US workers to environmental tobacco smoke. *Environ Health Perspec* 1999;**107**(suppl 2):329–40.

41 Nebot M, López MJ, Gorini G, Neuberger M *et al.* ETS exposure in a sample of European cities. *Tob Control* 2005;**14**:60–63.

42 National Cancer Institute. *Smoking and tobacco control monograph No. 10, Health effects of exposure to environmental tobacco smoke: the report of the California Environmental Protection Agency* NIH Pub. No. 99–4645. Bethesda, MD: National Cancer Institute, 1999.

43 Longo LD. The biological effects of carbon monoxide on the pregnant woman, fetus and newborn infant. *Am J Obstet Gynecol* 1977;**129**:69–103.

2 Health effects of environmental tobacco smoke

2.1 The range of ETS effects

Active smoking is an established cause of a wide range of diseases, of which the commonest fatal illnesses are lung cancer, cardiovascular disease and chronic obstructive pulmonary disease (COPD).[1,2] Since non-smokers exposed to ETS breathe the same chemicals as active smokers it is likely that they will be at increased risk for most, if not all, of the disorders linked to active smoking, though at a lower level of risk. Maternal smoking during pregnancy affects placental blood flow, nutrient supply and oxygen delivery, which affects fetal growth and development. It is plausible that maternal exposure to ETS has similar effects to active smoking, though again at a lower level of risk.

Evidence for the health effects of ETS exposure is more limited than for active smoking, and has focused to date on lung cancer, ischaemic heart disease, COPD and stroke in adults, and cot death, asthma, respiratory infections and ear disease in children. However, it is likely that the full range of ETS effects is much wider than this. ETS also causes subjective annoyance and sensory irritation to many people (Fig 2.1).[3]

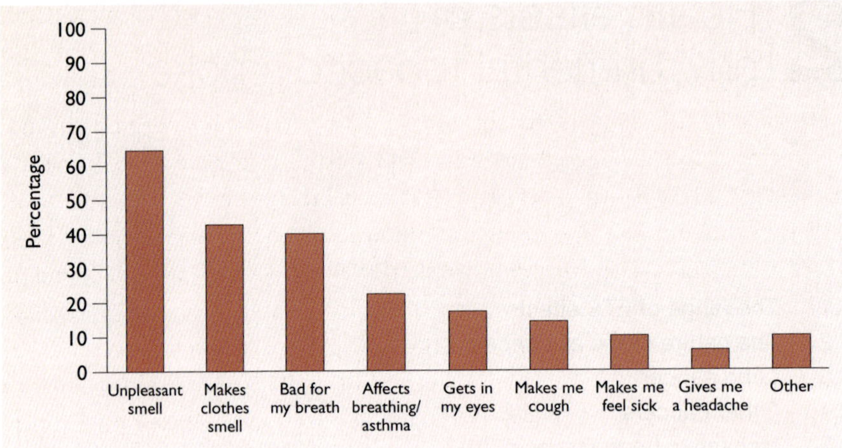

Fig 2.1 The nuisance effects of passive smoking: why people mind others smoking near them.[3]

2.2 The nature of the evidence

The direct evidence for ETS effects comes primarily from observational studies of never-smokers, either by retrospectively comparing exposure to ETS between people with and without the disease of interest (case-control studies), or comparing the incidence of disease in people with and without ETS exposure followed over time (cohort studies). Since smoking has tended to be much more common in men than women in the past, many studies have investigated ETS effects by comparing health outcomes in non-smoking women who live with a smoking partner with those who live with a non-smoker.

2.3 Lung cancer

The relation between ETS exposure and lung cancer has attracted more research attention than any other ETS effect. This is because active smoking has a particularly strong effect on lung cancer risk; smokers are about 15–20 times more likely than non-smokers to develop the disease.[4,5] Therefore, even at the lower levels of exposure to tobacco toxins resulting from ETS, it is relatively feasible for studies to detect an increase in risk of lung cancer in passive smokers in reasonably sized studies.

The first two studies to quantify the increase in risk of lung cancer associated with ETS were published in 1981;[6,7] both were large cohort studies and both showed an increased risk among never-smokers married to smokers. Since then, over 50 studies have been published on this topic and several meta-analyses reported. As the evidence has accumulated, many governmental, scientific and health professional bodies in the US, the UK and Australia, and also the World Health Organization, have concluded that ETS is a cause of lung cancer.[8–11]

Meta-analyses of ETS effects on lung cancer risk consistently show similar results.[11,12] A recent pooled analysis of 46 studies of female never-smokers, including 6,257 lung cancer cases,[11] yielded an increase in risk associated with ETS exposure from the spouse of 24% (95% confidence interval (CI) 14–34%) (Table 2.1). It has been shown previously that the effect of dietary confounding and other biases is small.[12] Furthermore, other measures of exposure also show an increased risk of lung cancer, including among non-smokers exposed in the workplace for whom there is an excess risk of 19% (Table 2.1). As the number of studies providing data on ETS risk has increased over time, the pooled estimate of excess risk associated with ETS exposure has remained remarkably stable, indicating that the evidence is consistent and strong.[12]

Table 2.1. Summary of meta-analyses of the relative risk of lung cancer in never-smokers according to specified sources of ETS exposure. (Data summarised from Ref 11.)

Source	No. of studies (No. of lung cancer cases)	Gender	Pooled relative risk (95% CI)
Spouse	46 (6,257)	Women	1.24 (1.14–1.34)
	11 (442)	Men	1.37 (1.02–1.83)
Workplace	19 (3,588)	Women	1.19 (1.09–1.30)
	6 (246)	Men	1.12 (0.80–1.56)
	7 (1,582)	Women & men	1.03 (0.86–1.23)
Childhood			
Mother	9 (2,085)	Women	1.50 (1.04–2.14)
Father	10 (2,274)	Women	1.25 (0.94–1.68)
Either parent	14 (2,576)	Women	1.11 (0.87–1.42)
Either parent	5 (252)	Men	0.86 (0.62–1.20)
Either parent	6 (1,306)	Women & men	1.14 (0.77–1.70)

As expected, the magnitude of this effect is small in relation to that of active smoking, but this is consistent with the evidence on the relation between exposure and risk in active smokers. In active smokers the relative risk of lung cancer increases in linear relation to the number of cigarettes smoked per day, up to about 25 cigarettes per day.[13] Given that the increase in relative risk in active smokers is about 15–20 fold,[4,5] and since passive smokers, on average, sustain tobacco smoke exposure equivalent to about 1% of that of a typical smoker (see Chapter 1), the expected increase in risk in passive smokers based on a linear interpolation would be about 14–19%. This indirect estimate is close to the direct estimate of 24% from the epidemiological studies, supporting the validity of the direct estimate.

Further support for a causal relationship comes from the demonstration of a dose-response effect in meta-analyses of the epidemiological studies: risk increases with the amount of exposure. Figure 2.2 shows the increase in risk according to the number of cigarettes smoked per day by the spouse (after, on average, about 30–40 years of marriage) and the number of years living with a smoker (who smokes, on average, about 20 cigarettes per day). For example, in someone exposed to about 10 cigarettes per day for 30–40 years, the risk of lung cancer is increased by about 20%.

In 2002, the International Agency for Research on Cancer (IARC), part of the World Health Organization, reviewed the full range of evidence on the carcinogenic components of ETS, and data from epidemiological, experimental and biomarker studies, and concluded that ETS is a human carcinogen.[11]

There have been attempts to cast doubt on the causal relationship between ETS exposure and lung cancer. A re-analysis of part of the American Cancer Society (cohort) study published in 2003 reported a relative risk of 0.99,[15] and so concluded that there was no evidence for a causal link. Although it received substantial media attention, the validity of this finding was widely criticised.[16] The UK Committee on Carcinogens reported that this study did not alter previous conclusions,[17] and even if the result was added to those from the IARC analysis the effect on the pooled relative risk is negligible.[18] New studies that claim to show that ETS is not associated with lung cancer should be interpreted alongside the existing significant body of evidence, bearing in mind that most studies on their own have insufficient power to detect excess risks of the magnitude associated with ETS exposure.

2.4 Other cancers

There have been epidemiological studies of never-smokers and exposure to ETS in relation to several cancers other than of the lung, including leukaemia, cancer of the nasopharynx, breast and cervix. These studies are sparse, so obtaining robust estimates of the excess risk is difficult. The few studies that have reported on the direct risk from ETS on cancer of the breast, cervix, nasopharyngeal and nasal sinus cavity, and leukaemia are reviewed in the IARC and the US Surgeon General reports.[11,19] Many of these studies have been small and have produced

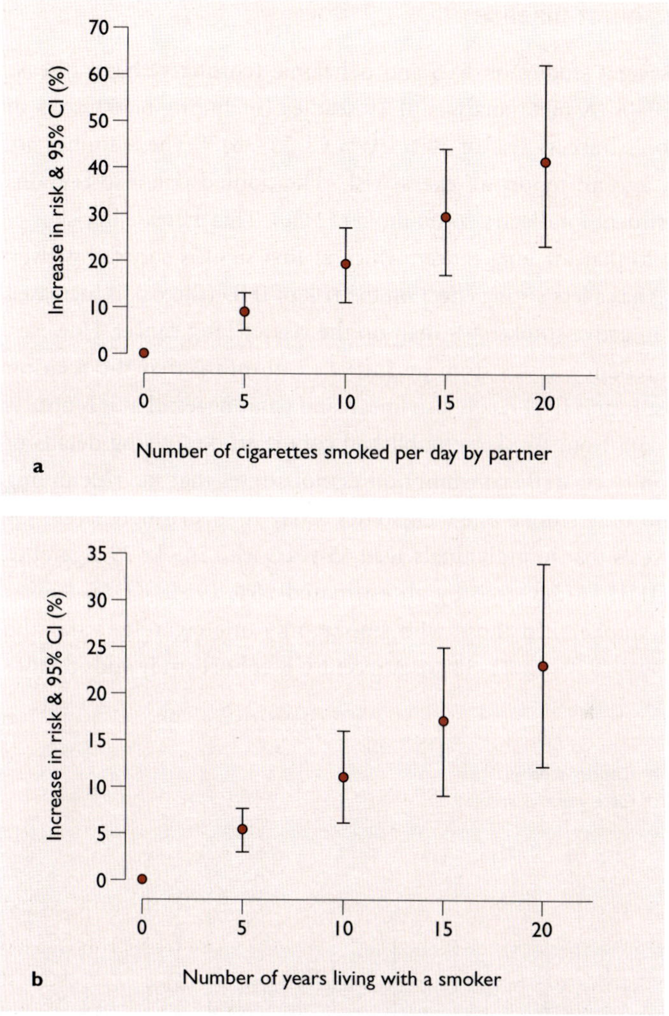

Fig 2.2 The increased risk of lung cancer in never-smokers estimated from a pooled regression analysis of 21 studies that each reported the risk according to (a) cigarette consumption of the partner, and (b) 18 studies that reported the risk according to duration of exposure (method described in Ref 14 using studies published up to 2001 in IARC.[11]

results that are not statistically significant; that is, the observed excess risk could be either real or due to chance. However, because carcinogens have no safe threshold below which there is no excess risk, it is reasonable to assume that if active smoking is a cause of a specific cancer then passive smoking will also impose some degree of increased risk.

2.5 Ischaemic heart disease

There have been several studies on ETS and ischaemic (coronary) heart disease (IHD) since the 1980s. A meta-analysis of 19 studies (including 6,600 cases of IHD) yielded a pooled excess risk of 30% (95% CI 22–38).[20] These studies are shown in Fig 2.3, and all report an excess risk. The pooled risk also remains elevated after adjustment for dietary confounding (23%). This increase in risk is of similar magnitude to that for lung cancer, which at first sight is surprising given that active smoking has a less strong effect on the risk of IHD (the risk is increased by about 60–90% in active smokers[4,5]) than on the risk of lung cancer. However, this apparent discrepancy arises from an initial assumption that the relation between ETS exposure and IHD risk is also linear, and data suggest that it is not.

An analysis of data from five large published cohort studies giving details of IHD risk in relation to cigarette consumption demonstrates that the risk among active smokers who only smoke a few cigarettes a day is surprisingly large.[20] A pooled analysis reveals that in individuals aged 65 years who smoke 29 cigarettes a day the risk of IHD is increased by an estimated 78% (95% CI 31–144%) compared to non-smokers. In those who smoke only one cigarette a day the increase in risk is 39% (95% CI 22–38%). A recent UK cohort study adds further

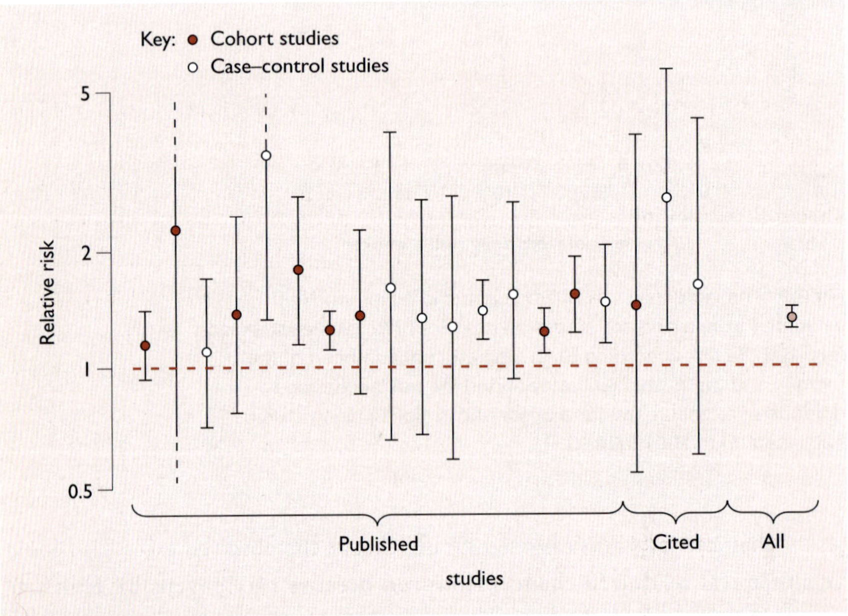

Fig 2.3 Estimates of the relative risk (& 95% CI) of ischaemic heart disease associated with exposure to ETS in never-smokers from 19 studies. There are 16 published studies and three with results cited in abstracts or theses.[20]

evidence in support of this conclusion, demonstrating that the risk of IHD in non-smokers exposed to ETS (defined as those having a serum cotinine concentration of 0.8–14.0 ng/ml) was similar to that in regular smokers who smoke one to nine cigarettes per day (Fig 2.4).[21]

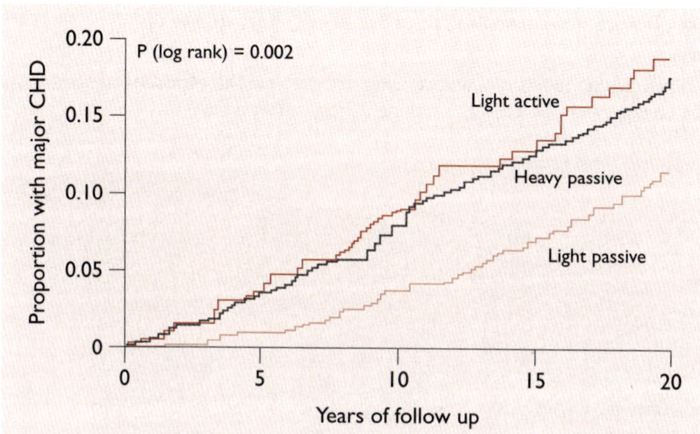

Fig 2.4 The proportion of men with major coronary heart disease from a UK cohort study of 4,729 subjects, with 20 years of follow up.[21] *Light active* refers to men who smoked one to nine cigarettes per day. *Heavy passive* are non-smokers who had serum cotinine concentrations of 0.8–14.0 ng/ml. *Light passive* are non-smokers with cotinine levels of 0–0.7 ng/ml.

These findings are consistent with an understanding of the pathogenesis of IHD and the role of platelet aggregation in precipitating episodes of IHD. Platelets are very sensitive to the effects of tobacco smoke, and experimental studies have shown that smoking one or two cigarettes per day has a similar effect on platelet aggregation to that seen in non-smokers exposed to ETS for 20 minutes.[20] It is plausible, therefore, that very low levels of ETS exposure could increase IHD risk to a degree equivalent to about one third of the effect of active smoking. This is illustrated in Fig 2.5, which demonstrates the relation between tobacco smoke exposure and the relative risk of ischaemic heart disease in active smokers and in ETS-exposed non-smokers. ETS exposure can also accelerate the formation of atherosclerotic lesions, increase tissue damage after a coronary event and reduce coronary blood flow.[22,23]

2.6 Stroke

Active smoking is associated with other cardiovascular diseases, including stroke, aortic aneurysm and peripheral vascular disease, but there are relatively few

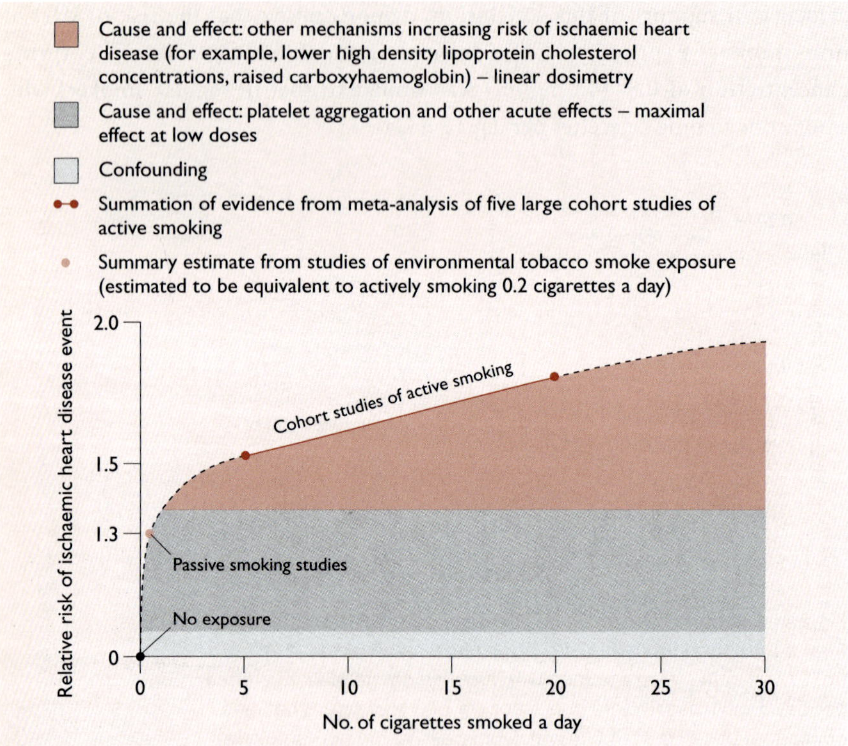

Fig 2.5 The relationship between tobacco smoke exposure and the relative risk of ischaemic heart disease.[23]

epidemiological studies of the effects of ETS on these outcomes in never-smokers. Table 2.2 shows the relative risk of stroke associated with ETS exposure in never-smokers in the studies that have been published.[21,24–30] Most show an increased risk, and the pooled estimate from the cohort studies suggest the excess risk could be about 27% (95% CI 10–46%). The excess risk in active smokers is about 60%[4] so it is possible that the association between tobacco smoke and the risk of stroke is non-linear, as with IHD, and that a small level of exposure can lead to an increase in risk greater than expected. The effect of ETS on the risk of stroke needs further investigation.

2.7 Chronic obstructive pulmonary disease

Chronic obstructive pulmonary disease (COPD) is the clinical condition arising from a combination of chronic bronchitis and emphysema. Smoking is the main cause of COPD; the risk of COPD is increased by a factor of 10–14 in active smokers compared to non–smokers.[4,5]

Table 2.2. The relative risk of stroke among never-smokers exposed to ETS.*

Study	No. of individuals (No. of stroke cases)	Gender	Relative risk (95% CI)+
Cohort studies			
Sandler *et al* 1989[24]	4,162 (33)	Men	0.97 (0.65–1.46)
	14,873 (297)	Women	1.24 (1.03–1.49)
Iribarren *et al* 2004[25]	10,482 (259)	Men	1.29 (0.75–2.20)
	17,216 (447)	Women	1.50 (1.07–2.09)
Whincup *et al* 2004[21]	945 (111)	Men	1.59 (0.90–2.81)
Pooled			**1.27 (1.10–1.46)**
Cross-sectional			
Iribarren *et al* 2001[26]	16,524 (42)	Men	0.25 (0.04–0.82)
	26,197 (95)	Women	1.23 (0.75–1.96)
Case-control			
Lee *et al* 1986[27]	24 cases, 133 controls	Men	0.78 (0.23–2.24)
	68 cases, 318 controls	Women	1.00 (0.54–1.91)
Bonita *et al* 1999[28]	265 cases, 1,336 controls	Men & women	1.82 (1.34–2.49)
You *et al* 1999[29]	154 cases, 213 controls	Men & women	1.70 (0.98–2.92)
Anderson *et al* 2004[30]	30 cases, 78 controls	Men	0.5 (0.2–1.3)
	105 cases, 168 controls	Women	1.3 (0.7–2.3)

* exposure from the spouse except Bonita *et al* which also included exposure at work
+ adjusted for various factors

There have been several epidemiological studies of ETS and COPD in non-smokers, based on either the occurrence of symptoms associated with COPD (chronic cough or phlegm, shortness of breath, wheeze) or a clinical diagnosis of COPD.[31,32] Most have shown an increased risk. In a review of eight studies of COPD and exposure to ETS in non-smokers (with exposure arising mainly from the spouse), all but one showed an increased risk (Fig 2.6). A meta-analysis of these studies yielded a pooled excess risk of 25% (95% CI 10–43%).[33] There have also been a number of studies that have shown a small but significant decrease in lung function among adult non-smokers exposed passively to ETS, consistent with an effect on COPD.[31]

2.8 Asthma and other respiratory illness

Studies of the incidence of wheezing illnesses in infancy,[34] the prevalence of wheeze and related symptoms among school children,[35] and the relative severity

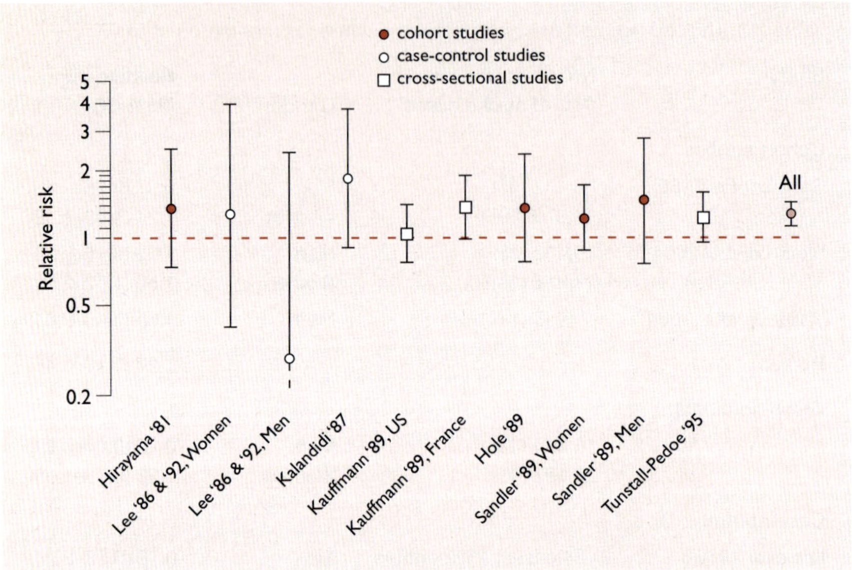

Fig 2.6 Relative risk (& 95% CI) of chronic obstructive respiratory disease in non-smokers exposed to ETS (mainly from the spouse). (Adapted from Ref 33).

of disease among children with physician-diagnosed asthma[36] consistently show that these conditions are increased in children with at least one parent who smokes. A recent series of meta-analyses included 38 studies of wheezing illness in infancy; 41 cross-sectional studies of asthma in school children; 62 studies of wheeze among school children; 11 longitudinal studies of asthma incidence; and 24 case-control studies of prevalent asthma.[37] Summary estimates indicate that children brought up in households where one or both parents smoke have a relative excess risk of 60% (95% CI 47–74%) for early lower respiratory illnesses (similar for wheezing and non-wheezing illnesses); 26% (20–33%) for wheezing at school age; 23% (14–33%) for asthma at school age; and 39% (19–64%) for 'clinically defined asthma' in case-control studies. A qualitative review of 16 case-series of asthmatic patients also suggests greater severity of disease in children exposed to smoking in the household, especially among asthmatics attending hospital as outpatients or inpatients.[37]

These findings are all important indicators of a substantial and potentially preventable public health burden. Whether or not the relation is causal in respect of the incidence of new cases of asthma, as opposed to exacerbation of existing disease, remains unresolved. In either case it is clear that ETS exposure is responsible for considerable morbidity due to asthma in children.

ETS is also associated with the onset of asthma in adulthood.[31,32] In a review of six studies that each looked at the onset of asthma among non-smoking adults exposed to ETS, all showed an increased risk. The excess risk is estimated to be at least 50%.[31] The same review also included studies that attempted to assess the effect on asthma exacerbation but these were too few in number and had too much variability in outcome measures to reach a clear conclusion. A large case-control study of adults in Finland has provided strong evidence of increased asthma incidence in adults exposed to ETS at work or at home.[38] It is likely, therefore, that ETS exposure contributes to the onset of asthma in both adults and children.

2.9 Sudden infant death syndrome (SIDS)

Sudden infant death ('cot death') occurs more commonly in babies whose parents smoke.[39] Although part of this increase in risk may be explained by associated socio-economic factors, much of the excess is caused by parental smoking. Maternal smoking approximately doubles the risk of sudden infant death, independent of other factors (CI 55–143% increase in risk). The balance of evidence suggests that at least some of this effect is due to postnatal (ie environmental) exposure, rather than prenatal exposure to maternal smoking during pregnancy. About a quarter of cot deaths in Britain are attributable to parental smoking.

2.10 Acute respiratory disease in infancy and childhood

The risk of bronchitis and pneumonia in infants during the first two to three years of life is 57% greater (CI 42–74%) if the parents smoke compared to non-smoking parents, based on a meta-analysis of 27 studies.[34] This increased risk applies to both hospitalised and community episodes, is dose-related, and is higher for smoking by the mother than by the father, suggesting that prenatal exposure may also be important. Since respiratory disease in infancy is associated with impaired respiratory function and chest disease in adulthood, the effect of this early ETS exposure may be life-long.

Parental smoking also increases the risk of cough, phlegm, wheeze and breathlessness in older children, although the effect is weaker than for infants (20–35% increase, depending on the symptom).[34,37] The severity of disease is greater in asthmatic children whose parents smoke. Although not all studies adjust for potential confounding variables, many do, and comparison of adjusted and unadjusted relative risks within each study suggests that it is the parental smoking, rather than other personal or family characteristics, which is most influential. As for infants, there is evidence of dose-response relationships to the amount of passive smoke exposure.

The balance of evidence thus supports a causal relationship between parental smoking and respiratory symptoms in children. The relative increases are of the order of 35% (27–43%) for chronic cough; 26% (20–33%) for wheeze; 35% (30–41%) for chronic phlegm; and 31% (14–50%) for breathlessness.[37] The numbers of attributable cases are not easily quantified but even these small relative excesses imply many additional children affected by these common diseases because of ETS exposure.

2.11 Ear disease

ETS is also a recognised risk factor for glue ear, a chronic middle ear disease which commonly causes deafness in children.[40] The risk is increased by about one-third (depending on the outcome measured) in children whose parents smoke. In the published studies, about 10% of surgical operations for glue ear are attributable to the effects of parental smoking. There is insufficient evidence to conclude that parental smoking increases the risk of acute otitis media (middle ear infection), or the risk of surgical removal of adenoids and/or tonsils, for reasons other than glue ear.

2.12 Effects on the fetus

It is already established that women who smoke during pregnancy can adversely affect their unborn baby, the main effects being low birth weight and miscarriage.[1] It is likely, therefore, that unborn babies in mothers who do not smoke but are exposed to ETS during pregnancy will also be affected, but to a lesser extent. A meta-analysis of 19 studies of non-smoking pregnant women suggests that the mean birth weight is, on average, 31 grams lower in ETS-exposed mothers compared to those who are unexposed.[41] There is also some direct evidence, though weak, that ETS exposure among non-smoking pregnant women increases the risk of fetal death and preterm delivery.[42]

2.13 Appraisal of the evidence

Most studies of ETS effects report relative risks of less than two, and it is sometimes argued (particularly by the pro-tobacco lobby) that effects of this magnitude cannot be causal. However, as argued in Chapter 1, the order of magnitude of the various relative risks of disease associated with ETS exposure are entirely consistent with the effects of active smoking, given the amount of ETS inhaled by non-smokers. Also, the evidence for ETS as a cause of disease comes from a wide range of sources, including epidemiological studies, animal studies and investigations of biological mechanisms. The particular value of epidemiological studies of non-smokers is to quantify the excess risk associated with exposure.

Epidemiological studies of ETS and health, like all epidemiological studies, are susceptible to bias. Biases may result in the true association between ETS and disease being over- or underestimated. Imprecision in exposure measurement is an important source of bias which will generally result in an underestimation of the risks from ETS. For example, defining ETS exposure status only by the smoking status of the spouse ignores ETS exposures in other settings such as the workplace, socially, and from other smokers in the home. Such misclassification of exposure status will usually reduce the observed level of association between ETS exposure and health effects. For example, subjects with a non-smoking spouse but with workplace exposure will be classified as unexposed, and health effects which may have been due to workplace ETS exposure will instead be included as occurring in the 'non-exposed' comparison group.

Other biases may cause overestimates of the level of association. In particular, people classified as non-smokers married to smokers could in fact be, or have been, smokers themselves. Such misclassification will tend to increase the apparent magnitude of the risk of living with a smoker. Confounding is another potential explanation for the observed association between ETS exposure and health effects. This could occur if other exposures, such as occupational risk factors or poor diet, which cause adverse health effects occur more frequently among individuals exposed to ETS.

For each of the health effects described above, the results of individual studies of ETS range generally from finding a weakly negative to moderately strongly positive association with ETS exposure. That there is discrepancy between the results of the available studies is not surprising because this is a well-recognised observation in the investigation of exposures associated with relatively low levels of risk. The problem can be addressed by examining all of the data available in systematic overviews and quantitative meta-analysis, as used in this chapter. Although these overviews are susceptible to publication bias (arising from the fact that, at least in the early stages of investigation, studies that find evidence of adverse effect are more likely to be published than those finding no effect), there are methods of detecting this bias and, in relation to ETS, it appears not to be a substantial problem. Not only is the balance of evidence usually determined by larger studies (which are less prone to publication bias), but also there are instances of large unpublished studies which yield similar estimates to those obtained from the peer-reviewed literature. For studies of ETS effects on health there is an overall consistency within the published literature, derived from diverse locations and a variety of study designs, which is impressive.

2.14 Summary

- ETS has been shown to cause lung cancer and ischaemic heart disease, and probably to cause COPD, asthma and stroke in adults.
- ETS is harmful to children, causing sudden infant death, pneumonia and bronchitis, asthma, respiratory symptoms and middle ear disease.
- Maternal exposure to ETS may also adversely affect the unborn child, causing low birth weight, fetal death and preterm delivery.
- For most of these effects the level of individual risk is low relative to active smoking, but the fact that large numbers of people are exposed results in a substantial burden of disease.
- Since non-smokers exposed to ETS inhale the same chemicals as active smokers, they probably also have an increased incidence of most other disorders linked to active smoking, though at a lower level of risk.
- The risk of ischaemic heart disease from passive smoking is disproportionately high, equivalent to approximately half that of an active smoker.

References

1 Boyle P, Gray N, Henningfield J, Seffrin J, Zatonski W (eds). *Tobacco: the public health disaster of the twentieth century.* Oxford: Oxford University Press, 2004.

2 Vineis P, Alavanja M, Buffler P, Fontham E *et al.* Tobacco and cancer: recent epidemiological evidence. *JNCI* 2004;**96**(2):99–106.

3 Lader D, Goddard L. *Smoking-related behaviour and attitudes, 2003.* London: Office for National Statistics, 2004.

4 Doll R, Peto R, Boreham J, Sutherland I. Mortality in relation to smoking: 50 years' observations on male British doctors. *BMJ* 2004;**328**:1519.

5 US Department of Health and Human Services. *Reducing the health consequences of smoking: 25 years of progress. A report of the Surgeon General.* DHHS Publication No. CDC 89–8411. Rockville MD: US DHHS, Public Health Service, Centers for Disease Control, Center for Chronic Disease Prevention and Health Promotion, Office on Smoking and Health, 1989.

6 Garfinkel L. Time trends in lung cancer mortality among nonsmokers and a note on passive smoking. *JNCI* 1981;**66**:1061–6.

7 Hiryama T. Nonsmoking wives of heavy smokers have a higher risk of lung cancer: a study from Japan. *BMJ* 1981;**282**:183–5.

8 US Department of Health and Human Services. *The health consequences of involuntary smoking. A report of the US Surgeon General.* DHHS Publication No. (CDC) 87–8398. Rockville, MD: DHHS, Public Health Service, Centers for Disease Control, Center for Health Promotion and Education, Office on Smoking and Health, 1986.

9 Australian National Health and Medical Research Council. *Effects of passive smoking on health.* Report of the NHMRC working party. Canberra, Australia: Government Publishing Service, 1987.

10 Department of Health; Department of Health & Social Services for Northern Ireland; Scottish Office Department of Health; Welsh Office. *Report of the Scientific Committee on Tobacco and Health.* London: HMSO, 1998.

11 International Agency for Research on Cancer. *IARC Monographs on the evaluation of carcinogenic risks to humans Vol 83: Tobacco smoke and involuntary smoking.* Lyon, France: WHO/IARC, 2004.

12 Hackshaw AK, Law MR, Wald NJ. The accumulated evidence on lung cancer and environmental tobacco smoke. *BMJ* 1997;**315**:980–988.

13 Law MR, Morris JK, Watt HC, Wald NJ. The dose-response relationship between cigarette consumption, biochemical markers and risk of lung cancer. *Br J Cancer* 1997;**75**:1690–3.

14 Hackshaw AK. Lung cancer and passive smoking. *Stat Methods Med Res* 1998;7(2):119–36.

15 Enstrom JE, Kabat GC. Environmental tobacco smoke and tobacco related mortality in a prospective study of Californians, 1960–98. *BMJ* 2003;**326**:1057–60.

16 Letters in response to Enstrom & Kabat. *BMJ* 2003;**327**:501–505.

17 Department of Health. Notes from the UK Committee on Carcinogens, June 2003. www.advisorybodies.doh.gov.uk/coc/meetings/coc032.htm

18 Hackshaw AK; International Agency for Research on Cancer. Paper does not diminish conclusion of previous reports. *BMJ* 2003;**327**:501–2.

19 Involuntary smoking and cancer among adults. In: Samet J (ed), *Health consequences of secondhand smoking. A report of the US Surgeon General,* 2005 (In press).

20 Law MR, Morris JK, Wald NJ. Environmental tobacco smoke and ischaemic heart disease: an evaluation of the evidence. *BMJ* 1997;**315**:973–80.

21 Whincup PH, Gilg JA, Emberson JA, Jarvis MJ *et al.* Passive smoking and the risk of coronary heart disease and stroke: prospective study with cotinine measurement. *BMJ* 2004;**329**:200–5.

22 Glantz S, Parmley WW. Passive smoking and heart disease; mechanisms and risk. *JAMA* 1995;**273**:1047–53.

23 Pechacek TF, Babb S. How acute and reversible are the cardiovascular risks of secondhand smoke? *BMJ* 2004;**328**:980–983.

24 Sandler DP, Comstock GW, Helsing KJ, Shore DL. Deaths from all causes in non-smokers who lived with smokers. *Am J Public Health* 1989;**79**:163–7.

25 Iribarren C, Darbinian J, Klatsky AL, Friedman GD. Cohort study of exposure to environmental tobacco smoke and risk of first ischemic stroke and transient ischemic attack. *Neuroepidemiology* 2004;**23**:38–44.

26 Iribarren C, Friedman GD, Klatsky AL, Eisner MD. Exposure to environmental tobacco smoke: association with personal characteristics and self reported health conditions. *J Epidemiol Comm Health* 2001;**55**:721–8.

27 Lee PN, Chamberlain J, Alderson MR. Relationship of passive smoking to risk of lung cancer and other smoking-related diseases. *Br J Cancer* 1986;**54**:97–105.

28 Bonita R, Duncan J, Truelson T, Jackson RT. Passive smoking as well as active smoking increases the risk of acute stroke. *Tob Control* 1999;**8**:156–60.

29 You RX, Thrift AG, McNeil JJ, Davis SM *et al.* Ischemic stroke risk and passive exposure to spouse's cigarette smoking. *Am J Public Health* 1999;**89**(4):572–5.

30 Anderson CS, Feifin V, Bennett D, Lin R-B, Hankey G, Jamrozik K. Active and passive smoking and the risk of subarachnoid hemorrhage. *Stroke* 2004;**35**:633–7.

31 Jaakola MS, Jaakola JJK. Effects of environmental tobacco smoke on the respiratory health of adults. *Scand J Work Environ Health* 2002;**28**(suppl 2):52–70.

32 Coultas DB. Passive smoking and risk of adult asthma and COPD: an update. *Thorax* 1998;**53**:381–387.

33 Law MR, Hackshaw AK. Environmental tobacco smoke. In: Doll R, Crofton J (eds), Tobacco and health. *Br Med Bull* 1996;**52**(1):22–34.

34 Strachan DP, Cook DG. Parental smoking and lower respiratory illness in infancy and early childhood. *Thorax* 1997;**52**:905–914.

35 Cook DG, Strachan DP. Parental smoking and prevalence of respiratory symptoms and asthma in school age children. *Thorax* 1997;**52**:1081–1094.

36 Strachan DP, Cook DG. Parental smoking and childhood asthma: longitudinal and case-control studies. *Thorax* 1998;**53**:204–212.c

37 Cook DG, Strachan DP. Parental smoking and children's respiratory health. In: Samet J (ed), *Health consequences of secondhand smoking. A report of the US Surgeon General*, 2005 (In press).

38 Jaakkola MS, Piipari R, Jaakkola N, Jaakkola JJK. Environmental tobacco smoke and adult-onset asthma: a population-based incident case-control study. *Am J Public Health* 2003;**93**:2055–60.

39 Anderson HR, Cook DG. Passive smoking and sudden infant death syndrome: review of the epidemiological evidence. *Thorax* 1997;**52**:1003–1009.

40 Strachan DP, Cook DG. Parental smoking, middle ear disease and adenotonsillectomy in children. *Thorax* 1998;**53**:50–56.a

41 Windham GC, Eaton A, Hopkins B. Evidence for an association between environmental tobacco smoke exposure and birthweight: a meta-analysis and new data. *Paediatr Perinat Epidemiol* 1999;**13**:35–57.

42 Kharrazi M, DeLorenze GN, Kaufman FL, Eskenazi B *et al.* Environmental tobacco smoke and pregnancy outcome. *Epidemiology* 2004;**15**:660–70.

3 | Exposure to passive smoking

3.1 Introduction

This chapter describes patterns of exposure to passive smoking in the general population of non-smokers in the UK. Data are presented on how measured exposure varies in children and adults according to age, sex, household circumstances and socio-economic status, and on changes in the extent of this exposure over time. Evidence for particular high-risk occupational groups is also presented. Cotinine concentrations in non-smokers are used as a quantitative guide to the extent of exposure. Much of the information reported is derived from large surveys of the general population, principally the Health Survey for England (HSE)[1] but also the Scottish Health Survey,[2] which employs a similar methodology to the HSE. The HSE is an annual survey based on a representative sample of households in England and has incorporated measures of cotinine in adults since 1993, and in children aged four and above since 1996. The HSE affords consideration of how exposure to passive smoking varies among individuals in a household, since both adults and children in the home are surveyed, and questionnaire responses and cotinines can be linked across members of the family.

3.2 Cotinine as a quantitative measure of smoke exposure in non-smokers

Cotinine is the principal proximal metabolite of nicotine. It is agreed to be the best available marker of exposure to passive smoking.[3,4] It is preferred to nicotine itself as a marker of smoke intake because it has a longer half life (16–20 hours compared to just two hours for nicotine in blood). A spot sample of cotinine will reflect nicotine intake over the past two or three days. As such, it is strictly an indicator of current rather than long-term exposure. However, studies in children show that spot samples of cotinine taken twelve months apart correlate closely,[5] indicating that the conditions governing exposure to other people's smoke tend to change rather little over time. In practice, therefore, cotinine is a good indicator of regular, long-term ETS exposure, as well as of current exposure.

Cotinine can be measured in any available body fluid, most commonly blood plasma or serum, urine, and saliva. Although absolute concentrations vary (they are four to five times higher in urine than in blood, and 25% higher in saliva than in plasma or serum[6]), the information provided on exposure is essentially the same. In the HSE, as in most field surveys, saliva cotinine is preferred because of its non-invasive nature. On average, about 80% of nicotine is metabolised to cotinine. However, genetic variation between individuals in the nicotine metabolic pathway means that, in the absence of more detailed information, in any given individual there is a degree of uncertainty about the nicotine intake that gave rise to a measured cotinine concentration. However, this is less of a problem in epidemiological surveys, where cotinines are analysed across demographic groups, since variation due to genetic factors will tend to average out.

Cotinine metabolism and excretion is reduced in neonates but otherwise varies little by age or sex in older children and adults, thereby allowing valid cotinine-based comparisons of the extent of exposure to passive smoking by age and by sex.

As a specific indicator of nicotine intake, cotinine may not necessarily give quantitative information on risk-relevant aspects of passive smoking dose, since it is unlikely that nicotine itself is responsible for many, if any, of the hazards to health incurred through breathing other people's smoke. However, it has been observed that measured cotinine concentrations correlate well with those of tobacco-specific nitrosamines, which are recognised carcinogens.[7] This suggests that measured cotinines may provide a reasonable surrogate indication of likely harm from passive smoking.

3.3 Exposure by age, sex and socio-economic status

Few non-smokers have undetectable concentrations of cotinine, which would indicate that they sustain no exposure at all to ETS. As shown in Fig 3.1, the percentage of such truly non-exposed non-smokers in the HSE (here defined as cotinine below 100 picograms per millilitre of saliva – the detection limit of the assay) varies systematically by age and by socio-economic status. Among those

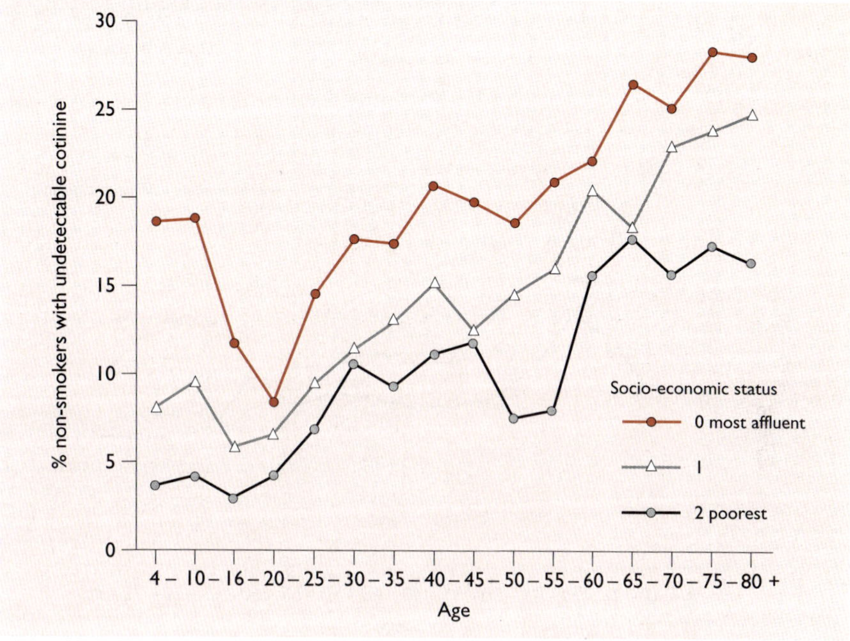

Fig 3.1 Incidence of non-detectable cotinine by age and socio-economic status. Health Survey for England 1996–2003 combined.[1]

from the most affluent backgrounds, just under 20% are classified as unexposed in childhood. This percentage drops to under 10% in early adulthood and then rises steadily with increasing age to about 30% among the oldest. At the other extreme of socio-economic deprivation, fewer than 5% of children from the poorest backgrounds have undetectable cotinine, rising to no more than 15% in the elderly.

Figure 3.2 shows how the population burden of measured exposure to passive smoking varies by age and by socio-economic background. There is an evident general trend for exposure to be highest in young children and to decline steadily with increasing age. This pattern is seen most clearly among non-smokers from poorer backgrounds. Among non-smokers from the most affluent backgrounds, measured exposure remains low across all ages, with the exception of a peak in those aged 16–30. It is plausible that this reflects primarily increased use of leisure facilities such as pubs, clubs and bars as adolescents emerge into adulthood.

Figure 3.3 illustrates the major significance of smoking in the home in determining non-smokers' exposure to passive smoking. Among non-smokers living in non-smoking households, cotinines decline with age through the childhood years, spike upwards in early adulthood, and then decline steadily into old age. However, at all ages, non-smokers living in smoking households have much higher measured exposures. Their cotinines show evidence of a decline

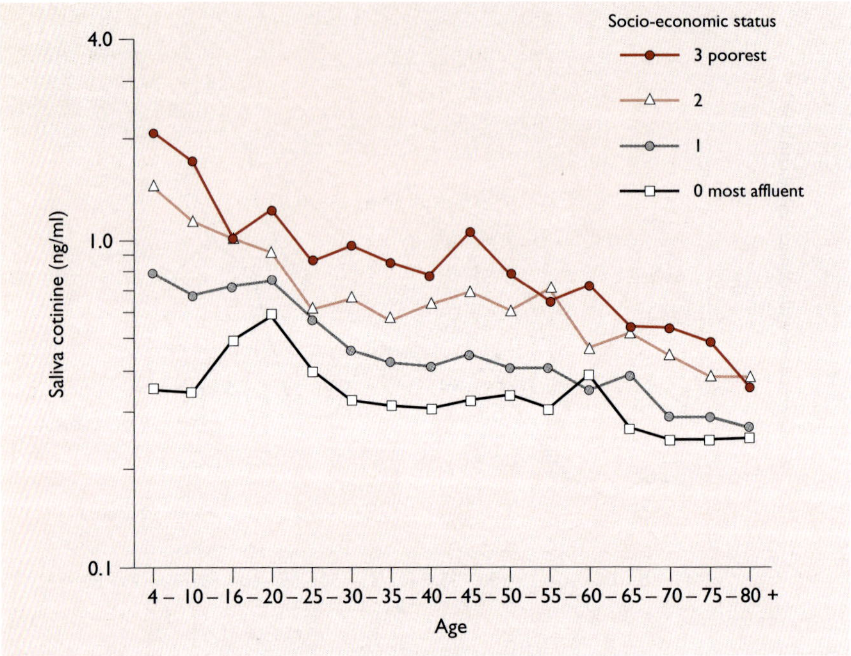

Fig 3.2 Geometric mean saliva cotinine in non-smokers by age and socio-economic status. Health Survey for England 1996–2003 combined.[1]

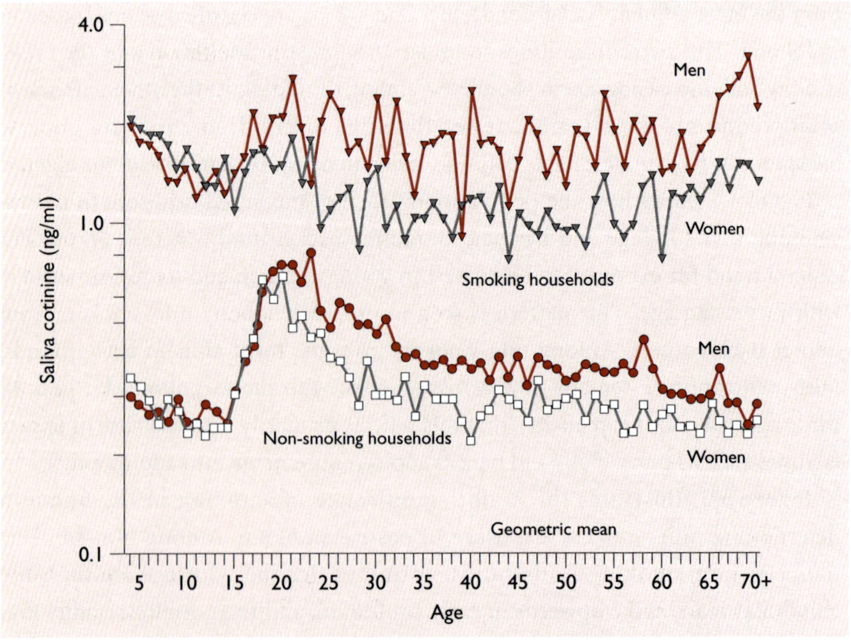

Fig 3.3 Geometric mean saliva cotinine in non-smokers by age and household smoking. Health Survey for England 1996–2003 combined.[1]

through childhood and an attenuated spike in young adulthood, but then remain high and essentially unchanged into old age. At all ages combined, the geometric mean saliva cotinine concentration in non-smokers from smoking homes, at 1.46 ng/ml, is nearly five times higher than in non-smokers living in non-smoking homes (0.31 ng/ml).

Figure 3.3 shows that there are systematic differences in measured exposure to passive smoking by sex. These sex differences are not evident in children and adolescents but emerge in young adults and persist throughout adult life into old age. Exposure in men is consistently higher than in women. This effect is seen both in those from non-smoking households and in homes where a smoker is present. This suggests that men may be exposed more heavily to tobacco smoke outside the home than women.

3.4 Parental smoking and exposure in children

Smoking by parents is the major determinant of measured exposure in non-smoking children. Numerous studies have shown that smoking by either parent raises cotinine concentrations in their children, with smoking by mothers being found consistently to have a greater effect than smoking by fathers.[5,8-11] In households where both parents are smokers, children's cotinines have been observed to be approximately the sum of father-only and mother-only effects.

There is evidence that children's exposure to ETS has been declining for some years. Data from 11–15 year olds surveyed in the Office for National Statistics national surveys of secondary school children showed that geometric mean cotinines in non-smoking children from non-smoking homes reduced by almost a half between 1988 and 1998.[12] Reductions in measured exposure among children with smoking parents were less clear in this analysis. More recent data from the HSE show that the decline in cotinines in children from non-smoking homes has continued, although at a slower rate (Table 3.1). However, with further data up to 2003 it is now clear that there have also been substantial declines where only the father is a smoker (1.15 ng/ml in 1988 down to 0.73 ng/ml in 2003); where only the mother smokes (1.91 ng/ml down to 1.34 ng/ml); and where both parents smoke (3.08 ng/ml down to 1.50 ng/ml). Among all children combined, geometric mean cotinine has declined by over 50% since 1988, from about 1 ng/ml to under 0.5 ng/ml.

There have been suggestions that the effects of parents' smoking on their children's exposure could be mitigated by the adoption of smoking policies to limit smoking to outside the home. No general population data to test this hypothesis were available prior to 1996. Since 1996 the HSE has included the

Table 3.1. Geometric mean saliva cotinine (ng/ml) in non-smoking children aged 11–15 by parental smoking habits.

		Mean age	Non-smoking parents			Father smokes			Mother smokes			Both parents smoke			Overall		
			No.	Mean	95%CI	No.	Mean	95%CI	No.	Mean	95%CI	No.	Mean	95%CI	No.	Mean	95%CI
ONS national	1988	13.6		.47	(.42–.54)		1.15	(.98–1.35)		1.91	(1.59–2.30)		3.08	(2.60–3.64)	1,228	.96	.83–1.11
surveys of	1990	13.4		.60	(.53–.67)		1.36	(1.17–1.6)		2.08	(1.77–2.45)		3.01	(2.59–3.50)	1,263	1.06	.92–1.23
smoking in	1992	13.4		.34	(.30–.39)		1.10	(.93–1.29)		2.34	(1.94–2.82)		3.33	(2.78–3.98)	1,334	.74	.63–.86
secondary	1993	13.4		.35	(.32–.40)		.90	(.74–1.09)		1.98	(1.61–2.43)		2.87	(2.33–3.53)	660	.66	.57–.78
school children	1994	13.4		.28	(.25–.32)		.87	(.73–1.03)		1.80	(1.49–2.19)		2.88	(2.37–3.50)	1,128	.58	.54–.63
	1996	13.4		.28	(.24–.33)		.71	(.56–.90)		1.47	(1.16–1.86)		2.25	(1.72–2.96)	593	.56	.51–.63
	1998	13.9													992	.52	.43–.62
Health	1996	12.8	583	.30	(.27–.33)	113	.97	(.78–1.22)	147	1.38	(1.15–1.66)	106	2.41	(2.06–2.82)	949	.55	(.50–.60)
Survey for	1997	12.8	331	.26	(.23–.30)	57	.62	(.44–.88)	72	1.68	(1.32–2.15)	55	2.10	(1.66–2.64)	515	.47	(.41–.53)
England	1998	12.8	498	.25	(.22–.28)	77	.71	(.55–.93)	141	1.42	(1.17–1.72)	76	2.14	(1.74–2.64)	792	.46	(.42–.51)
	2001	12.9	479	.24	(.21–.26)	73	.64	(.48–.87)	148	1.62	(1.38–1.90)	63	1.84	(1.47–2.32)	763	.45	(.41–.50)
	2002	12.8	259	.21	(.18–.25)	36	.72	(.50–1.05)	74	.80	(.59–1.08)	49	2.64	(2.04–3.42)	418	.40	(.35–.46)
	2003	12.9	718	.27	(.24–.30)	69	.73	(.54–.99)	127	1.34	(1.07–1.68)	66	1.50	(1.18–1.92)	718	.46	(.42–.51)
	1996–2003	12.8	2,606	.26	(.25–.27)	425	.75	(.68–.84)	709	1.38	(1.26–1.50)	415	2.08	(1.91–2.27)	4,155	.47	(.45–.49)

Top part of table, data from Ref 12
Bottom part of table, data from Ref 1.
ONS: Office for National Statistics

question, answered by all aged eight and above: 'Does anyone smoke *inside* this house/flat on most days? (Yes/No)'. Smoking homes with an apparent de facto non-smoking policy are then defined as those where the mother and/or the father report themselves to be smokers but the child reports that no one smokes in the home on most days.

Table 3.2 shows geometric mean cotinine concentrations according to whether smoking households appeared to have a policy restricting smoking in the home. Major reductions in exposure attributable to parental smoking are seen, with geometric mean cotinines of 0.44 ng/ml in children from homes with a non-smoking policy, compared with 2 ng/ml in those from homes without such a policy. Parents from homes with an apparent policy smoked significantly fewer cigarettes per day and were substantially more affluent than smoking parents from homes without such a policy. On average, across the years from 1996–2003, 32% of homes where only the father smoked appeared to have a policy, 16% where only the mother smoked, but only 9% where both parents were smokers.

These findings suggest that one explanation for the observed secular decline in children's measured exposure from smoking parents is that as smoking has become denormalised, and more restrictions on smoking in public places have been introduced, an increasing proportion of homes have followed suit by introducing their own household ban. The findings also indicate that any concern that tightening restrictions on smoking in the workplace could have an adverse impact on children's exposure by forcing more smoking to occur within the home is unfounded.

A number of other influences, additional to parental smoking habits, on children's measured exposure to passive smoking have been identified. These include day of the week (higher on Mondays); season of the year (higher in winter); the number of siblings in the home (lower exposure with more siblings); and the presence of other smokers within the home.[13] All of these effects are small in magnitude. Apart from parental smoking, by far the greatest influence is the socio-economic status of the child's home.[10] As shown in Fig 3.4, there is a clear gradient in exposure such that, at any level of parental cigarette consumption, children from poorer backgrounds have substantially higher cotinines. This effect is just as evident among children from non-smoking homes as in those from homes with low or high levels of smoking.

3.5 Determinants of exposure in adults

Adults' exposure to passive smoking, like children's, is influenced strongly by the smoking habits of other household members, particularly spouses. Clear dose-

Table 3.2. Geometric mean saliva cotinine concentrations in children with smoking parents according to whether children report smoking in the home most days.

	Father only smokes			Mother only smokes			Both parents smoke			Overall		
	No.	Mean (95%CI)		No.	Mean (95%CI)		No.	Mean (95%CI)		No.	Mean (95%CI)	
Smoking in home most days	717	1.15	(1.06–1.25)	1,629	2.16	(2.06–2.26)	981	2.65	(2.50–2.80)	3327	2.00	(1.94–2.07)
No smoking in home most days	335	0.33	(.29–.37)	321	0.46	(.40–.53)	101	0.94	(.76–1.17)	757	0.44	(.40–.48)
% of households with apparent policy	32			16			9			19		

Data from HSE 1996–2003 combined.[1]

Table 3.3. Geometric mean saliva cotinine concentrations in adults in the HSE since 1993 by partners' and others' smoking.[1]

	Adults with a partner												Other adults					
	Non-smoking partner			Partner smokes, but not in home			Partner smokes in home			All smoking partners			Partner smokes, but not in home			Smoking in home		
	No.	Geo-metric mean	95% CI	No.	Geo-metric mean	95% CI	No.	Geo-metric mean	95% CI	No.	Geo-metric mean	95% CI	No.	Geo-metric mean	95% CI	No.	Geo-metric mean	95% CI
1993	1,981	0.58	(.56–.61)							381	1.73	(1.56–1.93)	911	0.65	(.61–.70)	139	1.74	(1.47–2.07)
1994	3,951	0.37	(.36–.38)							744	1.29	(1.18–1.40)	2,002	0.46	(.43–.48)	382	.87	(.76–.98)
1996	4,998	0.43	(.42–.44)	192	.67	(.58–.79)	674	1.72	(1.60–1.84)	866	1.40	(1.30–1.50)	1,876	0.52	(.49–.55)	246	1.61	(1.41–1.84)
1998	4,513	0.27	(.26–.28)	178	.43	(.35–.52)	573	1.58	(1.44–1.72)	751	1.16	(1.06–1.27)	1,723	0.35	(.33–.37)	232	1.63	(1.43–1.87)
2000	1,127	0.28	(.26–.30)	38	.42	(.28–.63)	130	1.58	(1.33–1.88)	168	1.17	(.98–1.40)	603	0.38	(.35–.42)	81	1.56	(1.23–1.88)
2001	3,919	0.25	(.24–.26)	162	.41	(.34–.48)	379	1.58	(1.43–1.74)	541	1.05	(.95–1.16)	2,047	0.35	(.33–.37)	255	1.56	(1.35–1.79)
2002	2,123	0.23	(.22–.24)	80	.50	(.38–.65)	162	1.43	(1.21–1.70)	242	1.01	(.86–1.18)	1,132	0.32	(.30–.35)	129	1.29	(1.06–1.56)
2003	658	0.25	(.23–.27)	35	.50	(.34–.74)	59	1.84	(1.43–2.37)	94	1.13	(.87–1.45)	350	0.33	(.29–.38)	44	1.16	(.79—1.69)

Since 1996, it has been possible to identify households where partners smoke but not in the home. Partners who smoked but not in the home were more affluent than those who did smoke in the home, and also had lower cigarette consumption. The apparent proportion of partners who smoke but not in home was 1996: 22%; 1998: 24%; 2000: 23%; 2001: 30%; 2002: 33%; 2003: 37%.

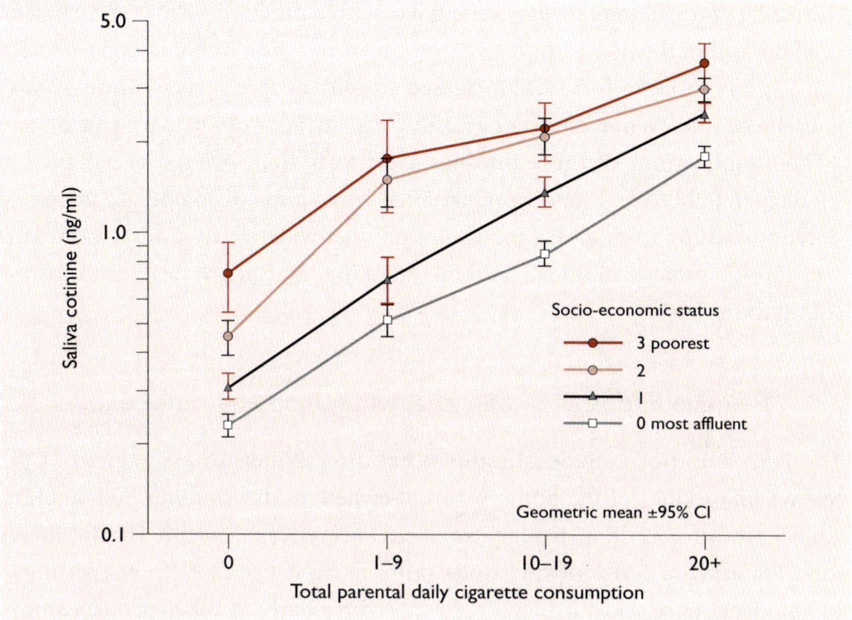

Fig 3.4 Geometric mean saliva cotinine in non-smoking children by total parental cigarette consumption and socio-economic status. Health Survey for England 1996–2003 combined.[1]

response relationships have been demonstrated between the number of cigarettes smoked by partners and cotinine concentrations in adults.[14] Of course, adults are exposed to other people's smoke not only in the home but also in the workplace and in pubs and bars. Jarvis[14] speculated that for most adults the home is now the biggest source of exposure to passive smoking, but definitive evidence on this point has been lacking. It is also important to document whether, as with children, there has been a secular trend of declining levels of exposure in adult non-smokers as smoking prevalence has declined and more restrictions on smoking in public places have been introduced.

Table 3.3 shows geometric mean cotinines in non-smoking adults surveyed in the HSE since 1993. Among adults with non-smoking partners, cotinines have approximately halved over 10 years (from 0.58 ng/ml in 1993 to 0.25 ng/ml in 2003). There has also been a major decline in non-smokers with smoking partners (1.73 ng/ml to 1.13 ng/ml). Similar declines have been observed in adults without marriage partners, both in homes where there is no smoking (0.65 ng/ml to 0.33 ng/ml) and where there are smokers present (1.74 ng/ml to 1.16 ng/ml). Further examination of the data for non-smokers with a smoking partner indicates that the decline in their measured cotinines is confined to those in households where there appears to be a ban on smoking inside the home (defined, as for children, by the non-smoker with a smoking partner reporting no smoking within the home on most days). The proportion of homes where such a ban appears to be in force has increased steadily in recent years, from 22% of households where a non-smoker has a smoking partner in 1996 to 37% in 2003.

The implications of these findings are clearly that lowered acceptance of smoking in public places and workplaces has led to lowered acceptance in homes. There is no support at all for the conjecture that wider restrictions on smoking outside the home would lead to more smoking, and hence heavier exposure, within the home.

3.6 Relative importance of home, workplace and other exposures

The HSE does not include questions that directly permit assessment of the relative importance of the home versus elsewhere in determining non-smoking adults' exposure to other people's smoke. However, the Scottish Health Survey for 1998 asked a series of questions probing exposure in different settings.[2] Respondents were asked if they were exposed regularly to other people's smoke in the home, at work, in other people's homes, on public transport, or in other

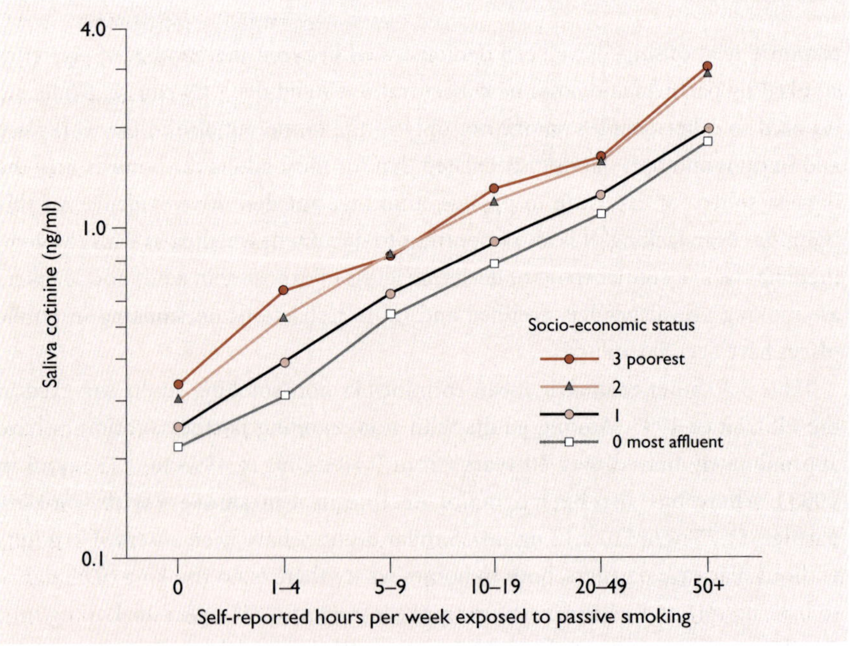

Fig 3.5 Geometric mean saliva cotinine in non-smoking adults by reported weekly hours of exposure by socio-economic status. Health Survey for England 1996–2003 combined.[1]

public places. When responses to these items were analysed by stepwise multiple regression to examine the relative importance of different potential determinants of exposure, smoking in the home emerged as by far the strongest predictor, followed by the respondent's socio-economic status and age and sex. Reported exposure in pubs and in the workplace contributed to the model, but only to a minor degree. There were no significant effects of reported exposure in other people's homes, on public transport, or in other public places. These findings illustrate the importance of addressing home exposure in public health measures to reduce the harm caused by passive smoking.

3.7 Evidence for occupational groups at risk for high exposure

While it is evident that the home is now the major source of exposure to other people's smoke for most non-smokers, and there have been substantial increases in restrictions on smoking in shops, public transport and many workplaces, some adults remain at risk of particularly high exposure because of the circumstances of their work. This is especially the case for workers in the hospitality industry employed in pubs, bars and clubs. Pubs have long been seen as a refuge for smokers, and few serious attempts have been made to restrict the exposure to passive smoking of either their clientele or staff. A study of non-smoking bar staff in London and Birmingham in the early 1990s found measured exposures which were much higher than those in either adults or children from smoking households.[15] A similar study of London bar staff in 2001 confirmed that exposure levels remain exceptionally high; the geometric mean cotinine levels in bar workers are three to four times higher than the average in non-smokers with smoking partners, and some 11–14 times higher than in non-smokers living in non-smoking households (Fig 3.6).[16]

3.8 Variation in adult exposure by socio-economic status

As with children, the most important determinant of adults' exposure to passive smoking, after household smoking, is socio-economic background. There is a systematic gradient of higher measured exposure with increasing social disadvantage. This is an effect of substantial magnitude, and one that is found across all levels of reported exposure. As shown in Fig 3.5, for any given duration of weekly exposure to passive smoking, there is a linear trend to higher measured cotinine with increasing social disadvantage. This suggests that as well as, and perhaps because of, living in generally smokier environments, poorer people's thresholds for reporting exposure to passive smoking have been raised.

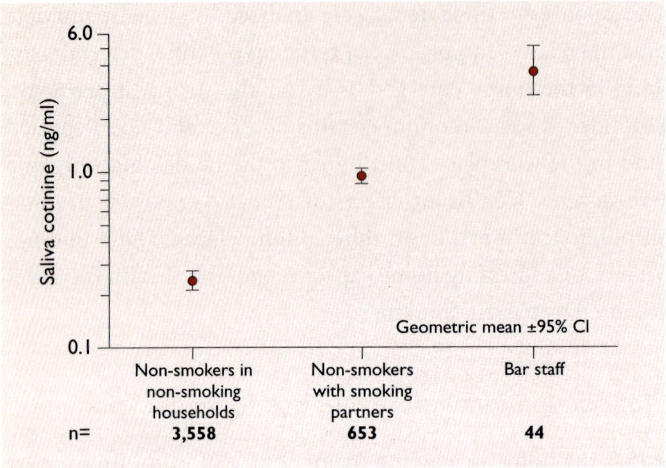

Fig 3.6 Geometric mean saliva cotinine in London bar workers[16] compared with non-smokers living with either non-smokers or smokers. Health Survey for England 1998.[1]

3.9 Summary

- Most non-smokers are exposed to ETS.
- Exposure is especially high in children and the relatively disadvantaged, and tends to be higher in men than in women.
- The strongest determinants of exposure in children are parents who smoke and low socio-economic status.
- In adults, the strongest determinants of exposure are living with a smoker and low socio-economic status.
- There has been a consistent trend towards lower levels of exposure in all groups over time.
- People who live in smoke-free homes have much lower levels of exposure.
- The proportion of smoking households that are smoke-free has increased from 22% in 1996 to 37% in 2003, and this is contributing to lowered exposures.
- While it is clear that the home is now the major source of exposure for most adults, occupational groups such as bar workers remain at risk for exceptionally high exposure.
- This suggests that lower levels of smoking in the general population, increased restrictions on smoking in public, and household smoking bans have all helped to reduce exposure.

References

1 Department of Health. *Health Survey for England.* www.dh.gov.uk/PublicationsAndStatistics/PublishedSurvey/HealthSurveyForEngland/fs/en

2 Scottish Executive. *Scottish Health Survey.* www.show.scot.nhs.uk/scottishhealthsurvey/index.htm

3 Benowitz NL. Cotinine as a biomarker of environmental tobacco smoke exposure. *Epidemiol Rev* 1996;**18**(2):188–204.

4 Jarvis MJ. Uptake of environmental tobacco smoke. In: O'Neill IK, Brunnemann KD, Dodet B, Hoffmann D, (eds) *Environmental carcinogens: methods of analysis and exposure measurement. Vol 9, Passive Smoking.* Lyon, France: International Agency for Research on Cancer, 1987.

5 Jarvis MJ, McNeill AD, Russell MAH, West RJ *et al.* Passive smoking in adolescents: one-year stability of exposure in the home. *Lancet* 1987;**1**(8545):1324–1325.

6 Jarvis MJ, Primatesta P, Erens B, Feyerabend C, Bryant A. Measuring nicotine intake in population surveys: comparability of saliva cotinine and plasma cotinine estimates. *Nicotine Tob Res* 2003;**5**:349–355.

7 Hecht SS, Ye M, Carmella SG, Fredrickson A *et al.* Metabolites of a tobacco-specific lung carcinogen in the urine of elementary school-aged children. *Cancer Epidemiol Biomarkers Prev* 2001;**10**(11):1109–1116.

8 Jarvis MJ, Russell MA, Feyerabend C, Eiser JR *et al.* Passive exposure to tobacco smoke: saliva cotinine concentrations in a representative population sample of non-smoking schoolchildren. *BMJ* 1985;5;291(6500):927–9.

9 Jarvis MJ, McNeill AD, Bryant A, Russell MA. Factors determining exposure to passive smoking in young adults living at home: quantitative analysis using saliva cotinine concentrations. *Int J Epidemiol* 1991;**20**(1):126–31.

10 Cook DG, Whincup PH, Jarvis MJ, Strachan DP *et al.* Passive exposure to tobacco smoke in children aged 5–7 years: individual, family, and community factors. *BMJ* 1994; **308**(6925):384–389.

11 Cook DG, Whincup PH, Papacosta O, Strachan DP *et al.* Relation of passive smoking as assessed by salivary cotinine concentration and questionnaire to spirometric indices in children. *Thorax* 1993;**48**(1):14–20.

12 Jarvis MJ, Goddard E, Higgins V, Feyerabend C *et al.* Children's exposure to passive smoking in England since the 1980s: cotinine evidence from population surveys. *BMJ* 2000;**321**:343–345.

13 Jarvis MJ, Strachan DP, Feyerabend C. Determinants of passive smoking in children in Edinburgh, Scotland. *Am J Public Health* 1992;**82**(9):1225–1229.

14 Jarvis MJ, Feyerabend C, Bryant A, Hedges B, Primatesta P. Passive smoking in the home: plasma cotinine levels in nonsmokers with smoking partners. *Tob Control* 2001;**10**:368–374.

15 Jarvis MJ, Foulds J, Feyerabend C. Exposure to passive smoking among bar staff. *Br J Addict* 1992;**87**(1):111–113.

16 Jarvis MJ; Smokefree London. *Quantitative survey of exposure to other people's smoke in London bar staff, 2001.* Report to Greater London Assembly inquiry into smoking in public places, September 2001. www.ash.org.uk/html/publicplaces/pdfs/sflsubmission.pdf

4 Deaths from exposure to environmental tobacco smoke in the UK

4.1 Introduction

Almost a quarter of a century has elapsed since publication of the first evidence that exposure to ETS increases the risk of lethal diseases in adults.[1,2] Since then, there has been a rapid expansion of the evidence base on the adverse health effects of exposure to ETS, and major independent reviews in several countries have affirmed that ETS is a serious danger to the health of adults as well as children.[3–5] Increased public awareness of the risks of smoking, and the progressive reduction in the prevalence of smoking during this period, have led to substantial changes in exposure to ETS at work and in public places. By 2003 in the UK, 50% of people in employment (other than those working alone) worked in an environment in which no smoking was allowed, an increase of 10% in eight years.[6] However, 38% of employees worked in places where smoking was only partially restricted, whilst 8% still worked in places with no restriction on smoking at all.

While the risk to the health of an individual associated with exposure to ETS at work is modest, the overall impact in the population is likely to be large as long as a sizeable proportion of employees continues to be exposed. It is also evident that substantially greater numbers of people are exposed to ETS at home, and therefore that domestic exposure generates a much larger burden of ill health across the population as a whole.

This chapter presents estimates of the likely impact of exposure to ETS at home and at work on mortality in the UK. The methods and calculations discussed have been published in the *British Medical Journal* following a process of independent peer review,[7] but are updated here by the inclusion of estimates of deaths from chronic obstructive pulmonary disease (COPD), and with a revision of the estimated number of deaths arising from ETS exposure at work in the light of a more recent estimate of that exposure.[6] The estimates presented here relate specifically to the United Kingdom, but the approach is widely applicable. It requires only reasonable estimates of the prevalence of exposure to tobacco smoke in particular settings, although it is useful to have some indication of the intensity of exposure.

4.2 Calculation

Assuming that a relationship of cause and effect exists between passive exposure to tobacco smoke and deaths from a particular cause, then the number of deaths attributable to passive smoking in a given population is obtained from the following formula:

$$\text{Attributable deaths} = \{[p.(RR\text{–}1)]/[1+p.(RR\text{–}1)]\}.D$$

Where p is the proportion of the population exposed, RR is the relative risk associated with exposure (in this instance, the ratio of the rate of deaths from the specific cause in passive smokers compared with the rate of deaths from that cause in persons not passively exposed to tobacco smoke) and D is the number of deaths from the cause at issue in the whole of the population.

4.3 Populations

As may be seen from Table 4.1, the starting point for the calculations is to estimate from official statistical sources the sizes of the general and employed populations, the former subdivided by age (<65 versus ≥ 65 years).[8,9] It is also assumed that the great majority of employed persons are aged 20–64 years.

4.4 Causes of death

The calculations summarised in Table 4.1 have been limited to four causes of death. Three of these – lung cancer, ischaemic heart disease (IHD) and stroke – have been included because the authoritative independent reviews mentioned earlier accept that each of these may be caused by passive smoking.[3–5] In view of growing evidence that a fourth major consequence of active smoking, COPD,

Table 4.1. Estimate of deaths attributable to passive smoking, UK, 2003.

		General population		
		20–64 years	All workforce	65+ years
Site		**Home**	**Work**	**Home**
Population (thousands)		35,056.6	29,847	9,429.7
Total Deaths (*n*)				
Lung cancer		7,317	6,230	25,032
IHD		14,949	12,727	97,380
Stroke		4,544	3,869	60,453
COPD		2,678	2,280	26,184
Attributed deaths	Lung cancer	594	117	778
	IHD	1,486	200	3,753
	Stroke	646	134	3,428
	COPD	226	45	846
Subtotal		**2,951**	**497**	**8,805**
Totals		**All aged 20–64**	**All aged 20–64 from workplace exposure**	**All aged 65+**
		3,448	**497**	**8,805**

Data adapted from Ref 7.
* Subtotals and totals may be affected by rounding in the component estimates

should be added,[10] we have included estimates of deaths from COPD in the present analysis. Non-fatal cases or episodes of illness are omitted because many of the original studies of the risks of passive smoking considered only effects on mortality, and because it is very difficult to obtain reliable data on numbers of new cases of heart attack, stroke or COPD in the UK each year.

The number of deaths (*D*) from particular conditions can be obtained either directly from official mortality statistics,[11] or by applying a pro rata correction to such data to obtain estimates for particular populations defined by geography. Such estimates are inevitably approximate, however. For example, because Scotland has higher rates of cardiovascular disease than England and Wales, deaths from IHD in Scotland are underestimated if English rates are applied. By contrast, applying national mortality figures for persons aged 20–64 years to employed populations is likely to overestimate the numbers of deaths because of the 'healthy worker effect'.

4.5 Magnitude of the risks

As all epidemiological studies are subject to error, studies of the risks associated with exposure to ETS are likely to provide different answers, even if the populations investigated, the levels of exposure to ETS, and the methods and degree of rigour used are identical. This probably accounts for some of the variation in published estimates of relative risks (RRs) for effects of ETS; other sources of error, including bias in the original studies and publication bias, probably also contribute. Nevertheless, calculations of the impact of passive smoking should employ 'typical' or representative figures for the risks. Such figures can be obtained from mathematical combinations (meta-analysis) of the results of individual studies[3] or, alternatively and more simply, by ranking the results of individual studies in terms of their estimates of risk and taking the middle (median) figure.[4]

Most studies of the risk associated with passive smoking have involved non-smokers who have a spouse or partner who is a smoker. More recently, there have been separate investigations of the risk associated with passive smoking at work. Meta-analyses are available for both sets of investigations. Following an approach developed in New Zealand,[12,13] the results in Table 4.1 are based on figures for relative risk for 'domestic' exposure of 1.24 for lung cancer and 1.30 for IHD. The corresponding figures for exposure at work are 1.24 and 1.20. In the case of stroke, however, the available evidence regarding risk from passive smoking is much less and the calculation is based on a median figure of 1.45. The same figure has been used for occupational exposure and stroke, as there are no published studies of stroke and passive smoking at work. The figure of 1.25 for risk of COPD associated with passive exposure to ETS in each setting is taken from Law and Hackshaw.[10]

4.6 Prevalence of passive smoking

The final element required to use the formula given above is the proportion of particular populations exposed to ETS. The most recent report from the Office for National Statistics indicates that at least 8% of the general workforce in the UK work in settings where there are no restrictions on smoking.[6] This figure has been used to derive the results presented in Table 4.1.

In the general population, 30% of adults of working age are active smokers,[14] and 42% of multiple-adult households include a smoker.[15,16] Allowing for people who live alone reduces the second figure to 37%. After the age of 65, 15% of individuals are active smokers, but 37% of people live alone, giving a corrected prevalence of domestic exposure to ETS of 13%.

4.7 Estimates of attributable deaths

The first part of Table 4.1 includes the sizes of various components of the population of the UK and the actual and estimated numbers of deaths from the four conditions of interest that occurred in each population in 2003 (see also Fig 4.1). Overall, in that year there were more than 3,000 deaths attributable to passive smoking at home among people aged 20–64 years, and another 8,800 such fatalities in people aged 65 or over. In 2003, there were an estimated 497 deaths from exposure to tobacco smoke in workplaces without any restriction on smoking.

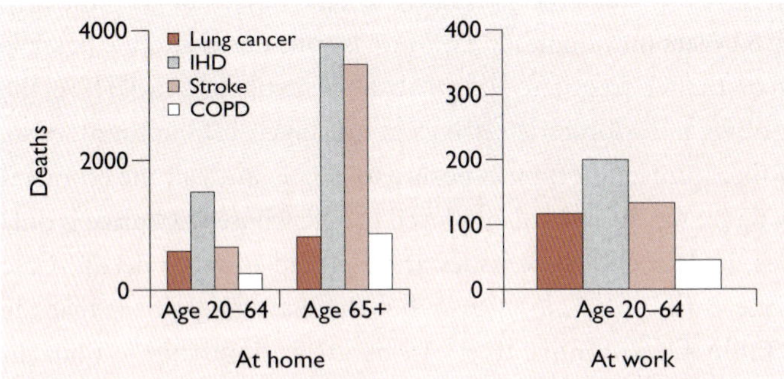

Fig 4.1 UK deaths from passive smoking by age and place of exposure 2003.

4.8 Interpretation

Calculation of attributable numbers of events is a well-established method for judging the impact of a particular exposure on a population as a whole. It does not identify individuals who have suffered as a result of being exposed to a particular risk (or who have benefited from exposure to a specified protective factor), but it is a useful method for informing the development of public policy. As has been made clear, the figures in Table 4.1 rest upon a number of assumptions, including one that the risks associated with passive smoking can be judged precisely. Thus, it is not the exact numbers in the table that are of central importance, but their general size. Confining the calculation to workplaces in which there is no restriction on smoking indicates that passive smoking at work appears to be causing around 10 deaths each week in the UK. As estimated previously, about 10% of deaths from exposure to ETS at work, or about 50 per year, occur in people employed in the hospitality industry.[7] The national annual total of deaths from passive smoking at home appears to be around 12,000. These figures exclude any contribution of passive smoking to deaths from many other conditions for which active smoking has long been accepted as a cause.

The present calculations assume that active and passive smoking have additive effects and, therefore, that there would be fewer deaths from lung cancer, IHD, stroke and COPD in active smokers if they were not also exposed to other people's smoke. Biologically this is defensible – the risks associated with active smoking increase with lifetime consumption of tobacco – but epidemiologically this is very difficult to demonstrate.

In the main, the other assumptions relevant to Table 4.1 have been deliberately conservative. For example, non-smokers whose workplaces become smoke-free are assumed to have shed their excess risk associated with passive smoking immediately, when in reality this process is likely to take rather longer. Similarly, for those aged over 65 years only domestic exposure is considered and the possible cumulative effect of earlier frequent and protracted exposure to ETS in the workplace and in other non-domestic settings is not taken into account. Also, since the extent of their protection from exposure to ETS is unclear, the estimates do not include any figure for the 38% of employed people whose workplace is only partially smoke-free, and so on. These issues are explored in more detail in the original report in the *British Medical Journal*,[7] but the essential point is that the figures given in Table 4.1 are more likely to be an underestimate than an overestimate. Thus, one can be confident that passive smoking is a major public health problem in the UK. Since there is no industrial process in which the generation of tobacco smoke is intrinsic, there would appear to be no reason why all workplaces should not be smoke-free. The issue of preventing harm from smoking at home is addressed in more detail in Chapter 6.

4.9 Summary

- ETS exposure caused approximately 12,200 deaths in the UK in 2003. This estimate is likely to be conservative.
- The great majority of these deaths (over 95%) occurred as a result of exposure to ETS at home.
- Preventing exposure to ETS at home would have significant benefit to public health.
- A minimum of approximately 500 deaths were caused by exposure to ETS at work, including 50 deaths among employees in the hospitality industry.
- Deaths from exposure to ETS at work would be prevented by making all workplaces smoke-free.

References

1 Hirayama T. Non-smoking wives of heavy smokers have a higher risk of lung cancer: a study from Japan. *BMJ* 1981;**282**:183–5.

2 Trichopoulos D, Kalandidi A, Sparros L, MacMahon B. Lung cancer and passive smoking. *Int J Cancer* 1981;**27**:1–4.

3 Office of Environmental Health Hazard Assessment. *Health effects of exposure to environmental tobacco smoke. Final report September 1997.* Sacramento, US: California Environmental Protection Agency, 1997.

4 National Health and Medical Research Council Working Party. *The health effects of passive smoking: a scientific information paper.* Canberra, Australia: NHMRC, 1997.

5 Scientific Committee on Tobacco and Health. *Report of the Scientific Committee on Tobacco and Health.* London: The Stationery Office, 1998.

6 Lader D, Goddard E. *Smoking-related behaviour and attitudes, 2003.* London: Office for National Statistics, 2004.

7 Jamrozik K. Estimate of deaths among adults in the United Kingdom attributable to passive smoking; database analysis. *BMJ* 2005;**330**:812.

8 Office for National Statistics. *Mid-2002 population estimates; United Kingdom; estimated resident population by single year of age and sex – provisional results from the Manchester matching exercise (with armed forces correction),* May 2004. www.statistics.gov.uk

9 Office for National Statistics. *Employment: workforce jobs by industry*, May 2004. www.statistics.gov.uk/pdfdir/lmsuk0404.pdf

10 Law MR, Hackshaw AK. Environmental tobacco smoke. *Br Med Bull* 1996;**52**:22–34.

11 Office for National Statistics. *Deaths by age, sex and underlying cause, 2003 registrations*, June 2004. www.statistics.gov.uk/STABASE/Expodata/Spreadsheet/D8257.xls

12 Kawachi I, Pearce NE, Jackson RT. Deaths from lung cancer and ischaemic heart disease due to passive smoking in New Zealand. *NZ Med J* 1989;**102**:337–40.

13 Woodward A, Laugesen M. *Deaths in New Zealand attributable to second-hand cigarette smoke: a report to the New Zealand Ministry of Health.* Wellington: Wellington School of Medicine, 2000.

14 Office for National Statistics. *General Household Survey, Living in Britain, 2002* (Table 8.5: Cigarette-smoking status by age and marital status), May 2004. www.statistics.gov.uk

15 Jarvis MJ, Goddard E, Higgins V, Feyerabend C *et al.* Children's exposure to passive smoking in England since the 1980s: cotinine evidence from population surveys. *BMJ* 2000;**321**:343–5.

16 Kurukulaaratchy RJ, Matthews S, Arshad SH. Does environment mediate the earlier onset of the persistent childhood asthma phenotype? *Pediatrics* 2004;**113**:345–50.

5 Control of environmental tobacco smoke exposure in the workplace

5.1 Background

Workplaces are an important source of ETS exposure for many people. In businesses that have little or no direct contact with the public, the main source of ETS is likely to be smoking by staff, whilst in businesses with higher levels of public contact, ETS exposure is also likely to arise to varying degrees from smoking by customers, clients or visitors. In some workplaces, particularly pubs, bars, casinos and other hospitality industry venues, ETS arises predominantly from smoking by customers, and levels can be very high (see Chapter 3). Staff employed in these venues are therefore potentially at particularly high risk.

Although exposure to occupational health hazards in the workplace is generally subject to strict legal controls, ETS exposure is excluded from such regulation in the UK and most other countries. This chapter describes the options for controlling ETS exposure in the workplace, and reviews the evidence relating to their effectiveness.

5.2 What are the options?

There are four main, practically viable options for reducing ETS pollution in the workplace:

- To make workplaces partially smoke-free. Options range from allowing smoking throughout the workplace with the exception of one or more designated non-smoking areas or rooms, to making the workplace predominantly smoke-free but allowing smoking in one or more designated areas or rooms.

- To allow smoking in some or all areas, and use ventilation to remove ETS.
- To make the indoor workplace environment completely smoke-free, with no smoking allowed anywhere in any enclosed buildings within the workplace, but allow smoking on the outdoor premises.
- To make the entire workplace premises, both indoor and outdoor, completely smoke-free.

A further theoretical option of providing personal protective equipment (for example, respirators) to staff exposed to ETS is impractical and inappropriate for almost all workplaces in which ETS exposure occurs.

5.3 What are the current regulations and standards for ETS exposure at work?

In the UK

There is no specific regulatory framework for occupational ETS exposure in the UK. The Health and Safety at Work Act (1974) includes the general requirement for employers, 'To provide and maintain a safe working environment which is so far as reasonably practicable, safe, without risks to health…',[1] whilst the 2002 Control of Substances Hazardous to Health (COSHH) Regulations state that employers should prevent exposure of their employees to substances hazardous to health or, where this is not reasonably practicable, ensure that exposures are adequately controlled.[2] The COSHH regulations also state that if substances cannot be eliminated, then control measures should be implemented to reduce occupational exposure, for example enclosure of the source, localised ventilation or, as a last resort, providing respiratory protection.

Since the publication of the Government White Paper *Smoking kills* in 1998, the UK hospitality industry has pursued a voluntary, self-regulatory 'Public Places Charter' as a means of controlling ETS exposure in pubs, bars and other venues.[3] One of the options included in the Charter is to allow smoking and provide ventilation.[4] However, this option is expressed in the Charter as a means of minimising customer or staff discomfort, rather than the threat to health. The good practice standard specified in the Charter is a minimum of $30m^3$ per person, per hour, of fresh air entering the venue and the same quantity of stale air extracted. This is intended to prevent 'a visible smoke haze, the smell of smoke on clothes, and stinging eyes and irritated throats'[5] – that is, to prevent the nuisance effects of ETS. There is no mention of protecting staff or customers from serious health effects, and the standard does not specify air quality outcomes, such as target concentrations of ETS constituents.

There are no agreed UK air quality standards to define the level of ETS in the environment at which health risks are removed or minimised. The Health and Safety Commission (HSC) publishes Occupational Exposure Standards (OESs) and Maximum Exposure Limits (MELs) for pollutants[6] but, as stated above, there is no occupational exposure standard for ETS. Some constituents of ETS, such as benzene, have OESs or MELs, but these are limits for the pollutant encountered as an individual exposure, for example as a consequence of a manufacturing process. Hence, they do not represent safe levels for occupational ETS pollution where individual pollutants occur in association with the large number of other pollutants and toxins, and where the exact pollutant or mixture of pollutants responsible for the observed adverse health effects is not known.

In the USA

The American Society of Heating, Refrigerating and Air-Conditioning Engineers (ASHRAE) issues ventilation standards for indoor air quality. The stated aim is to specify minimum ventilation rates and indoor air quality that will be acceptable to human occupants and minimise the potential for adverse health effects. Indoor air quality standards (Standards 62–1999 and 62–2001) prescribe ventilation rates for indoor environments, but only apply to indoor areas that are smoke-free. Section 6.1.3.5 (Addendum 62o) states that 'Specific ventilation rate requirements cannot be determined until cognizant authorities determine the concentration of smoke that achieves an acceptable level of risk'. Despite this statement, ASHRAE have also issued an 'Informative Appendix' providing guidelines for ventilation in smoking-permitted areas. These are based on avoidance of nuisance effects rather than protecting health, and have been much criticised for this reason.[7]

The US National Ambient Air Quality Standards (NAAQS) are sometimes applied to indoor air quality. These set air quality levels to protect the public health. The standards for respiratory suspended particles (RSPs) of ≤2.5 μg diameter ($PM_{2.5}$) are 15 $\mu g/m^3$ for the annual arithmetic mean and 65 $\mu g/m^3$ for a 24-hour average.

Others

The most important international tobacco control instrument is the World Health Organization (WHO) Framework Convention on Tobacco Control, which came into force in February 2005.[8] Article 8 states that each party shall:

Adopt and implement in areas of existing national jurisdiction as determined by national law and actively promote at other jurisdictional levels the adoption and implementation of effective legislative, executive, administrative and/or other measures, providing for protection from ***exposure to tobacco smoke in indoor workplaces****, public transport, indoor public places and, as appropriate, other public places.* [Emphasis added]

The WHO Air Quality Guidelines (2000) note that there is no evidence for a safe exposure level for ETS. They state that ETS has been found to be carcinogenic and cause other serious health effects at levels of 1–10 μg/m³ of nicotine found in homes of smokers and workplaces where smoking is allowed, and to cause acute and chronic respiratory health effects in children even in homes of occasional smokers with levels of 0.1–1 μg/m³ of nicotine.[9]

5.4 Range of ETS levels in workplaces

Several constituents of ETS have been used to provide objective measures of ETS levels in the ambient air of workplaces or the personal breathing zones of staff, and hence to evaluate the effectiveness of measures to control workplace ETS exposure. Commonly used markers include carbon monoxide, vapour phase nicotine (VPN), RSPs such as $PM_{2.5}$ and PM_{10}, tobacco-specific particles such as solanesol, and total or particulate polycyclic aromatic hydrocarbons (PPAHs) which include a range of known carcinogens such as benzo(α)pyrene.

Several reviews have summarised the levels of ETS found in the atmosphere of different homes and workplaces where unrestricted smoking is allowed.[10–12] Typical values for VPN from one of these reviews are shown in Table 5.1. Similar values for bars and restaurants were found in a recent study from seven European cities.[13]

Reviews of studies of workplaces where smoking is permitted have typically found mean VPN levels between 1–10 μg/m³, and levels of between 1–3 μg/m³ in the homes of smokers.[10] Levels are far higher in bars (Table 5.1).

5.5 Impact of smoke-free policies on ETS levels

Partial smoke-free policies

There is some evidence that partial smoke-free policies reduce ETS pollution exposure, but not to the levels achieved in smoke-free workplaces. The evidence also suggests that in environments with high levels of ETS, such as pubs and bars, partial restrictions are ineffective and can result in levels in non-smoking areas that are greater than in other workplaces with unrestricted smoking.

Table 5.1. Levels of ETS in different settings with unrestricted smoking – review of US studies. Data adapted from Ref 12.

	No. studies	No. venues	Weighted mean vapour phase nicotine (μg/m³)	Range vapour phase nicotine (μg/m³)
Offices	22	940	4.1	0.8–22.1
Residences	7	91	4.3	1.6–21.0
Restaurants	17	402	6.5	3.4–34.0
Bars	10	27	31.1	7.4–104.5

For example, Fig 5.1 shows mean nicotine concentrations in office areas and non-office work areas (such as production areas, laboratories and fire stations) from a US study in which 467 measurements were taken in 25 workplaces of widely varying types and with different smoking policies.[14]

In this study, 82% of smoke-free offices had nicotine concentrations less than 1 μg/m³, compared with 45% where there were partial restrictions on smoking and 13% where smoking was unrestricted. These findings are supported by studies of self-reported ETS exposure, which is reduced by partial smoking restrictions by between about 20–95%.[15]

Levels of ETS are generally much higher in hospitality sector venues such as bars, clubs and pubs. Comparisons of smoke-free areas and unrestricted smoking areas between venues may be confounded by occupancy levels, smoking intensity, ventilation arrangements, room volumes and room configuration. The

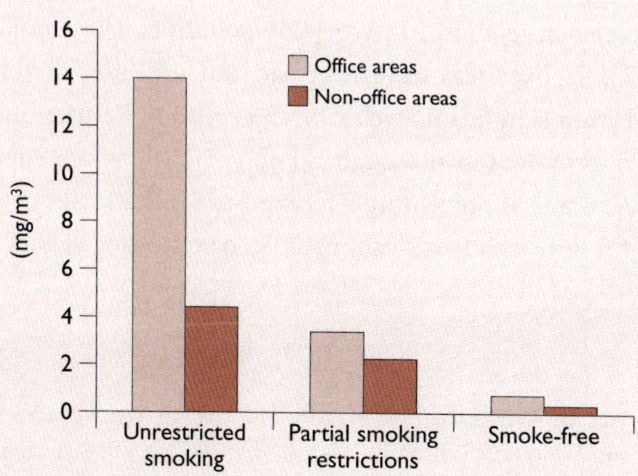

Fig 5.1 Mean nicotine levels in office and non-office workplaces by level of smoking restrictions. Data from Ref 14.

best way to evaluate the effectiveness of non-smoking areas is to compare levels in smoking and non-smoking areas within the same establishment. Several studies have carried out such comparisons.

In a recent study of seven hospitality venues in Australia,[16] mean VPN concentrations in smoking areas were 15 μg/m^3 and mean PM_{10} concentrations 255 μg/m^3. This compared with mean levels of 7.5 μg/m^3 for VPN and 192 μg/m^3 for PM_{10} in non-smoking dining areas. Another Australian study found ETS levels were approximately halved in social and gaming clubs. For example, from a mean VPN of 100.5 μg/m^3 in the smoking areas to 41.3 μg/m^3 in non-smoking areas or rooms.[17]

A larger study of 59 pubs in Manchester included 23 pubs which had non-smoking areas.[18] Mean VPN levels were 75.3 μg/m^3 in the smoking areas and 27.8 μg/m^3 in non-smoking sections of these pubs.[19] These reductions in nicotine levels, though substantial, still leave the 'smoke-free' areas with ETS levels well over typical mean levels found in other workplaces where unrestricted smoking is allowed (see Table 5.1). In fact, using nicotine as a marker may underestimate the level of ETS in 'smoke-free' areas, as the reduction in mean $PM_{2.5}$ level in the smoke-free compared to smoking areas in this study was far less (74.0 versus 97.7 μg/m^3). This may reflect the high level of local adsorption, and hence limited mobility of nicotine, in contrast to other ETS constituents. In restaurants, one study found no difference in nicotine concentrations between smoking and 'smoke-free' areas,[20] whilst another found reductions in RSPs of 40% and VPN of 65% in non-smoking areas.[21]

Overall, this evidence indicates that even when using VPN as a specific marker of ETS exposure, smoke-free areas in pubs and restaurants reduce exposure only to levels that are still very high in relation to other workplaces. The reductions achieved may be even smaller in relation to particulate pollution. These policies, including banning smoking in bar areas to protect bar staff, will not, therefore, protect customers or staff from significant levels of ETS exposure. Restrictions on smoking near bar areas, as proposed in the English Public Health White Paper,[22] will also be ineffective as a means of preventing ETS exposure in staff who have to move into smoking areas for duties such as cleaning tables or collecting glasses.

Ventilation

There are three main types of ventilation available for use in workplaces and other public places:

1. *Local exhaust ventilation* employs mechanical extraction ventilation to capture emissions at source. For ETS this includes enclosure hoods such as

ashtray exhaust systems; capture hoods, where air is passed from the source to the hood to capture emissions; and receiving hoods, where rising warm air is used to convey ETS to a hood for removal.[23] Such systems are partially reliant on smoker cooperation in where they exhale their smoke, and configuration of the system needs careful consideration to achieve maximum efficiency.

2. *Dilution ventilation* involves the supply of external air through natural or mechanical means, to mix with and dilute ETS pollutants in the indoor space, usually in combination with extraction. The mechanical option includes air-conditioning systems which aim to control internal temperature and relative humidity. Apart from the filtration of supply air, air-conditioning systems have no enhanced capability to reduce the concentration of indoor air pollutants.
3. *Displacement (or 'supply and extract') ventilation* combines the introduction of external air at low velocity at one or more points and high-level extraction to establish an air flow. This entrains and hence carries away ETS pollutants. Such systems are more complex than simple dilution ventilation, but have greater ventilation efficiency in appropriate circumstances.

There are other approaches, such as the use of air filtration systems, which reduce levels of particles, but these do not generally remove gaseous pollutants unless combined with complex chemical cleaning systems. Such approaches are costly, difficult to maintain and there is no evidence of their effectiveness in reducing ETS pollutants in real settings.

There is little doubt that ventilation can reduce to some degree the concentration of ETS pollutants in indoor environments. Of the approaches outlined above, ventilation specialists generally argue that displacement ventilation offers the most feasible solution to ETS pollution.[24] However, the question remains whether ventilation can reduce ETS levels sufficiently in venues where smoking is allowed to remove the health hazard posed by ETS, and do so sustainably. The evidence to date is that it cannot.

There are few published peer-reviewed studies of the effectiveness of ventilation in real settings. The study of Manchester pubs categorised the ventilation systems used into 'natural', 'simple extractor fans', and 'mechanical ventilation', which included a range of dilution ventilation, electrostatic filtration, and air-conditioning systems.[18] Mean nicotine levels in the pubs with smoking and non-smoking areas by ventilation type are shown in Table 5.2.[19] Regardless of ventilation type, the levels of VPN in both smoking and smoke-free areas are well above those found in other workplaces and homes where smoking is allowed (Table 5.1), and which are associated with adverse health effects.

Table 5.2. Mean levels (µg/m³) of ETS markers in smoking and non-smoking areas in 23 Manchester pubs with restricted smoking – by ventilation type.

	Mechanical ventilation		Simple extractor fan		Natural	
	Smoking area (n=11)	Non-smoking area (n=6)	Smoking area (n=25)	Non-smoking area (n=12)	Smoking area (n=6)	Non-smoking area (n=5)
RSP	87.9	78.7	107.2	77.5	76.6	62.8
VPN	56.7	27.0	88.0	31.9	60.1	20.9

RSP: respiratory suspended particles; VPN: vapour phase nicotine
Data adapted from Ref 18.

Further analysis of the data from all 59 pubs revealed that bar areas in pubs with mechanical ventilation had higher levels of ETS markers than the general smoking areas.[19] This suggests that the effect of some of the ventilation systems was to increase ETS exposure and consequent health hazard to staff in these pubs. This may have occurred as a result of placing extractor systems close to the bar area, thus drawing ETS towards rather than away from staff.

In a US study in six bars, a casino and a pool hall in Delaware, all of which had mechanical ventilation and/or air conditioning systems (James Repace, personal communication), the mean $RSP_{3.5}$ levels were 231 µg/m³.[25] The estimated achieved ventilation rates in air changes per hour were less than a tenth of that recommended in the ASHRAE Informative Appendix described above. These RSP levels in the hospitality venues compared with a background level of 11 µg/m³. Levels of PPAHs in the hospitality venues exceeded levels measured on heavily trafficked interstate highways and urban neighbourhoods.

Studies conducted in controlled environments, such as the European Union's INDOORTRON 'environmental chamber' have found that changes in ventilation rates made little difference to peak levels of a range of ETS constituents from controlled smoking of cigarettes.[26]

Typical ventilation systems in public places do, however, improve subjective impressions of air quality. For example, in a study carried out for the Atmosphere Improves Results initiative among 45 staff and 246 customers in pubs and bars in ventilated premises in London, 69% of staff thought the atmosphere 'less' or 'much less' smoky than at other venues they had worked, and 58% of customers thought them 'less' or 'much less' smoky than other pubs and bars.[27] However, the studies described above show that ventilation is not effective at removing ETS or improving air quality to anything like a level which would protect against health effects of exposure, particularly in heavily polluted premises in the hospitality business. This, and the fact that ventilation systems are expensive to install and maintain, and require an extensive inspection and monitoring infrastructure, is a strong argument against ventilation as an acceptable solution to ETS exposure.

Smoke-free workplaces

In contrast to the other proposed solutions, there is substantial evidence that smoke-free workplaces achieve considerable improvements in air quality and hence protect health. The cross-sectional evidence, such as the US study of 25 workplaces described above, shows clearly that ETS levels are very low in smoke-free offices;[14] further evidence is available from studies of workplaces in which air quality measurements were taken before and after becoming smoke-free.

An early demonstration from the hospitality industry was a study from a single Californian sports bar in which a series of 76 measurements of RSPs were made before and after a smoke-free policy was introduced.[28] The mean increase in RSP concentration in the bar relative to outdoor levels was 56.8 $\mu g/m^3$ before the policy was introduced, and 5.9 $\mu g/m^3$ immediately afterwards. On a series of visits later in the year, matched for day of the week, season and time of day with the pre-legislation measurements, the mean level was 12.9 $\mu g/m^3$, thus confirming a sustained substantial reduction in exposure.

More recently, measurements in the Delaware study were repeated after the introduction of smoke-free legislation. The RSP and PPAH levels were reduced on average to less than 10% and 5% of pre-legislation levels, and were virtually indistinguishable from outdoor levels except in a pool hall where RSP levels remained above 100 $\mu g/m^3$ (17% of pre-legislation levels), possibly due to the effect of chalk dust.[25] A similar study from western New York State found a 90% reduction in $RSP_{2.5}$ levels (from mean of 412 $\mu g/m^3$ to 27 $\mu g/m^3$) at 14 bars and restaurants where active smoking had been allowed pre-legislation (Fig 5.2).[29] A study carried out in 40 pubs before and one year after the smoke-free legislation in Ireland found a reduction in mean levels of PM_{10} from 79 to 37.4 $\mu g/m^3$ (53% decrease), and in $PM_{2.5}$ from 40.2 to 5.0 $\mu g/m^3$ (88% decrease).[30]

The effect of smoke-free legislation on exposure of staff has also been assessed. Another study from New York State measured exposure before and after smoke-free legislation in non-smoking non-hospitality; hospitality non-casino; and hospitality casino workers.[31] Casino workers were included because casinos were exempt from the legislation. Self-reported ETS exposure over a four-day period decreased from a median of over 20 hours to six hours in non-casino hospitality workers, but was 18 and 19.8 hours respectively in casino workers. There was no

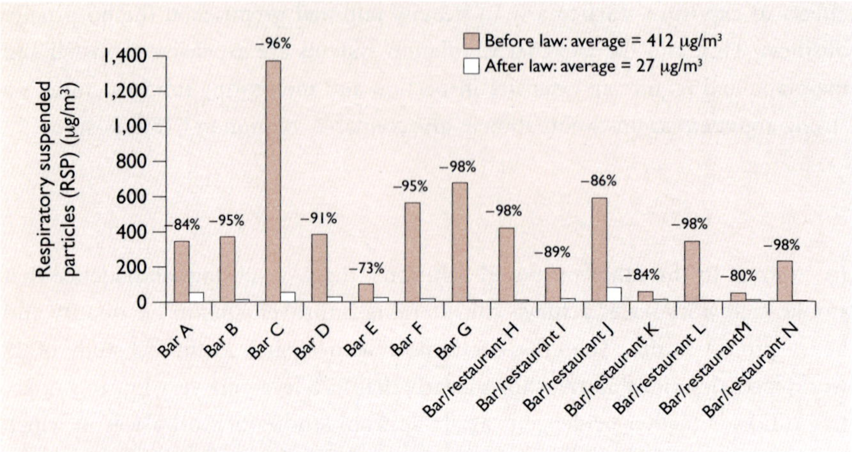

Fig 5.2 Change in air quality in western New York bars and restaurants after implementation of the New York Clean Indoor Air Law. Data from Ref 29.

significant change in non-hospitality workers, who had low self-reported exposure at the outset. Mean urinary cotinine values fell from 4.9 ng/ml to 0.1 ng/ml in the non-casino hospitality workers and from 2.0 ng/ml to 0.1 ng/ml in the non-hospitality workers. There was only a modest and not statistically significant change in cotinine levels among casino workers (8.4 ng/ml versus 6.5 ng/ml).

In Ireland, a study of carbon monoxide levels in 56 non-smoking bar workers demonstrated that levels had decreased by 45% one year after the implementation of smoke-free legislation.[30]

Finally, a study of bar-tenders from San Francisco before and after smoke-free legislation reported reductions in median self-reported ETS exposure over the previous seven days from 28 to two hours,[32] together with large decreases in the occurrence of respiratory symptoms (from 74% to 32%) and sensory symptoms (from 77% to 19%), and significant improvements in lung function.

5.6 Summary

- Partial restrictions on smoking and/or ventilation can reduce the nuisance effects of ETS, but do not reduce levels sufficiently to protect the health of staff.
- Even if these measures were more effective, a safe level for ETS in the environment has not been defined. The precautionary principle of removing the source of the pollutant should apply.

- Smoke-free policies improve air quality dramatically, minimise ETS exposure, and have significant health benefits.
- There is, therefore, a strong scientific and moral case that smoke-free policies in the workplace are the only method that can currently be recommended to protect staff.

References

1 Health and Safety at Work Act 1974.

2 Health and Safety Executive. *Control of substances hazardous to health regulations 2002. Approved code of practice and guidance. L5.* London: HSE Books, 2002.

3 Secretary of State for Health. *Smoking kills.* A White Paper on tobacco. London: The Stationery Office, 1998.

4 Atmosphere Improves Results. *A guide to the public places charter on smoking,* 2003. www.airinitiative.com

5 Atmosphere Improves Results. *A fresh look at air quality.* London: AIR, 2004.

6 Health and Safety Executive. *EH40/2002 Occupational exposure limits 2002.* London: HSE Books, 2002.

7 Glantz SA, Schick S. Implications of AHSRAE's guidance on ventilation for smoking-permitted areas. *ASHRAE Journal* 2004;54–9.

8 World Health Organization. *WHO Framework convention on tobacco control.* Geneva: WHO, 2003.

9 World Health Organization. *WHO Air quality guidelines* (2nd edition). Copenhagen: WHO Regional Office For Europe, 2000.

10 Hammond SK. Exposure of US workers to environmental tobacco smoke. *Environ Health Perspect* 1999;**107**(Suppl 2):329–40.

11 Siegel M. Involuntary smoking in the restaurant workplace. A review of employee exposure and health effects. *JAMA* 1993;**270**:490–3.

12 Siegel M, Skeer M. Exposure to secondhand smoke and excess lung cancer mortality risk among workers in the '5Bs': bars, bowling alleys, billiard halls, betting establishments, and bingo parlours. *Tob Control* 2003;**12**:333–8.

13 Nebot M, Lopez MJ, Gorini G, Neuberger M *et al.* Environmental tobacco smoke exposure in public places of European cities. *Tob Control* 2005;**14**:60–3.

14 Hammond SK, Sorensen G, Youngstrom R, Ockene JK. Occupational exposure to environmental tobacco smoke. *JAMA* 1995;**274**:956–60.

15 Hopkins DP, Briss PA, Ricard CJ, Husten CG *et al.* Reviews of evidence regarding interventions to reduce tobacco use and exposure to environmental tobacco smoke. *Am J Prev Med* 2001;**20(2S)**:16–66.

16 Cenko C, Pisaniello D, Esterman A. A study of environmental tobacco smoke in South Australian pubs, clubs and cafes. *Int J Environ Health Res* 2004;**14**:3–11.

17 Cains T, Cannata R, Poulos R, Ferson MJ, Stewart BW. Designated 'no smoking' areas provide from partial to no protection from environmental tobacco smoke. *Tob Control* 2004;**13**:17–22.

18 Carrington J, Watson AFR, Gee IL. The effects of smoking status and ventilation on environmental tobacco smoke concentrations in public areas of UK pubs and bars. *Atmos Environ* 2003;**37**:3255–66.

19 Unpublished findings from further analysis of Carrington *et al* study data.

20 Moshammer H, Neuberger M, Nebot M. Nicotine and surface particulates as indicators of exposure to environmental tobacco smoke in public places in Austria. *Int J Hyg Environ Health* 2004;**207**:337–43.

21 Lambert WE, Samet JM, Spengler JD. Environmental tobacco smoke concentrations in no-smoking and smoking sections of restaurants. *Am J Public Health* 1993;**83**:1339–41.

22 Department of Health. *Choosing health: making healthier choices easier.* London: The Stationery Office, 2004.

23 Burton DJ. Ventilation control of environmental tobacco smoke. In: Watson RR, Witten M (eds), *Environmental tobacco smoke*, pp 349–73. London: CRC Press, 2000.

24 Guffey SE. *Proceedings of the workshop on ventilation engineering controls for environmental tobacco smoke in the hospitality industry.* Cincinnati, USA: American Conference of Governmental Industrial Hygienists (ACGIH), 1998.

25 Repace J. Respirable particles and carcinogens in the air of Delaware hospitality venues before and after a smoking ban. *J Occup Environ Med* 2004;**46**:887–905.

26 Kotzias D, Geiss O, Leva P, Bellintani A, Arvanitis A. *Report on preliminary results on the impact of various air exchange rates on the levels of environmental tobacco smoke (ETS) components.* Ispra: JRC–IHCP Physical and Chemical Exposure Unit, 2003.

27 Corporate Responsibility Consulting. *Acceptability of hospitality 'Ventilated premises standard': UK market research report.* London: Atmosphere Improves Results, 2002.

28 Ott W, Switzer P, Robinson J. Particle concentrations inside a tavern before and after prohibition of smoking: evaluating the performance of an indoor air quality model. *Air Waste* 1996;**46**:1120–34.

29 Travers M, Cummings KM, Hyland A, Repace J *et al.* Indoor air quality in hospitality venues before and after the implementation of a Clean Indoor Air Law – Western New York, 2003. *Morb Mortal Wkly Rep* 2004;**53**(44):1038–41.

30 Office of Tobacco Control. *Smoke-free workplaces in Ireland: a one-year review.* Clane, Ireland: Office of Tobacco Control, 2005.

31 Abrams SM, Mahoney MC, Hyland A, Cummings KM, Davis W, Song L. Early evidence on the effectiveness of Clean Indoor Air Legislation in New York State. Submitted to *Tob Control,* 2004.

32 Eisner MD, Smith AK, Blanc PD. Bartenders' respiratory health after establishment of smoke-free bars and taverns. *JAMA* 1998;**280**:1909–14.

6 | Control measures in the home – effects on exposure

6.1 Introduction

Smoking in public and workplaces, and the effects of the involuntary exposure to ETS that arise from it, has been recognised as a major public health concern for many years. However, measures to reduce exposure to ETS in the home have received relatively little attention. This is despite the fact that most of the evidence on the harm caused by ETS comes from studies carried out on exposure in the home, which is also the location of the greatest exposure for the most vulnerable group, infants and young children.

This is a contentious area of public policy, for which the primary health objective is to identify and, where possible, implement strategies that are effective in protecting children, but are also proportionate, acceptable and workable. It is also necessary to encourage adults to understand the risks and to protect themselves and those around them from ETS.

6.2 The rights of children to be protected from ETS

Adults are able generally to exercise choice about their exposure to ETS in the home, and are able to take steps to avoid exposure if they wish. Children, and particularly younger children, do not typically enjoy this freedom. However, under the terms of the UN Convention on the Rights of the Child, the Government has legally binding international obligations to protect children from harm. Article 3 states:

> *In all actions concerning children, whether undertaken by public or private social welfare institutions, courts of law, administrative authorities or legislative bodies, the best interests of the child shall be a primary consideration.*[1]

Although the Convention does not explicitly declare a right to protection from the harm caused by ETS exposure, official interpretation of the articles of the Convention demonstrates that tobacco is a human rights issue. In the 1997 Declaration of the Environment, under the section on Children's Environmental Health, the Leaders of the G8 stated:

> *We affirm that environmental tobacco smoke is a significant public health risk to young children and that parents need to know about the risks of smoking in the home around their young children. We agree to co-operate on education and public awareness efforts aimed at reducing children's exposure to environmental tobacco smoke.*[2]

According to the World Health Organization (WHO):

> *Because of the enormous potential harm to children from tobacco use and exposure, States have a duty to take all necessary legislative and regulatory measures to protect children from tobacco and ensure that the interests of children take precedence over those of the tobacco industry.*[3]

The UK has now ratified the WHO Framework Convention on Tobacco Control (FCTC),[4] the first international health treaty designed to reduce the devastating health and economic impacts of tobacco. However, on second-hand smoke the FCTC sets out conditions only for public places and workplaces, committing parties under Article 8 to:

> *...the adoption and implementation of effective legislative, executive, administrative and/or other measures, providing for protection from exposure to tobacco smoke in indoor workplaces, public transport, indoor public places and, as appropriate, other public places.*[4]

The FCTC does not address the problem of ETS exposure at home.

Similarly, the UK Government has not, to date, attempted to legislate to try to control exposure to ETS in children's own homes. The need to protect children from ETS is recognised clearly by Government, which introduced restrictions on smoking in day care settings other than the home in 2001[5] and, after heavy lobbying from childcare and health organisations, extended these to cover paid childminders working in their own homes in 2003.[6] The Health Minister at the time, Alan Milburn, commented that, 'This measure is not about telling parents how to bring up their kids, but equally there has got to be some protection for children.'[7] As yet, however, there are no other controls on children's exposure to ETS in the home. In the US, legal sanctions have been employed to limit child custody/visitation rights in divorce cases and to disqualify adoption applicants, but there are no laws controlling ETS exposure of children at home. However, these established legal sanctions set precedents and may be forerunners of community ordinances to protect children in homes.[8]

6.3 Extent of exposure to tobacco smoke in the home

Around 45% of British children in 1996 lived in a home where at least one person smoked.[9] The proportion of children exposed to ETS is high because smoking is most common in the age groups most likely to have young children. In 2003, 36% of those aged 20–24, and 34% of those aged 24–35, were smokers. The average smoking prevalence for the adult population is only 26%.[10] There is also a great deal of variation in ETS exposure in relation to socio-economic status; children of parents with routine and manual occupations are more likely to live in households where they are exposed to tobacco smoke than those of parents with professional and managerial backgrounds because their parents and carers are more likely to smoke.[10] They are also more likely to be exposed to ETS outside the home.[11] These variations help to perpetuate the intergenerational impact of social inequalities in health, not only because of the direct effect of ETS on child health, but also because children are three times as likely to become smokers themselves if their parents smoke.[12]

ETS at home is the main source of exposure for children, particularly very young children, as they spend most of their time at home and indoors. Maternal smoking also tends to have a greater influence on exposure than paternal smoking because of the cumulative effect of exposure during pregnancy and the mother being the most common primary caregiver in early life. Cotinine levels in children indicate that exposure in households where the mother smokes is equivalent to approximately 50 cigarettes a year; where both parents smoke this rises to 80 cigarettes a year.[13] ETS exposure in the home is a significant source of ETS exposure throughout childhood (see also Chapter 3).[14,15]

6.4 Direct impact of ETS on child health

The direct health impacts of ETS in children are summarised in Chapter 2, and are substantial. In addition to the recognised adverse effects of maternal smoking on the fetus (low birth weight, premature birth, spontaneous abortion and stillbirth),[16,17] ETS exposure of non-smoking pregnant women has also been linked to adverse pregnancy outcomes,[18–21] particularly low birth weight,[22–24] and, in one study, is estimated to account for 10% of fetal deaths, preterm deliveries and low birth weight babies.[25] ETS exposure after birth is well established as a cause of sudden infant death syndrome (SIDS or cot death),[26] lower respiratory tract infections such as bronchitis, pneumonia and bronchiolitis,[27] asthma,[28–31] middle ear disease[31] and impaired olfactory function,[32] reduced lung function in adulthood,[33] and chronic obstructive airway disease and cancer as adults.[34] A previous RCP report, *Smoking and the young*, estimated that in 1992, 17,000 children a year under the age of five were admitted to hospital with illnesses resulting from passive smoking.[34] A review by the BMA's Board of Science concluded that there is no safe level of exposure to tobacco smoke for children and adverse effects can be seen at low levels of exposure.[35] Preventing the ETS exposure currently experienced at home by over 40% of UK children is therefore an important health priority.

6.5 Impact of parental smoking on uptake in young people

Uptake of smoking in adolescence is a very strong determinant of smoking as an adult; almost 80% of all regular smokers start at or before the age of 19.[10] One-third of children have experimented with smoking by the age of 11, and two-thirds by the age of 16.[36] One study found that adolescents in smoke-free homes were less likely to smoke themselves, and the same was true for adolescents employed in smoke-free workplaces.[37]

On the other hand, children growing up in households where those around them smoke are much more likely to become smokers. Children are three times more likely to smoke if both parents smoke, and their likelihood of smoking is also affected by parental approval or disapproval.[38] It is not clear whether this increased risk of uptake results only from role modelling and access to cigarettes, or whether factors such as a genetic predisposition to smoke, or conditioning of nicotine receptors from passive exposure to tobacco smoke in utero, also have an effect.[39,40] However, whatever the reasons, it is clear that the uptake of smoking in adolescence is a key determinant of adult smoking and that exposure to ETS at home is a substantial determinant of uptake.

6.6 Awareness of the health risks to children from ETS

The general public recognise that ETS is harmful, and the majority of smokers report that they try not to smoke in the presence of children. The 2003 ONS Omnibus survey found that 68% of smokers said they do not smoke at all when they are in a room with children, and 24% said they would smoke fewer cigarettes in the presence of a child.[41]

The same survey found a high level of knowledge about the effects of passive smoking. Ninety per cent of respondents thought that a child's risk of getting chest infections was increased by passive smoking; 84% thought that passive smoking would increase a child's risk of asthma; and 56% thought it would increase a child's risk of cot death. However, the answers were prompted (that is, the interviewer asked the respondent whether ETS would increase a child's risk of the medical condition in question). As a result, these figures may not give a true indication of the real level of knowledge about passive smoking. For example, the survey included a question asking whether passive smoking increases the risk of developing diabetes. There is no medical evidence that it does, yet one respondent in six (17%) thought that the risk of becoming diabetic would be increased by passive smoking. The figures for the other conditions are likely, therefore, to overestimate the true level of awareness of possible smoking risks.

In contrast, a poll conducted for SmokeFree London revealed very low unprompted awareness of the impact of passive smoking on children among parents of children under 10.[42] Only 26% identified asthma and 22% respiratory illness or lung infections as a likely impact. Two of the most common ailments linked to passive smoking – cot death and glue ear – were identified by only 3% and 1% of parents respectively. This implies that more needs to be done to raise parents' awareness of the risks of ETS. However, awareness of the risks of ETS exposure alone may not necessarily lead to parents reducing the amount they smoke in front of their children. To be effective, interventions need to lead to behaviour change, as well as improve knowledge and understanding.

6.7 What interventions are required?

Studies involving measurements of ETS exposure in rooms of different sizes, and with different ventilation systems, show that the most reliable means of reducing ETS exposure is to stop smoking indoors.[43] This is supported by research showing that the levels of cotinine in children's urine only declines when parents prohibit all smoking in the home, in contrast with lesser measures such as not smoking in front of children inside the home.[44] Therefore, whilst the objective of interventions to reduce ETS exposure at home is ideally to encourage complete smoking cessation by parents, the next best outcome would be to make the indoor environment of the home smoke-free.

6.8 Individual or family-level interventions

A number of programmes have been developed to reduce smoking at home, using theories of behaviour change,[45] clinical interventions, and health promotion techniques. In relation to children's exposure in the womb and in early years, smoking cessation interventions for women who are pregnant or have young children can be effective in terms of reducing smoking,[46] although post-natal relapse rates among women who have quit in pregnancy are high.[47] Prevention of relapse amongst this group is an obvious means of preventing ETS exposure for their children.

Systematic reviews have demonstrated that individual counselling increases cessation rates,[48] and simple advice from a physician has a positive effect in triggering quit attempts.[49] However, a Cochrane Review of family and carer smoking control programmes for reducing children's exposure to ETS found that in only four out of 18 studies which met the selection criteria was there a statistically significant intervention effect.[50] The authors concluded, therefore, that there was little evidence that such programmes are effective. This suggests that attempts to reduce ETS exposure in the home through measures targeted only at instigating smoking behaviour change at individual level are unlikely to have a major impact.

Even where studies have reported successful outcomes, all too often there has been no objective validation of parental reports of reduction in exposure.[51] Thus, only one of the four successful studies in the Cochrane review included objective validation which corroborated the self-reported reductions in exposure.[50,52] In that study, 291 smoking parents or grandparents living with a child under three were given a 30–45 minute motivational interview at the carer's home by a trained health educator. [52] This was followed up by four telephone counselling calls of approximately 10 minutes each. The aim was to reduce household ETS exposure and increase the smoker's level of readiness for change. Feedback was given of baseline household air nicotine, parental carbon monoxide level and smoking-related respiratory symptoms. Self-help materials targeting ETS reduction and smoking cessation strategies were provided. The control group were given only self-help materials, including a cessation manual, ETS reduction tip sheet and a resource guide. Subjects were recruited from hospital labour and delivery logs, community health centres and healthcare providers. The results showed reduced household air nicotine measurements six months after the interventions, as measured by passive sampling diffusion monitors in the kitchen and one other room in the home.

In the study by Wahlgren *et al*[51] (another of the successes reported in the Cochrane review[50]), there was little objective corroboration of self-reported success. Families with asthmatic children aged six to 17 years old attending paediatric allergy clinics were assigned to one of three groups: behavioural counselling to reduce ETS exposure, self-monitoring control, and usual medical care control. Measures of parent-reported exposure to cigarette smoking were obtained at a baseline home visit, a pre-intervention clinic visit, and at intervals up to two years after the completion of the intervention phase. Sustained and significantly greater self-reported change in exposure occurred in the counselling intervention group, thought the effect size was small. There was no significant change in pulmonary function between the different groups over time. The children's exposure to ETS was not validated using cotinine measurements.

Since parent-reported smoking in front of children has been found to significantly underestimate exposure when compared with estimates derived from objective measures such as urine cotinine levels,[53,54] it is clear that the success of interventions such as that reported by Wahlgren[51] must be verified by objective measures such as cotinine levels. Self-report is particularly likely to be compromised when parents have been encouraged to reduce the exposure of their children to tobacco smoke for health reasons.

This is illustrated by the results of the study by Hovell *et al*,[55] another of the four successful studies reported in the Cochrane review.[50] This measured exposure by urine cotinine samples and by self report in a group of 108 mothers of children aged under four. The mothers were recruited from a supplemental nutrition programme in San Diego, so were on low incomes. Seven individualised counselling sessions were given over three months (three sessions in person and four on the telephone). The control group received the usual nutritional counselling and brief advice to quit smoking and not expose their children to environmental tobacco smoke. Counselling was based on shaping procedures in which complex smoking practices were gradually altered to reduce exposure to the child.[56] The interventions were extensive. At the first session the mothers had to set long-term goals for reducing their children's exposure to ETS and sign contracts. Fortnightly objectives were set, and mothers had to record their smoking and their child's exposure on pictorial charts between sessions. They were given 'No smoking' signs and stickers to serve as cues. At each session the counsellors reviewed progress and negotiated possible solutions to barriers to reducing the children's exposure. In the last session, mothers were helped to write final goals and objectives for maintaining low exposure, or for further decreasing exposure.

Mothers in both the intervention and control groups reported falls in the number of cigarettes smoked in the presence of the child, from 3.9 to 0.5 (intervention) and from 3.5 to 1.2 (control) per day over 12 months. However, there was no change in the cigarette smoke absorption as measured by children's urinary cotinine for the intervention group (10.9 ng/ml at baseline and 10.5 ng/ml after 12 months, see Fig 6.1). Cigarette smoke absorption for the control group continued to increase from 9.4 ng/ml at baseline to 17.5 ng/ml after 12 months. In this study, counselling does seem, at the very least, to have prevented an increase in the exposure to ETS. Hovell *et al*[55] suggest that the inconsistency between parental reports and levels of exposure could be because parents were smoking in a different room, but still close enough for the child to inhale the smoke, or that as the children became more mobile over the 12-month period they were exposed to nicotine from dust on floors and furniture. However, data on cotinine levels in childhood shown in Chapter 3, and from other research into cotinine levels in infants,[57] does not lend support to this hypothesis since they suggest that, if anything, cotinine levels fall as children grow older.

The final successful study in the Cochrane Review was a community-based intervention in China.[58] This achieved a reduction in fathers' reported smoking in the intervention group, but no change in the control group, eight months after children wrote letters home from school to their fathers, urging them to quit smoking. However, it is unclear whether this effect was culturally specific, or whether it even occurred given that it was based on self-report.

The remaining 14 studies included in the review found no evidence of a reduction in ETS exposure. In 12 studies, children's ETS exposure was reduced in both intervention and control groups, showing a possible research effect. A lack of effect was found even when the children concerned were already suffering from illnesses exacerbated by tobacco smoke. There was also no clear evidence for differences in the effectiveness of interventions to reduce ETS exposure delivered in the context of respiratory childhood illness, other non-respiratory illness, around birth, or at times when the child is well.

Interventions were more successful in changing participants' knowledge of the effect of ETS, but change in smoking behaviour or reduction in children's ETS exposure did not necessarily follow. Interventions that focus on change in attitudes and behaviour rather than knowledge have been found to be more successful.[59] The overall conclusion was that the effects of brief counselling interventions, successful in the adult health setting when coming from physicians, cannot be extrapolated to adults in the setting of child health.

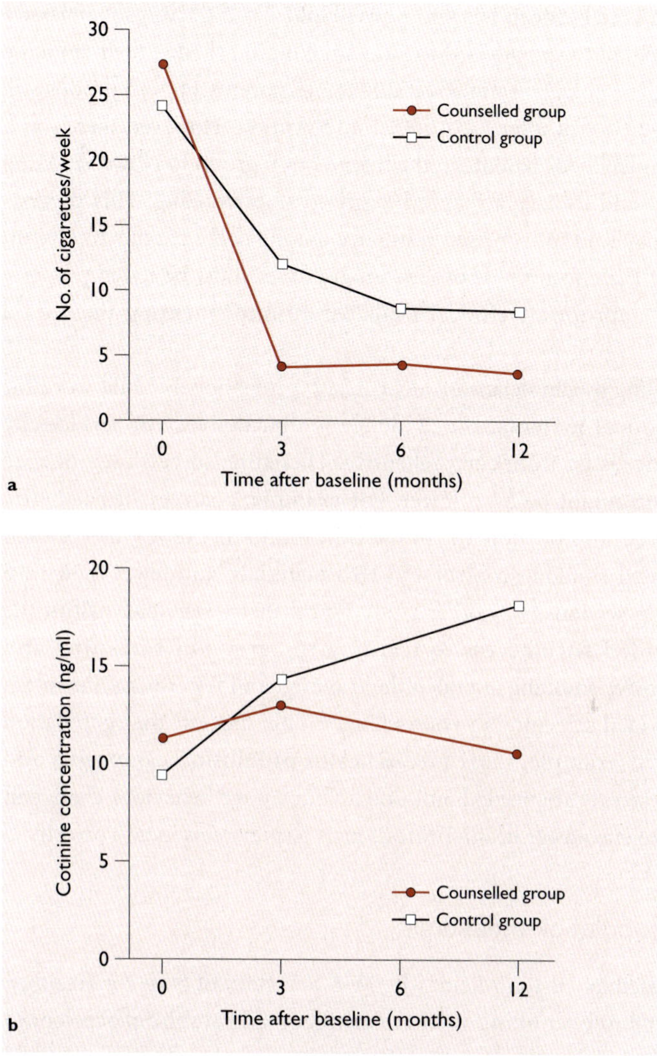

Figure 6.1 Effect of counselling mothers on their children's exposure to tobacco smoke, (a) as reported by the mother, and (b) as objectively validated by urinary cotinine level.[55]

Whilst it remains possible that better designed and implemented counselling interventions may have a modest effect, care needs to be taken in designing and testing new approaches to consider the possibility raised by one study that there may be potential to cause harm.[60] In this case, a randomised controlled trial examined the effect of intensive counselling to give up smoking delivered by a nurse in the home, plus the provision of printed cessation information materials, compared with participants who received only printed materials. Parents of asthmatic children aged between two and 12 were told about the impact of passive smoking on asthma and were advised to stop smoking or change their smoking habits to protect their child's health. Overall, 98% of parents in both groups still smoked at follow-up a year after the original intervention. However, there was a non-significant tendency for parents in the intervention group to report smoking more at follow-up and to have a reduced desire to stop smoking. This suggests that counselling may lead to increased resistance among some parents to give up smoking, and that the effectiveness of new programmes must be tested properly in the context of appropriate clinical trials before implementing them on a widespread basis.

Even if counselling by physicians or other health professionals could work for a small proportion of patients, the evidence is that delivery of services by clinicians in practice is far from comprehensive. Therefore, success rates outside of research settings might be even lower. For example, a survey of paediatric office-based interventions on smoking in the USA found that fewer than 50% of clinicians distributed smoking control and ETS materials, and fewer than 12% provided follow-up sessions.[61] Another study found that fewer than half of the physicians provided with access to training to carry out screening and counselling for passive smoking attended the training, and fewer than one in ten subsequently provided screening or counselling.[62] This suggests that population level changes – for example, mass media health promotion campaigns and smoke-free workplaces – are needed, not only to encourage behaviour change in smokers but also to encourage health professionals to make this issue a priority.

6.9 Impact of population measures

Concerns were raised by Dr John Reid, when UK Secretary of State for Health,[63] that preventing people smoking in the workplace and public places could encourage smokers to smoke more in the home, and thereby expose their families and children to harm. This explanation was used by Dr Reid to justify exemptions in the Government's proposed legislation on smoke-free public places for pubs that do not serve food, and private clubs. However, there is no evidence that this is the case; in fact the reverse seems to be true.

As shown in Chapter 3, population level research has shown that exposure of children in England to ETS, objectively measured by cotinine levels, halved in the decade between 1988 and 1998, and that this decline has continued in recent years. This was mainly due to decreases in the percentage of parents who smoked and the exposure of children from non-smoking households.[9] However, there was also some reduction in exposure of children living with mothers or fathers who smoked and certainly no evidence that growing restrictions on smoking outside the home had led to increased exposure within the home. In addition, at any level of parental cigarette consumption, children from poorer backgrounds have substantially higher cotinines and this is just as evident in children from non-smoking homes. The implication is that children from poorer homes are exposed to higher levels of ETS outside the home and so will benefit to a greater extent from comprehensive smoke-free legislation than children from better off homes.

It is clear, therefore, that the most effective means of protecting children from tobacco smoke is encouraging parents to give up smoking or, if they carry on smoking, to not smoke in the home. A systematic review of 26 studies on the effects of smoke-free workplaces found that totally smoke-free workplaces are associated with reductions in prevalence of smoking of around 4%.[64] For those who carried on smoking, smoke-free workplaces were associated with an average of three fewer cigarettes per day per smoker. It is likely, therefore, that smoke-free legislation in workplaces and public places will have a secondary protective effect on harm caused by ETS, by reducing smoking prevalence and cigarette consumption.

Research shows that where smoke-free workplaces and enclosed public places are the norm, parents report that they are more likely to try to prevent smoking in the home.[65,66] As shown in Fig 6.2, being employed in smoke-free workplaces increased the likelihood of smoke-free homes for both current and past smokers,[67,68,69] and smoke-free workplaces and public places have also been linked to lower exposure of children to tobacco smoke pollution in the

Figure 6.2. Trends in the percentage of adults reporting workplace smoking restrictions,[68] and of adult smokers who report that they always smoke outside the home,[69] in the State of Victoria, Australia, 1988 to 2001 (smoking restriction data interpolated for 1996 and 2000).

home.[69–70] The key, however, is that in these cases the introduction of smoke-free workplaces went hand in hand with comprehensive health promotion campaigns involving advertising and education.[70,71,72] A recent study of a national representative sample of smokers in Ireland surveyed both before and after the implementation of smoke-free legislation in March 2004 found that there was a statistically significant increase in the percentage of smokers who banned smoking in their own homes after the law was introduced.[73]

In England, too, health promotion campaigns have been linked to behaviour change in adults. In summer 2003, the Department of Health ran a heavy weight media campaign to raise general public awareness of the health risks of smoking around children. The aim was to encourage any adults who currently smoke around children to change their behaviour. The campaign was backed up by widely distributed education materials promoted by healthcare professionals, including midwives, health visitors and smoking cessation counsellors, to new parents and families. Prior to the campaign, 28% of respondents stated spontaneously that second-hand smoke was a risk to children's health. This rose to 50% after the campaign with 3% of smokers claiming they had given up as a result of the advertising, and 19% of smokers claiming that they had stopped smoking around children.[74] However, evidence from elsewhere shows that a one-off campaign such as this is unlikely to have a long-term impact and needs to be part of an overall long-term strategy for reducing smoking around children. Objective evidence from the Health Survey for England shows that cotinine exposures for both children and adults living with smokers are significantly lower in homes with an apparent smoking ban than for homes where smoking is allowed (see Chapter 3). The proportion of homes where such a ban appears to be in force has increased steadily in recent years (see Chapter 3), in line with the increase in non-smoking workplaces[41] and public places, but is still a minority of smokers' homes. There is, therefore, clear evidence that the most effective way to increase the proportion of smoke-free homes would be to introduce comprehensive legislation to enforce smoke-free workplaces and enclosed public places, without the exemptions envisaged by the Government in the White Paper.[75]

6.10 Summary

- ETS exposure in the home is particularly harmful for young children.
- Awareness of the health risks of ETS exposure in children is relatively low.
- The most effective control measure is for parents and carers to quit smoking entirely.

- Alternatively, making homes completely smoke-free reduces ETS exposure significantly.
- Attempts to reduce ETS exposure by limiting smoking to parts of the home away from children have not proved successful.
- Measures targeted at individuals or households and intended to reduce smoking in the home while stopping short of making the home smoke-free are unlikely to have a major impact on ETS exposure at home.
- Smoke-free public places reduce the exposure of children to tobacco smoke outside the home.
- There is no evidence that smoke-free workplaces and enclosed public places increase the exposure of children to ETS at home.
- Smoke-free workplaces and enclosed public places lead to reductions in smoking prevalence and also to reduced smoking and, therefore, reduced ETS exposure at home, particularly if backed up by comprehensive health education programmes.
- Population and individual-level interventions to encourage smoking cessation, including smoke-free public places, are, therefore, the most effective means of reducing ETS exposure at home.

References

1 United Nations Office of the High Commissioner for Human rights. *Convention on the rights of the child* (adopted by the UN General Assembly November 1989; entry into force September 1990). www.unhchr.ch/html/menu3/b/k2crc.htm

2 Environment Leaders' Summit of the Eight. *1997 Declaration of the Environment Leaders of the Eight on Children's Environmental Health.* www.g8.utoronto.ca/environment/1997miami/children.html

3 World Health Organization. *Tobacco and the rights of the child.* (WHO/NMH/TFI/01.3 WHO), 2001. www.who.int/tobacco/resources/publications/rights_child/en/

4 World Health Organization. *WHO Framework convention of tobacco control.* Geneva: WHO, 2003 www.who.int/tobacco/framework/download/en/

5 Action on Smoking and Health. Press release: Research highlights parents' ignorance of health effects of passive smoking on children, May 2001. www.ash.org.uk/html/press/010531.html

6 news.bbc.co.uk/1/hi/uk/3000035.stm

7 Alan Milburn on Breakfast with Frost, 4 May 2003

8 Ezra D. Sticks and Stones can break my bones but tobacco smoke can kill me: can we protect children from parents that smoke? *St Louis U Pub L Rev* 1994;13:547–90

9 Jarvis MJ, Goddard E, Higgins V, Feyeraband C *et al.* Children's exposure to passive smoking in England since the 1980s: cotinine evidence from population surveys. *BMJ* 2000;321:343–345.

10 Office for National Statistics. *2003/4 General Household Survey.* www.statistics.gov.uk/ghs/

11 Jarvis MJ, Strachan D, Feyeraband C. Determinants of Passive Smoking in Children in Edinburgh, Scotland. *Am JP Health.* 1992;**82**:1225–1229.
12 Jarvis, L. *Teenage smoking attitudes in 1996.* London: ONS, 1997.
13 Jarvis MJ, Russell MA, Feyeraband C, Eiser JR *et al.* Passive exposure to tobacco smoke: saliva cotinine concentrations in a representative population sample of non-smoking schoolchildren. *BMJ* 1985;**291**:927–929.
14 Blackburn CM, Spencer N, Bonas S, Coe C *et al.* Parental smoking and passive smoking in infants: fathers matter too. *Health Educ Res.* 2005 Apr;**20**(2):185–94.
15 Cook DG, Whincup PH, Jarvis MJ, Strachan DP *et al.* Passive exposure to tobacco smoke in children aged 5-7 years: Individual, family and community factors. *BMJ* 1994; **308**(6925):384–389.
16 Eskenazi B, Bergmann JJ. Passive and active maternal smoking during pregnant, as measured by serum cotinine and postnatal smoke exposure. Effects on physical growth at age 5 years. *Am J Epidemiol* 1995;**142**:S10–S18.
17 Windham GC, Hopkins B, Fenster L, Swan SH. Prenatal active or passive tobacco smoke exposure and the risk of preterm delivery or low birth weight. E*pidemiology* 2000;**11**: 427–433.
18 Goel P, Radotra A, Singh I, Aggarwal A, Dua D. Effects of passive smoking on outcome in pregnancy. *J Postgrad Med* 2004:**50**:12–16.
19 Barber K, Mussein E, Taylor DK. Fetal exposure to involuntary maternal smoking and childhood respiratory disease. *Ann Allergy Asthma Immunol* 1996;**76**:427–430.
20 Venners SA, Wang X, Chen C, Wang L *et al.* Paternal smoking and pregnancy loss: a prospective study using a biomarker of pregnancy. *Am J Epidemiol* 2004;**159**:993–1001.
21 Lodrup CK, Jaakkola JJ, Nafstad P, Carlsen KH. In utero exposure to cigarette smoking influences lung function at birth. *Eur Respir J* 1997;**10**:1774–1779.
22 Mainous AG, Hueston WJ. Passive smoke and low birth weight. Evidence of a threshold effect. *Arch Fam Med* 1994;**3**:875–878.
23 Misra DP, Nguyen RH. Environmental tobacco smoke and low birth weight: a hazard in the workplace? *Environ Health Perspect* 1999;**107**(Suppl 6):897–904.
24 Rebagliato M, Florey CV, Bolumar F. Exposure to environmental tobacco smoke in non-smoking pregnant women in relation to birth weight. *Am J Epidemiol* 1995;**142**:531–537.
25 Kharrazi M, DeLorenze GN, Kaufman FL, Eskenazi B *et al* Environmental tobacco smoke and pregnancy outcome. *Epidemiology* 2004;**15**:660–670.
26 Anderson HR, and Cook DG. Passive smoking and sudden infant death syndrome: review of the epidemiological evidence. *Thorax* 1997;**52**:1003–9.
27 Strachan DP, Cook DG. Parental smoking and lower respiratory illness in infancy and early childhood. *Thorax* 1997; **52**:905–914.
28 California Environmental Protection Agency Office of Environmental Health Hazard Assessment. *Health effects of exposure to environmental tobacco smoke.* California: EPA, 1997.
29 Asthma UK. National Asthma Panel Survey 2004. Stratified sample of 1,500 people with asthma across the UK. Unpublished, personal communication from Martin Dockrell, Asthma UK.
30 Mannino DM, Moorman JE, Kingsley B, Rose D, Repace J. Health effects related to environmental tobacco smoke exposure in children in the United States. *Arch Pediatr Adolesc Med.* 2001;**155**:36–41.
31 World Health Organization. *International consultation on environmental tobacco smoke (ETS) and child health.* Consultation report. WHO, 1999.
32 Nageris B. Effects of passive smoking on odour identification in children. *J Otolaryngol.* 2001;**30**(5):263–5.

33 Gilliland FD, Berhane K, McConnell R *et al.* Maternal smoking during pregnancy, environmental tobacco smoke exposure and childhood lung function. *Thorax.* 2000;**55**:271–276.

34 Royal College of Physicians. *Smoking and the young.* London: RCP, 1992.

35 British Medical Association Board of Science and Education & Tobacco Control Resource Centre. *Towards smoke-free public places.* London: BMA, 2002.

36 Goddard, E. *Drug use, smoking and drinking among young teenagers in 1999.* London: Office for National Statistics, 2000.

37 Farkas AJ, Gilpin EA, White MM, Pierce JP. Association between household and workplace smoking restrictions and adolescent smoking. *JAMA* 2000;**284**:717–722.

38 Office for National Statistics. *Teenage smoking attitudes in 1996.* London: Office for National Statistics, 1997.

39 Kandel DB, Wu P, Davies M. Maternal smoking during pregnancy and smoking by adolescent daughters. *Am J Public Health* 1994;**84**:1407–1413.

40 Cornelius MD, Leech SL, Goldschmidt L, Day NL. Prenatal tobacco exposure: is it a risk factor for early tobacco experimentation? *Nicotine Tob Res* 2000;**2**:45–52.

41 Lader D, Goddard E. *Smoking related behaviour and attitudes, 2003.* London: Office for National Statistics, 2004.

42 British Market Research Bureau. Telephone survey of 2,040 adults, January 2001.

43 Repace J. Risk Management of passive smoking at work and at home. *St Louis U Pub L Rev* 1994;**13**:763–85.

44 Winkelstein M, Tarzian A, Wood R. Parental smoking behaviour and passive smoke exposure in children with asthma. *Ann Allergy Asthma Immunol* 1997;**78**:419–23.

45 Borland R. *Theories of behaviour change in relation to ETS control to protect children.* Background paper for World Health Organization International consultation on environmental tobacco smoke and child health WHO/NCD/TFI/99.11, 1999.

46 Lumley J, Oliver S, Waters E. Individual behaviour counselling for smoking cessation (Cochrane Review) In: *The Cochrane Library, 4.* Oxford: Update Software. CD001055, *2002.*

47 Lelong N, Kminski M, Saurel-Cubizolles MJ, Bouvier-Colle MH. Postpartum return to smoking among usual smokers who quit during pregnancy. *Eur J Public Health* 2001;**11**:334–9.

48 Lancaster T, Stead LF. Individual behavioural counselling for smoking cessation (Cochrane Review). In: *The Cochrane Library, 4.* Oxford: Update Software. CD001292, 2002

49 Silagy C, Stead LF. Physician advice for smoking cessation (Cochrane Review). In: *The Cochrane Library, 4.* Oxford: Update Software. CD000165, 2002.

50 Roseby R, Waters E, Polnay A, Campbell R *et al.* Family and carer smoking control programmes for reducing children's exposure to environmental tobacco smoke (Cochrane Review). In: *The Cochrane Library, 3.* Chichester, UK: John Wiley & Sons, Ltd, 2004

51 Wahlgren D, Hovell F, Meltzer S, Hofstetter R, Zakarian M. Reduction of environmental tobacco smoke exposure in asthmatic children: a two-year follow-up. *Chest* 1997;**111**;81–88.

52 Emmons KM, Hammond SK, Fava JL, Velicer WF *et al.* A randomised trial to reduce passive smoking exposure in low-income households with young children. *Pediatrics* 2001;**108**(1):18–24.

53 Matthews F. Birth outcome predicted by cotinine level. *Ann Clin Biochem* 1999;**36**:468–76.

54 Jarvis MJ, Tunstall-Pedoe H, Feyerabend C, Vesey C, Saloojee Y. Comparison tests used to distinguish smokers from nonsmokers. *Am J Public Health* 1987:77:1435–38.

55 Hovell MF, Zakarian JM, Matt GE, Hofstetter CR *et al.* Effects of counselling mothers on their children's exposure to environmental tobacco smoke: randomised controlled trial. *BMJ* 2000;**321**:337–342.
56 Mattanini MA, Thuer B (eds). *Finding solutions to social problems: behavioural strategies for change.* Washington DC: American Psychological Association, 1996.
57 Peterson EL, Johnson CC, Ownby DR. Use of urinary cotinine and questionnaires in the evaluation of infant exposure to tobacco smoke in epidemiological studies. *J Clin Epidemiol* 1997;**8**:917–923.
58 Zhang D, Qiu X. School-based tobacco use prevention. People's Republic of China, May 1989–January 1990. *MMWR Morb Mortal Wkly Rep* 1993;**42**(19):370–371.
59 Gehrman CA, Hovell MF. Protecting children from environmental tobacco smoke (ETS) exposure: a critical review. *Nicotine Tob Res* 2003;**5**:289–301.
60 Irvine L, Crombie IK, Clark RA, Slane PW *et al.* Advising parents of asthmatic children on passive smoking: randomised controlled trial. *BMJ* 1999;**318**:1456–1459.
61 Hymowitz N. A survey of pediatric office-based interventions on smoking. *New Jersey Med* 1995;**92**:657–60.
62 Narce-Valente S, Kligman E. Increasing physician screening and counselling for passive smoking. *J Fam Practice* 1992;**34**:722–8.
63 Evidence to the Health Select Committee into the Government's Public Health White Paper, 23 February 2005. www.publications.parliament.uk/pa/cm200405/cmselect/cmhealth/358/5022301.htm
64 Fichtenberg C, Glantz S, Effects of smoke-free workplaces on smoking behaviour: a systematic review. *BMJ* 2002;**325**:188–91.
65 Borland R, Mullins R, Trotter L, White V. Trends in environmental tobacco smoke restrictions in the home in Victoria, Australia. *Tob Control* 1999;**8**:266–271.
66 Soliman S, Pollack H, Warner K. Decrease in prevalence of environmental tobacco smoke exposure in the home during the 1990s in families with children. *Am J Public Health* 2004;**94**(2):314–20.
67 Merom D, Rissel C. Factors associated with smoke-free homes in NSW: results from the 1998 NSW Health Survey. *Aust NZ J Public Health* 2001;**254**:339–345.
68 Letcher T, Borland R. Smoking bans in Victorian workplaces: 2001 update. In: Letcher T, Trotter L (eds), *Quit Victoria research and evaluation studies No. 11: 2000–2001.* Melbourne: Victorian Smoking and Health Program, 2003.
69 Trotter L, Mullins R. Environmental tobacco smoke: Public opinions and behaviour in 2000–01. In: Letcher T, Trotter L (eds), *Quit Victoria research and evaluation studies No. 11: 2000-2001.* Melbourne: Victorian Smoking and Health Program, 2003.
70 Levy DT, Romano E, Mumford EA. Recent trends in home and work smoking bans. *Tob Control* 2004;**13**:258–263.
71 Hill DJ, White VM, Scollo MM. Smoking behaviour of Australian adults in 1995: trends and concerns. *Med Aus* 1998;**168**:209–13.
72 Koh HK Accomplishments of the Massachusetts Tobacco Control Programme. *Tob Control* 2002;**11**(Supp 2):1–3.
73 Fong GT, Hyland A, Borland R, Hammond D *et al. Initial evaluation of the comprehensive smoke-free workplace legislation in the Republic of Ireland: findings from the ITC-Ireland/UK Survey.* Presentation at the meeting of the Society for Research on Nicotine and Tobacco. Prague, March 22, 2005.
74 British Market Research Bureau. *Tracking of Department of Health Tobacco Education Campaign, 2003.*
75 Department of Heath. *Choosing health: making healthy choices easier.* London: DH, 2004.

7 The impact of partial and complete smoke-free policies on the prevalence of smoking and consumption of tobacco

7.1 Introduction

The introduction of smoke-free policies at work confers several benefits. Principal among these is the protection of the health of staff, clients and visitors against harm caused by ETS, though in many cases it is likely that smoke-free policies were introduced to avoid immediate nuisance effects, rather than to protect against longer-term health risks. However, smoke-free policies have important effects on smoking behaviour, which also deserve to be recognised and considered in assessing their impact. There is now increasing evidence that when workplaces go smoke-free, employees who smoke are likely at least to reduce their cigarette consumption and, more importantly, a substantial proportion will quit smoking completely. There is also evidence that smoke-free policies in schools and private homes can help to reduce the uptake of smoking by adolescents.

7.2 Comprehensive versus partial smoke-free policies

Substantial evidence from many different countries (based on self-reported exposure and consequent reactions and symptoms,[1–3] or on air-sampling[4] and measurement of bio-markers[5–7]) demonstrates that in the absence of protection by comprehensive smoke-free policies, exposure to ETS in the workplace is common and, in some circumstances, very intense (see Chapters 3 and 5). As well as preventing exposure to ETS, comprehensive smoke-free policies have the advantage of being unambiguous, which can facilitate compliance.[4] They have, therefore, become the gold standard public health response to the hazard of passive smoking. Policies based on courtesy, segregation or ventilation are regarded as distinctly inferior and, if acceptable at all, they could be adopted only as a time-limited 'stepping-stone' towards the introduction of comprehensive smoke-free provisions in particular settings.

7.3 Short-term compliance with smoke-free policies

Almost every extension of smoke-free policies to a new setting is greeted initially with disbelief that it can be made to work. However, it is also clear that there are many places, such as cinemas, theatres and the London Underground, in which smoking was commonplace in the relatively recent past and yet is now almost unthinkable. In its time, extension of smoke-free policies to public transport was contentious; doubt was expressed, for example, that smokers would be able to refrain from lighting up when travelling by air, particularly during long-haul flights. While anticipated difficulties with compliance and a consequent need for official enforcement are frequently advanced as reasons not to introduce smoke-free policies, deliberate breaches of smoke-free policies on aircraft have rapidly become so rare as to be newsworthy. More recently, smoke-free policies have become increasingly common in outdoor sports venues, and, once again, compliance has been found to be high[8] and the need for official enforcement low.

Smoke-free policies in hospitals have also been contentious in the past because they can require smokers admitted to hospital as patients to abstain from smoking for several days or more. Such policies have often been introduced only after claims relating to the 'comfort' and immobility of patients who wish to smoke have been dismissed in favour of concerns about the rights of other patients, protection of the health of staff, the exemplar role of health services or issues of fire safety. Making hospitals smoke-free can cause problems for patients who are smokers, and compliance can be incomplete, but being obliged not to smoke while in hospital is strongly predictive of continuing abstention after discharge.[9] This provides a hint regarding the impact of adopting smoke-free policies in workplaces on smoking among employees.

7.4 Effects on smoking of smoke-free policies in workplaces

It has been shown repeatedly that making workplaces smoke-free produces a measurable decrease in the prevalence of smoking among employees, and that those who continue to smoke tend to consume fewer cigarettes each day. The most authoritative source of information in this area is the systematic review and meta-analysis by Fichtenberg and Glantz of twenty-six studies performed in three continents.[10] Additional supportive evidence recently became available from evaluation of a package of tobacco control initiatives in New York.[11]

Effects on prevalence

Fichtenberg and Glantz found that if workplaces that do not restrict smoking implement a completely smoke-free policy, the absolute prevalence of smoking among employees falls on average by 3.8 (95% confidence interval (CI): 2.8–4.7) percentage points.[10] Implementing restrictions on smoking but stopping short of becoming completely smoke-free achieves about half of this effect. This impact is apparent very quickly, and is substantially greater than the average annual absolute decline in the prevalence of smoking in the UK.[12] However, making all workplaces smoke-free would not result in a reduction of 3.8 percentage points in the prevalence of smoking across the whole of the UK population because not all adults are employed, and because a sizeable proportion of workplaces are already partially or completely smoke-free. In 2003, only 8% of people who worked with others were subject to no restrictions on smoking, 38% were subject to partial restrictions, and half were already protected by complete smoke-free policies at work.[12]

The likely impact of implementing universal smoke-free policies at work in the UK can be estimated by allowing a four percentage point fall in the prevalence of smoking in those currently working without restrictions on smoking, and of two percentage points in those subject to partial restrictions. This suggests that the overall national impact might be a reduction in the population-wide prevalence of smoking of about one percentage point. Such a change would be important in terms of public and individual health, the more so because there has been a significant slowing in the long downwards trend in smoking in the community. However, the estimate of 1% may be unduly conservative; many workplaces are also public places and restrictions on smoking may reduce consumption and prompt cessation among the public. For example, there is evidence that making the subset of workplaces that are hospitality venues smoke-free is likely to prompt a proportion of 'occasional' smokers among the patrons to give up the habit entirely.[13]

Effects on consumption

The introduction of smoke-free policies in workplaces is also followed by a reduction in the number of cigarettes consumed by continuing smokers.[10]

Chapman *et al* estimated that the introduction of comprehensive smoke-free policies in all workplaces in Australia would result in a reduction of 3.4% in national sales of cigarettes.[14]

While there is abundant epidemiological evidence that risks to health increase progressively with the amount that an individual smokes, the benefits of a modest reduction in consumption in response to one's workplace becoming smoke-free are less certain. Smokers may compensate for their reduced opportunities to smoke by consuming more of each cigarette, taking more and larger puffs, and holding each puff for longer. Thus, the likely impact of smoke-free policies on sales of tobacco is unlikely to be reflected completely in reduced exposure to tobacco smoke among continuing smokers.[15] As it is the continuation of any smoking rather than the amount smoked that poses the greater threat to health in the longer term,[16] the modest reduction in consumption by continuing smokers in response to smoke-free policies may in itself have little impact on health.

Effects on uptake of smoking

Combining data from national surveys conducted in the US in 1992–3 and 1995–6, Farkas *et al* reported that among 4,231 15- to 17-year-olds who had a paid job outside the home, the prevalence of ever-smoking was 32% lower (95% CI: 10–49%) in those employed indoors in a smoke-free workplace compared with those in jobs with partial restrictions on smoking.[17] This observation may, to some extent, arise from selection bias whereby teenagers who have chosen not to smoke or who have given up smoking may seek smoke-free workplaces preferentially. However, having made that choice, the prevailing policy might have protected them from pro-smoking influences.

7.5 Effects of smoke-free policies in schools

In contrast to substantial evidence on the impact of school-based anti-smoking education programmes, relatively little is known about the effect of whole-of-school smoke-free policies on smoking behaviour of school pupils. As in other settings, it is useful to separate feasibility of implementation and apparent impact when considering smoke-free policies in schools.

All public and state-supported schools in California were obliged to adopt comprehensive smoke-free policies in 1995. Based on four cycles of the large California Tobacco Survey, Trinidad *et al* reported that the proportion of secondary school pupils who perceived complete compliance by students with school-wide no-smoking policies increased from 44% to 72% between 1993 and 2002, while perceived compliance among teachers rose from 81% in 1996 to 87% in 2002.[18] Thus, policies that prohibit smoking anywhere within school premises appear feasible.

Such policies are apparently the exception in Denmark where Poulsen *et al* report that 61% of 15-year-olds see their teachers smoking in the school grounds, and 87% report seeing teachers smoking within school buildings.[19] Reports of seeing teachers smoking in the school grounds were associated with an 80% (95% CI: 20–180%) increase in the chance of the pupil themself being a smoker, after taking into account parental smoking, smoking by best friends and classmates, and the individual student's sex. There was no significant relationship between smoking habits of pupils and their teachers smoking inside school buildings.

Using cross-sectional data from a national survey of 17,287 secondary students in the United States, and after allowing for smoking in a child's family, Wakefield *et al* found that the chance of a young person having smoked in the previous 30 days was reduced by 14% (95% CI: 6–23%) if he or she attended a school in which a no-smoking rule for students was strongly enforced.[20] This criterion was judged from high reported compliance with the rule by the student body. The published report gives no indication about smoking behaviour among teachers or its relationship to the adolescents' smoking habits.

Each of these reports is open potentially to some degree of both observer bias and selection bias. Students who smoke may be more likely to notice teachers smoking and less likely to report that no-smoking rules are upheld. Families with strong negative views about smoking may systematically seek out schools with congruent policies, even if one or both of the parents smoke. But these caveats are speculative, and, taken at face value, both surveys suggest that adoption of comprehensive smoke-free policies in schools – policies that apply indoors and outdoors, to students, teaching and other staff, and to all visitors to the school – could help to reduce the uptake of smoking by young people.

7.6 Effects of smoke-free policies at home

It has long been established that the children of non-smokers are less likely to take up smoking. More recently, there has been interest in whether adoption of smoke-free policies in private homes might have a similar effect.

In smoke-free homes, smokers in the household, and all visitors, are obliged to smoke outside. There is no doubt that such policies are now widespread in both Australia and the United States; 55% of homes in the US were smoke-free in the mid-1990s,[17] while the equivalent figure for New South Wales in 1998 was 72%.[21]

Based on the two national surveys conducted in 1992–3 and 1995–6 by the US Census Bureau, Farkas *et al* reported that the prevalence of having ever smoked among 15- to 17-year-olds was 26% lower (95% CI: 12–38%) in the 8,756 living in smoke-free homes, compared with the 4,549 from households with no restrictions on smoking.[17] Living in a home with partial restrictions on smoking appeared to have no impact on the prevalence of ever-smoking among a further 3,880 teenagers.

In the survey analysed by Wakefield *et al*,[20] which was conducted in 1996 using schools rather than the general population as the sampling frame, 48% of US homes were described as prohibiting smoking overtly. Such policies were associated with a 21% (95% CI: 9–33%) reduction in the 30-day prevalence of smoking among the adolescent respondents. The equivalent figures for teenagers living in homes with policies that limited smoking to special guests or areas was 15% (5–26%), providing some evidence of a 'dose-response' effect.

A survey of 4,495 college students in the US revealed an even stronger association between living in smoke-free accommodation and being a current smoker oneself. The prevalence of smoking was 31% lower among students in smoke-free housing, 21% of whom were smokers, compared with those living in settings where smoking was not restricted (30.6% smokers).[22] Despite this pattern obviously being open to bias related to self-selection – the same way non-smoking adolescents may choose to work in smoke-free jobs – the decision to live in smoke-free premises may have helped to reduce any late uptake of smoking among never-smokers and lowered the chance of relapse among ex-smokers.

7.7 Effects of smoke-free policies on morbidity and mortality

Smoke-free policies self-evidently prevent the nuisance effects of ETS, but will also reduce morbidity and mortality, both directly, by preventing exposure to ETS, and indirectly, through their effect on the prevalence of smoking. The magnitudes of these direct and indirect effects are difficult to estimate precisely but both are likely to be substantial in the longer term (see Chapter 4).[23,24] Evidence of the more immediate impact of preventing exposure to ETS on health outcomes is relatively limited. An ecological study from the small community of Helena in Montana suggests that admission to hospital for acute myocardial infarction (heart attack) fell appreciably in Helena residents, but not in persons who worked in Helena and were resident outside, during a six-month period in which all public places and workplaces were smoke-free (see Fig 7.1).[25] More direct evidence of benefit to health from adopting smoke-free policies is available

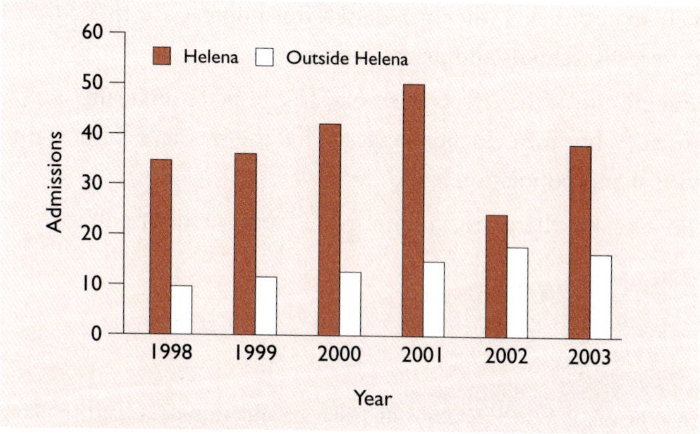

Fig 7.1 Admissions for acute myocardial infarction in June-November before, during and after smoke-free law in Helena on 5 June 2002, in persons resident in Helena (and thus benefiting from the smoke-free policy) and those resident outside Helena.[25]

from a small study of bar staff in California, in whom improvements in objective measures of lung function that were both clinically and statistically significant were observed when their workplaces became smoke-free.[26]

7.8 Effect of smoke-free policies on public opinion

As stated above, extensions of smoke-free policies to new settings are often contentious when they are first proposed, but more often than not their implementation proves easier than anticipated, and both initial and sustained requirements for enforcement are negligible. The available evidence from published studies confirms that support for smoke-free policies increases after their introduction (See also Chapter 15).[27,28]

7.9 Summary

- Comprehensive smoke-free policies can be implemented successfully in a wide variety of settings, in private as well as public venues, are generally well accepted, and achieve high levels of compliance.
- Making workplaces and other public places smoke-free is the best way to prevent the harmful effects of exposure to ETS.
- Smoke-free policies reduce the prevalence and uptake of smoking, and hence indirectly reduce smoking-related harm. Smoke-free policies also reduce consumption of cigarettes in those who continue to smoke. These

effects are likely to be realised wherever smoke-free policies are applied, including workplaces, schools and private homes.

- The precise magnitude of the effects of smoke-free policies on health is difficult to quantify, but the evidence suggests that the impact is important at both individual and population levels.
- Smoke-free policies are, therefore, an important component of public health policy.

References

1 Brenner H, Born J, Novak P, Wanek V. Smoking behavior and attitude toward smoking regulations and passive smoking in the workplace. A study among 974 employees in the German metal industry. *Prev Med* 1997;**26**:138–43.

2 Willemsen WM, de Vries H, Genders R. Annoyance from environmental tobacco smoke and support for no-smoking policies at eight large Dutch workplaces. *Tob Control* 1996;**5**:132–8.

3 Mizoue T, Reijula K, Yamato H, Iwasaki A, Yoshimura T. Support for and observance of worksite smoking restriction policies A study of municipal employees at a city office in Japan. *Prev Med* 1999;**29**:549–54.

4 Jenkins RA, Maskarinec MP, Counts RW, Caton JE *et al.* Environmental tobacco smoke in an unrestricted smoking workplace: area and personal exposure monitoring. *J Expo Anal Environ Epidemiol* 2001;**11**:369–80.

5 Wortley PM, Caraballo RS, Pederson LL, Pechacek TF. Exposure to secondhand smoke in the workplace: serum cotinine by occupation. *J Occup Environ Med* 2002;**44**:503–9.

6 Bates MN, Fawcett J, Dickson S, Berezowski R, Garrett N. Exposure of hospitality workers to environmental tobacco smoke. *Tob Control* 2002;**11**:125–9.

7 Al-Delamy W, Fraser T, Woodward A. Nicotine in hair of bar and restaurant workers. *NZ Med J* 2001;**114**:80–3.

8 Pikora T, Phang JW, Karro J, Corti B *et al.* Are smoke-free policies implemented and adhered to at sporting venues? *Aust NZ J Public Health* 1999;**23**:407–9.

9 Rigotti NA, Arnsten JH, McKool KM, Wood-Reid KM *et al.* Smoking by patients in a smoke-free hospital: prevalence, predictors, and implications. *Prev Med* 2000;**31**:159–66.

10 Fichtenberg CM, Glantz SA. Effect of smoke-free policies on smoking behaviour: systematic review. *BMJ* 2002;**325**:188–94.

11 Frieden TR, Mostashari F, Kerker BD, Miller N, Hajat A, Frankel M. Adult tobacco use levels after intensive tobacco control measures: New York City, 2002–2003. *Am J Public Health* 2005;**95**:1016–23.

12 Lader D, Goddard L. *Smoking-related behaviour and attitudes, 2003.* London: Office for National Statistics, 2004.

13 Philpot SJ, Ryan SA, Torre LE, Wilcox HM *et al.* Effect of smoke-free policies on the behaviour of social smokers. *Tob Control* 1999;**8**:278–81.

14 Chapman S, Borland R, Scollo M, Brownson RC *et al.* The impact of smoke-free workplaces on declining cigarette consumption in Australia and the United States. *Am J Public Health* 1999;**89**:1018–23.

15 Chapman S, Haddad S, Sindhusake D. Do work-place smoking bans cause smokers to smoke 'harder'? Results from a naturalistic observational study. *Addiction* 1997;**92**:607–10.

16 Peto R, Roe FJ, Lee PN, Levy L, Clack J. Cancer and ageing in mice and men. *Br J Cancer* 1975;**32**:411–26.

17 Farkas AJ, Gilpin EA, White MM, Pierce JP. Association between household and workplace smoking restrictions and adolescent smoking. *JAMA* 2000;**284**:717–22.

18 Trinidad DR, Gilpin EA, Pierce JP. Compliance and support for smoke-free school policies. *Health Educ Res* 2004 Nov 30; [Epub ahead of print].

19 Poulsen LH, Osler M, Roberts C, Due P *et al.* Exposure to teachers smoking and adolescent smoking behaviour: analysis of cross sectional data from Denmark. *Tob Control* 2002;**11**:246–51.

20 Wakefield MA, Chaloupka FJ, Kaufman NJ, Orleans CT *et al.* Effect of restrictions on smoking at home, at school, and in public places on teenage smoking: cross sectional study. *BMJ* 2000;**321**:333–7.

21 Merom D, Rissel C. Factors associated with smoke-free homes in NSW: results from the 1998 NSW Health Survey. *Aust NZ J Public Health* 2001;**25**:339–45.

22 Wechsler H, Lee JE, Rigotti NA. Cigarette use by college students in smoke-free housing: results of a national study. *Am J Prev Med* 2001;**20**:202–7.

23 Lewis S, Arnott D, Godfrey C, Britton J. Public health measures to reduce smoking prevalence in the United Kingdom: how many lives could be saved? *Tob Control* (In press)

24 Ong MK, Glantz SA. Cardiovascular health and economic effects of smoke-free workplaces. *Am J Med* 2004;**117**:32–8.

25 Sargent RP, Shepard RM, Glantz SA. Reduced incidence of admissions for myocardial infarction associated with public smoking ban: before and after study. *BMJ* 2004;**328**:977–80.

26 Eisner MD, Smith AK, Blanc PD. Bartenders' respiratory health after establishment of smoke-free bars and taverns. *JAMA* 1998;**280**:1909–14.

27 Miller C, Wakefield M, Kriven S, Hyland A. Evaluation of smoke-free dining in South Australia: support and compliance among the community and restaurateurs. *Aust NZ J Public Health* 2002;**26**:38–44.

28 Giles-Corti B, Clarkson JP, Donovan RJ, Frizzell SK *et al.* Creating smoke-free environments in recreational settings. *Health Educ Behav* 2001;**28**:341–51.

8 The legal perspective on work and leisure exposure to environmental tobacco smoke

8.1 Introduction

The evidence reviewed in the earlier chapters of this book make it clear that ETS exposure is harmful. This, in turn, raises important questions as to the legal rights and responsibilities of the public as well as of employees and employers in relation to limiting or preventing ETS exposure. However, ETS is exempt currently from UK legislation designed to protect employees from hazardous occupational exposures on the grounds that ETS exposure does not arise from manufacturing or other processes that are fundamental to the occupation itself, but from smoking by other staff, customers or visitors. At present, there is no legislation in the UK or decided case law that creates a clear duty upon employers to protect employees from ETS exposure in the workplace. Unless this regulatory approach changes, employers must deal with the hazard presented by ETS in the context of their general duties to safeguard their workforce. The legal implications of exposure are likely to relate to claims by employees for compensation for damage to health as a result of ETS exposure at work. This chapter summarises the current status of the law relating to ETS exposure in the UK, reviews the legal basis on which individual cases can be made, and provides examples of progress with current case law in the UK and elsewhere.

8.2 What does a claimant need to prove?

To succeed in a claim for compensation in a UK court, a claimant needs to prove all of the following:

- He/she has an illness that can be caused by exposure to ETS (Injury).
- The claimant's work posed a real risk of causing this type of illness and his/her employer knew (or ought to have known) that the claimant was exposed to that risk (Foreseeability).
- Given the foreseeable risk, the employer failed to take adequate steps to prevent or reduce the risk, as far was reasonably practicable, of the claimant suffering from this type of illness (Breach of Duty).
- The claimant's illness was caused, or materially contributed to, by exposure to ETS at work and by the employer's breach of duty (Causation).
- The claim must be also brought in time (Limitation).

Each of these elements will now be considered in turn.

Injury

The scientific evidence reviewed in Chapter 2 demonstrates that ETS is an independent risk factor for a number of conditions and diseases in adults. In particular, ETS is now a recognised cause of lung cancer, heart disease and exacerbation of asthma in adults.[1,2] These are the injuries most likely to be accepted by a court as being caused by ETS exposure at work.

Foreseeability

There are two elements to foreseeability:

- 'guilty knowledge' of the risks of passive smoking in general, and
- a risk of employees being exposed to ETS in the workplace.

Guilty knowledge refers to the general knowledge about a particular risk, and it can be argued that there has been general knowledge that ETS exposure comprises a health risk for many years. In a report published in 1998, the UK Government Scientific Committee on Tobacco and Health concluded that passive smoking was a cause of lung cancer and ischaemic heart disease;[3] the US Surgeon General concluded that ETS exposure was a cause of lung cancer as early as 1986;[4] and these conclusions have been reiterated in many other reports.[1,2,5–7] It is evident, therefore, that employers can no longer use the excuse that there is 'scientific uncertainty' as to whether ETS exposure constitutes a health risk.

Further, given the publicity over recent years about the dangers, it is almost impossible for any employer to argue that they were not aware of the risk. The employer cannot simply wait for an employee to be ill before the employer is on notice of a problem. If ETS exists in the workplace, the employer is required to assess the risk and determine the possible danger that might arise (see below). The employer does not have to foresee the exact illness, only that some form of illness can be caused by the exposure to ETS at the workplace. It is sufficient that some illness of the general type is foreseeable (see *Hughes* v *Lord Advocate* [1963] Appeals Cases 837).

Breach of duty

The existence of a duty of care between an employee and employer has been established for many years (see *Wilsons & Clyde Coal Co Ltd* v *English* [1938] Appeals Cases 57). Section 2 of the Health and Safety at Work Act 1974 (HSWA) requires an employer to ensure, so far as is reasonably practicable, the health, safety and welfare of employees at work.[8]

The test as to what is reasonably practicable was set out in the case of *Edwards* v *National Coal Board* ([1949] 1, All England Law Reports 743). This case established that the risk must be balanced against the 'sacrifice', whether in money, time or trouble, needed to avert or mitigate the risk. By carrying out this exercise the employer can determine what measures are reasonably practicable to take. This is effectively an implied requirement for a risk assessment. Failure to provide relief against tobacco smoke has been found to be a breach of an implied term in the contract of employment, based on the duty in the HSWA 1974 s2(1), in a recent case (Karen Whitehead, see below) in the Employment Appeal Tribunal.

The general duty upon an employer to carry out risk assessments of health and safety hazards involved in its business is set out in Regulation 3 of the Management of Health and Safety at Work Regulations 1999 (MHSWR). Regulation 3 states:

> *Every employer shall make a suitable and sufficient assessment of*
> *(a) the risks to the health and safety of his employees to which they are exposed whilst they are at work; and*
> *(b) the risks to the health and safety of persons not in his employment arising out of or in connection with the conduct by him of his undertaking for the purpose of identifying the measures he needs to take to comply with the requirement and prohibitions imposed upon him, by or under the relevant statutory provision and by Part II of the Fire Precautions (Workplace) Regulations 1997.*[9]

It was established by the Court of Appeal in *R* v *The Board of Trustees of the Science Museum* ([1993] 3, All England Law Reports 853) that risk means the possibility of danger, and not just actual danger.

Breach of Regulation 3 of the MHSWR does not give rise to civil liability (although the Health and Safety Commission is proposing to remove this exclusion) but it can be relied upon to prove a breach of an employer's 'common law' duty to take care of its employees. In a personal injury case concerning a claim for repetitive strain injury (*Lindsay & Johnson* v *Claremont Garments Ltd*, Newcastle Upon Tyne County Court, January 1998) the trial judge made the following observation about Regulation 3 (in relation to the 1992 regulations of the same name which introduced the general requirement for risk assessment):

> *...although the absence of a necessary risk assessment is not itself actionable as a breach of statutory duty, it is so central to the whole scheme that it should be considered important evidence of a failure to provide a safe system of work in all the circumstances, and therefore common law negligence. This argument is also applicable to other parts of the [MHSWR], such as health surveillance, the need for procedures to deal with serious and imminent dangers and the principles of prevention.*

Regulation 4 of the MHSWR sets out the priority to be given to measures to deal with the hazards that have been risk assessed where action is required. The hierarchy of measures is as follows:

(a) Avoid risks
(b) Evaluate the risks which cannot be avoided
(c) Combat the risks at source
(d) Adapt the work to the individual, especially as regards the design of workplaces, the choice of work, equipment and the choice of working and production method, with a view, in particular, to alleviating monotonous work and work at predetermined work rate and to reducing their effect on health
(e) Adapt to technical process
(f) Replace the dangerous by the non-dangerous or the less dangerous;
(g) Develop a coherent overall prevention policy that covers technology, organisation of work, working conditions, social relationships and the influence of factors relating to the working environment
(h) Give collective protective measures priority over individual protective measures, and
(i) Give appropriate instructions to employees.[9]

Since the object of these regulations is the avoidance of risk, the safest course of action an employer can take is to prevent ETS exposure by making all indoor areas of the workplace smoke-free. The provision of indoor smoking areas or rooms would need to comply with Regulation 6(1) of the Workplace (Health Safety and Welfare) Regulations 1992 (the Workplace Regulations),[10] which requires employers to make 'effective and suitable provision' for the workplace to be 'ventilated by sufficient quantity of fresh or purified air'. The quality of the ventilation would need to be sufficient to prevent harm, rather than simply remove nuisance effects (see Chapter 5), to avoid giving rise to civil liability. This obligation extends, under Regulation 25 of the Workplace Regulations, to facilities for rest and to eat meals.

Causation

To establish causation it must be proved that the claimant's illness was caused not only by exposure to ETS at work, but also that the employer was in breach of duty by failing to have in place reasonably practicable measures to deal with the risk of ETS. This is essentially an issue that will be decided by reference to expert medical evidence.

The onus is on the claimant to prove causation on the balance of probabilities (see *Bonnington Castings* v *Wardlaw* [1956] Appeals Cases 613 and *Pickford* v *Imperial Chemical Industries* [1998] 1, Weekly Law Reports 1189). A claimant will not recover compensation if the damage would have occurred anyway. An example of this is *Barnett* v *Chelsea and Kensington Hospital* ([1969] 1, Queens Bench Reports 428), in which a person who drank arsenic was treated negligently in hospital. The evidence in this case was that even with proper treatment the person would have died, so the negligent treatment was not relevant.

However, to succeed in a claim, the claimant does not need to prove that the employer's breach of duty which caused him/her to be exposed to ETS at work was the sole cause of his/her illness. In these circumstances, the claimant will succeed if the breach of duty made a material contribution (see *Bonnington Castings* v *Wardlaw* [1956] Appeals Cases 613, concerning a claim for pneumoconiosis) to the illness. The claimant will also succeed if he/she can prove the breach of duty was capable of causing the illness, and materially increased the risk of the condition occurring (see *McGhee* v *National Coal Board* [1973] 1, Weekly Law Reports 1 concerning a claim for dermatitis where the court found that the risk of dermatitis had been increased materially because there were inadequate washing facilities in the factory).

The question that follows is whether the claimant can recover compensation on a 100% basis where 'material contribution' is involved. To answer this it needs to be determined whether the illness is indivisible or divisible. *Indivisible* means it is not possible to attribute one part of the illness to one cause and other parts to other causes. If this is the situation, the claimant will recover in full against the employer (see *Bonnington Castings* v *Wardlaw* [1956] Appeals Cases 613). If the illness is *divisible*, that is different parts of the illness can be attributed to different causes, then the claimant will only recover compensation for that caused by the defendant's breach of duty. In the case of *Holtby* v *Brigham and Cowan (Hull) Ltd* (Court of Appeal 6 April 2000), the occurrence of pleural plaques caused by asbestos exposure was found to be divisible and, as a consequence, the claimant only recovered for that part of the condition caused by the defendant's breach of duty.

Limitation

In a passive smoking case, the claimant has three years to issue court proceedings from the date he/she knew, or ought to have known, that his/her illness was caused by exposure to ETS at work. If court proceedings are not issued in this period then the claimant will not normally be allowed to bring a claim. In some circumstances, however, the court may allow the case to proceed even if the limitation period has expired if there is a good reason why court proceedings were not issued in time.

8.3 What evidence is required in practice?

Individuals who seek to claim compensation need to demonstrate the following:

(a) That the employers knew, or should reasonably have known, that ETS exposure presented a risk of injury to their non smoking employees, and that the employers had this knowledge at the time the relevant exposure took place. Many claims may involve historical exposure going back over many years, so recent developments and reports may be of limited assistance.

(b) That the employer knew not only of the general risk from ETS, but also that the individual employee was being exposed to dangerous levels of smoke in their day-to-day work. This requires evidence from work colleagues, and would require the Court to make the best assessment it can on the basis of the evidence of what the exposure levels were. Only where it is decided that the exposure levels were high enough that the employer should have done something about it at the time would the exposure potentially found a claim.

(c) That the medical condition he or she developed had been caused by the exposure at work, rather than by any exposure he/she may have had outside work. A claimant who lives with a smoker is, therefore, likely to encounter significant difficulties, as is someone who regularly socialises with smokers or who is an ex-smoker themselves. These factors would be matters of evidence requiring a detailed analysis of the claimant's lifestyle and consideration by medical experts. It may be sufficient to prove that the occupational exposure made a material contribution to the development of the condition, rather than being its sole cause, but the hurdles will be high.

8.4 Progress with UK legal cases to date

There have been six notable cases to date in which individuals have claimed compensation for damage caused by ETS at work:

Veronica Bland

In January 1993, Veronica Bland, a local government employee, reached an out-of-court settlement of £15,000 with her employers after suing them for exposure to ETS at work that, she argued, caused chronic bronchitis.

Beryl Roe

In July 1995, Beryl Roe, who worked at the Stockport Metropolitan Borough Council, reached an out-of-court settlement of £25,000 with her employers in relation to her claim for passive smoking at work. She retired in 1987 before the Council had introduced a smoking policy. Her case was that she had suffered eye, nose and throat symptoms as well as bronchitis from exposure to ETS at work.

Agnes Rae

Agnes Rae's case came before Lord Bonomy in the Court of Session in Scotland in March 1997. She sued her employer Glasgow City Council for compensation on the basis that they should have warned her about the dangers of exposure to ETS, and for failure to have adequate ventilation, pursuant to Section 7 of the Office Shops and Railway Premises Act 1963. The case failed. The judge said that the series of reports of medical and non-medical bodies cited on her behalf did not identify a risk of lung disease or respiratory disease being 'contracted at work as a result of passive smoking'. In relation to Section 7 of the Act he concluded,

'There is nothing on record to indicate that effective and suitable provision was not being made for the ventilation of [Agnes Rae's] workplaces.'

However, Lord Bonomy also said of the section that it was, '...plainly directed at the mischief of foul air in the atmosphere of the workplace; tobacco smoke which fouled up the atmosphere clearly fell within that mischief.'

Sylvia Sparrow

Sylvia Sparrow's case came before the Manchester High Court in May 1998. This case also failed. Sylvia Sparrow worked at a residential nursing home, St Andrew's Homes. Her claim was for exacerbation of asthma caused by ETS. The judge accepted that, in principle, employers have to take reasonable steps to protect employees from the hazard of tobacco smoke but, in this case, found that the provision of separate smoking rooms by the employer constituted reasonable steps to prevent exposure to ETS.

Mickey Dunn

Mickey Dunn claimed he had contracted asthma after breathing in the smoke of customers' cigarettes and cigars while working in a casino. In 2003, he was awarded over £50,000 in an out-of-court settlement, though this was on the basis that the employer did not accept liability for his illness.

Karen Whitehead

The most recent case is that of Karen Whitehead who has asthma and who, in 2003, won £17,000 compensation for being sacked unfairly when smoking by workmates made her ill. An employment tribunal ruled that Karen, who was off sick for 16 of the 45 days she worked at a community centre in Plymouth, was discriminated against because of her asthma disability.

8.5 Experience of legal cases outside the UK

Several cases of claims for compensation have progressed in other countries.

Owen Brown (Australia)

In July 2001, the official Australian compensation agency paid compensation to Mr Brown, a teacher, who claimed that smoke-filled staffrooms at work had contributed to chronic lung disease. He received A$100,000 compensation.

Marlene Sharp (Australia)

In May 2001, Marlene Sharp, a former barmaid in Australia who had never smoked, won damages of A$450,000 from her ex-employer for lung cancer caused by exposure to ETS at work.

Norma Broin (USA)

Norma Broin worked as an airline attendant. In 1990, US Congress banned smoking on domestic flights. Norma Broin, who had never smoked, developed lung cancer which she argued had been caused by her exposure to ETS at work. Her claim was part of a successful class action in America which won compensation of US$350 million in 1991.

Heather Crowe (Canada)

In October 2002, Heather Crowe, a former waitress and non-smoker, was exposed to ETS as a result of working for 12 hours a day, six days a week, in restaurants, bars and hotels for 40 years. She developed lung cancer, which she claimed was caused by ETS, and was awarded compensation (amount unknown) by the Ontario Workplace Safety and Insurance Board.

8.6 Levels of compensation

Effectively, any personal injury claim is two separate claims for compensation: 'general damages' and 'special damage'. Typical levels of compensation vary from country to country, and from case to case.

General damages

This is compensation that cannot be calculated, for example for an injured person's pain and suffering and loss of amenity. Loss of amenity is the inability of the claimant to do things after the contraction of the illness that they could do before. It is also possible to recover general damages for future financial losses, such as loss of earnings or the cost of future care when the claimant is likely to be ill for some time.

As an approximate guide, general damages for pain, suffering and loss of amenity in a lung cancer case in the UK would be in the region of £40,000–£50,000. Bronchitis and wheezing not causing serious symptoms would provide damages of around £10,000–£15,000. Temporary aggravation of bronchitis or other respiratory problems resolving within a few months would provide damages in the region of £1,000–£2,500.

Special damage

This is compensation that can be calculated, and relates to losses that the claimant has incurred to the date of trial or settlement. The amount of damages awarded for financial losses and expenses will vary from case to case, according to the losses incurred.

8.7 The future for smoking at work

Reasonable and responsible employers have now known for several years that ETS represents a health hazard, and that they have a responsibility to protect their employees from the harm ETS can cause. In the special case of the hospitality industry, Action on Smoking and Health wrote (with appropriate legal support and advice) to the human resources directors and chief executives of about 150 leading UK hospitality trade employers, pointing out their obligations to protect the health of employees in hospitality venues (see Box 8.1). It is likely that in the relatively near future, many more personal compensation claims will succeed and, depending on the pace of legislative change in the UK, may actually pre-empt the introduction of comprehensive smoke-free policies before any legal requirements come into force.

In the meantime, what can employers reasonably be expected to do about smoky workplaces? Hopefully, good employers will treat the issue proactively as one of industrial relations, which requires the active involvement of the workforce and their unions in finding a solution. For enclosed workplaces, the implementation of comprehensive smoke-free policies is the best and most likely outcome. It is also hoped that more forward-looking employers will combine this with providing support and assistance for those employees who do smoke but who wish to give up. There are some workplaces where the issues are more complicated, and reasonable policies for some of these are discussed in Chapter 14.

One thing is certain: the employer who does nothing at all to deal with the health hazards of passive smoking among their workforce is storing up significant problems for the future. Compensation claims may always remain difficult but there will be those that can succeed. Employers who do nothing to address the problem are those most likely to be at risk from such claims in the future.

Box 8.1. Text of letter to leading UK hospitality industry employers, sent 7 January 2004

Dear

Re: The law and passive smoking

We are writing to ask you to consider your policy on passive smoking in the workplace, in view of what we believe to be your duties as an employer under the Health and Safety at Work Act. We hope to persuade to you that a smoke free workplace is in the interests both of your company and of its employees. In any event, we wish to draw your attention to the serious legal risks now being run by any employer that chooses to allow smoking at work.

Secondhand smoke contains over 4,000 chemicals, including benzene, formaldehyde, arsenic, ammonia and hydrogen cyanide. The US Environmental Protection Agency has classified environmental tobacco smoke as a known human (class A) carcinogen. The immediate effects of inhaling secondhand smoke include eye irritation, headache, cough, sore throat and nausea. Exposure for just 30 minutes to secondhand smoke has been shown to reduce coronary blood flow. Long-term inhalers of secondhand smoke suffer an increased risk of a range of smoking-related diseases. The Government appointed Scientific Advisory Committee (SCOTH) concluded that secondhand smoke is a cause of lung cancer and ischaemic heart disease in adult non-smokers and a cause of respiratory disease, cot death, middle ear disease and asthma in children. The British Medical Association estimates that secondhand smoke causes at least 1,000 premature deaths a year. The dangers of secondhand smoke have also been well publicised by the heads of all the Royal Colleges of Medicine and by the Government's Chief Medical Officer.

Because of the widespread publicity the scientific evidence on secondhand smoke has now received, it is our view that the date of "guilty knowledge" under the Health and Safety at Work Act 1974 has passed. Indeed, we believe that employers should have known of the risks by the early 1990s at the very latest. Therefore, in the event of claims for compensation for health damage, employers will be expected by the courts to know of the health effects of exposing employees and others to secondhand smoke and to take reasonable steps to eliminate it.

Conclusion

It should not be surprising to anyone that secondhand smoke is a killer. In addition to your employees, particular groups of your customers are particularly vulnerable. In particular children suffer more than adults from the effects of secondhand smoke. The Department of Health is currently running a major national advertising campaign to draw to parents' attention the risks of exposing their children to secondhand smoke: you should therefore expect the level of concern among your customers over this issue to continue to rise.

ASH intends to keep a formal record of this letter and its recipients, which we will make available to any future claimants in court cases for compensation. We are also copying this letter to the TUC and relevant trade unions. We intend to use our campaigning work

continued over

Box 8.1. Text of letter to leading UK hospitality industry employers, sent 7 January 2004 – *continued*

to inform customers of premises which expose staff and public to secondhand smoke of the risk they are running, and we will working with major firms of employment and personal injury lawyers to publicise what we believe to be the legal rights of employees in this area. In the meantime, we warmly welcome decisions by employers such as Pizza Hut, which announced in August that its 500 restaurants would be fully smoke free. We would certainly encourage parents to take their children to such restaurant chains in preference to those that still permit smoking on the premises.

There really is no satisfactory alternative to fully smoke free workplaces. Some employers have chosen to spend heavily on ventilation systems for example; yet there is clear evidence from the World Health Organisation that ventilation systems and smoke free areas do not sufficiently protect employees, because there is simply no safe level of exposure to secondhand tobacco smoke.

Finally, smoke free workplaces are known to be a major factor in encouraging smokers to quit. This in turn could have a major positive impact on your business, by reducing illness and absenteeism and increasing productivity. Research for Health Canada suggests that the average cost to employers of each smoker employed is as much as £1,400 a year. Introducing full smoke free workplaces and helping staff who wish to quit smoking to do so (excellent support services are now available through the NHS) could be an excellent business decision. It will protect your employees and customers. It could well attract new business. It would certainly avoid a growing legal risk.

We would be pleased to discuss any of the contents of this letter with you further, and to offer any advice and encouragement we can if you are considering smoke free policies. We look forward very much to hearing from you.

Yours sincerely,

Deborah Arnott
Director

8.8 Smoking at home

The discussion above relates to the effect of ETS exposure at work but, as outlined in earlier chapters, the majority of ETS exposure and consequent damage to health occurs at home. For adults able to exercise choice as to whether they allow themselves to be exposed to ETS there would be no grounds for legal redress against individuals causing the exposure (usually their partner or other family members). However, in the case of individuals unable to avoid or prevent ETS exposure, including children, there is a potential for legal action against those causing the exposure. This has not yet been tested in the UK courts.

8.9 Summary

- Employers have a general duty to safeguard their workforce.
- ETS exposure is known to be harmful but is not subject currently to specific workplace legislation.
- Employers who continue to allow employees to be exposed to ETS are at increasing risk of being found liable for personal injuries sustained by employees.
- Employers who do nothing to protect their workforce are those most at risk from legal action in the future.

References

1 Scientific Committee on Tobacco and Health (SCOTH). *Secondhand Smoke: Review of evidence since 1998.* London: Department of Health, 2004.

2 Samet J (ed). *Health consequences of secondhand smoking.* A report of the US Surgeon General, 2005 (In press).

3 Department of Health; Department of Health & Social Services for Northern Ireland; Scottish Office Department of Health; Welsh Office. *Report of the Scientific Committee on Tobacco and Health.* London: HMSO, 1998.

4 US Department of Health and Human Services. *The health consequences of involuntary smoking. A report of the Surgeon General.* DHHS Publication No. (CDC) 87-8398. Rockville, MD: DHHS, Public Health Service, Centers for Disease Control, Center for Health Promotion and Education, Office on Smoking and Health, 1986.

5 Australian National Health and Medical Research Council. *Effects of passive smoking on health.* Report of the NHMRC Working Party on the effects of passive smoking on health. Canberra, Australia: Australia Government Publishing Service, 1987.

6 US Environmental Protection Agency. *Respiratory health effects of passive smoking: lung cancer and other disorders.* US EPA Document No.EPA/600/6-90/006F, 1992.

7 International Agency for Research on Cancer. *IARC Monographs on the evaluation of carcinogenic risks to humans, Vol 83: Tobacco smoke and involuntary smoking.* Lyon, France: WHO/IARC, 2004.

8 Health and Safety at Work Act, 1974.

9 Management of Health and Safety at Work Regulations, 1999.

10 Workplace (Health Safety and Welfare Regulations), 1992.

9 | Public attitudes to smoke-free policy

9.1 Introduction

International experience suggests that successful implementation of smoke-free policies requires a reasonable level of both public awareness of the health risks of second-hand smoke and of public support for measures to control exposure. This chapter summarises current information on the status of knowledge and attitudes to smoking in public places in the UK, trends in these attitudes, and support for government action to improve and protect health.

The main source of data on trends in public attitudes to smoking in the UK is the government-funded Office for National Statistics (ONS) annual survey, *Smoking related behaviour and attitudes.*[1] The survey has collected information on smoking behaviour, public knowledge of the health risks of second-hand smoke, and support for smoking restrictions in various settings in a nationally representative UK population sample since 1996.

This chapter also draws on data from other objective surveys in the UK, and explores international experience of public responses to the implementation of smoke-free policies, particularly in New York and in Ireland.

9.2 Public awareness of the health effects of passive smoking

In 2003, more than half (56%) of British non-smokers said that they object if people smoke near them. Nuisance effects were cited most often as the reason for this objection, but 40% also had concerns over the effect on health (see Chapter 2,

Fig 2.1).[1] There is widespread acceptance among the British public that passive smoking harms health. For example, in the ONS survey, more than 8 out of 10 people agreed that breathing someone else's smoke increases the risk of lung cancer (85%), bronchitis (85%), and asthma (81%); 69% agreed that it increased the risk of heart disease. However, recognition of the health effects of passive smoking is lower among smokers than among non-smokers; while 92% of non-smokers believe that passive smoking can cause lung cancer, only 75% of smokers agree.[1]

Other surveys have assessed public attitudes to the health risks of passive smoking in the workplace. In a 2002 Cancer Research UK/MORI survey, just over half (52%) of the respondents said they were concerned about the risk of developing lung cancer as a result of passive smoking in the workplace.[2] A more recent survey by BBC/ICM in 2004 found that 70% of respondents were worried personally about the health risks of breathing other people's smoke.[3]

9.3 Public support for smoke-free public and workplaces

Internal documents made public as a result of legal action against the tobacco industry in the USA show that tobacco companies were monitoring attitudes to smoking in public places in Europe as early as the 1980s. In a document from 1989 comparing public attitudes to a range of tobacco control measures in 10 European countries and the USA, Philip Morris found that 70% of adults in the UK (40–84% across the 10 countries) believed that government should pass laws to restrict smoking in public places (Fig 9.1).[4]

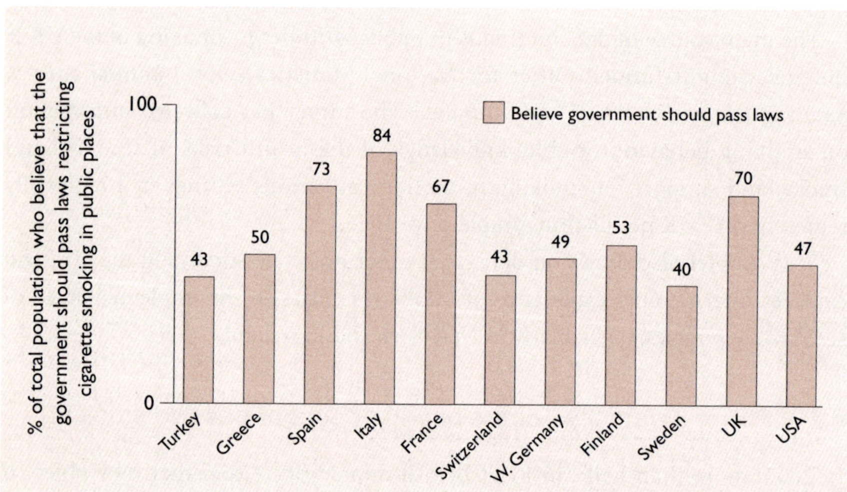

Fig 9.1 Data from Philip Morris on support for restrictions on smoking in public places in Europe and the USA, 1989.[4]

Trends documented in the annual ONS surveys demonstrate a consistently high level of public support for smoking restrictions in the workplace and in most public facilities, including restaurants. Support for restrictions in pubs has grown over the years, reaching 56% in 2003, but lags behind that for restrictions in other settings (Fig 9.2).[1] Support for smoking restrictions in public places varies substantially within the population, being higher among those who are aware of the health risks of passive smoking, and higher among non-smokers relative to smokers, with ex-smokers intermediate between these two groups. Supporters of smoking restrictions are also more likely to be women, to be in professional or managerial occupations, and to be aged 35 or over.[1]

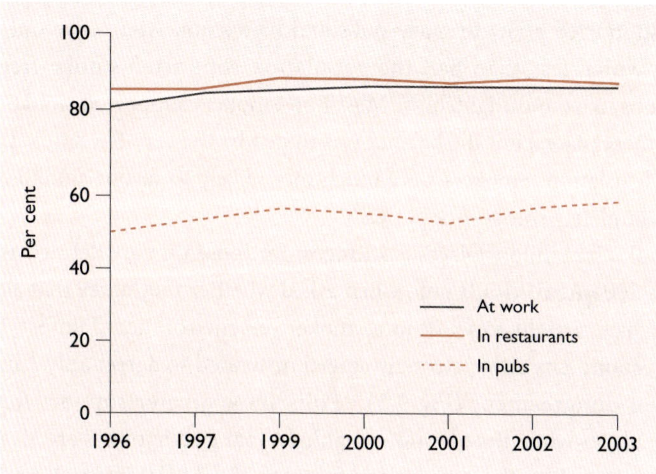

Fig 9.2 UK public support for restrictions on smoking at work, in restaurants and in pubs 1996–2003.[1]

The questions used in the ONS surveys have focused on assessing support for unspecified restrictions on smoking in public places, rather than specifically on support for smoke-free public or workplaces, or for smoke-free legislation. However, several other recent surveys have assessed public support for fully smoke-free workplaces and public places.[3,5–7] When comparing the results of these polls, it is important to be aware that the framing and phrasing of questions can have a substantial effect on responses. For example, the term 'smoke-free' is clear in meaning and positive in tone. In contrast, the term 'smoking-ban' has more negative associations in its suggestion of authoritarianism and coercion. It may also be misinterpreted as meaning that smoking itself may be made illegal, or that smoking may not be permitted anywhere except in the home. The term 'smoking restrictions', used in the ONS survey and others, is imprecise and may be understood differently by respondents. Hence, the interpretation of responses is difficult. Carefully worded survey questions avoid this potential confusion, and give a clearer picture of the true level and strength of public support for evidence-based measures to protect against the harmful effects of second-hand smoke.

The independent polls all confirmed, however, that the majority of the population, ranging from 52%[6] to 73%,[5] supports a ban on smoking in public, or a law to make all enclosed public places smoke-free. Support varied according to the phrasing used in the survey questions, but was consistently highest for smoke-free policies among non-smokers and lowest among smokers. For example, in the Action on Smoking and Health (ASH)/Mori poll, 62% of non-smokers but only 17% of smokers supported a law to make pubs and bars smoke-free.[5] The only public places for which less than half the population supported smoke-free legislation were pubs, bars and nightclubs. Most non-smokers supported smoke-free legislation in these places, but the balance was tipped by the very few smokers in favour of such legislation. Smokers were much more likely to favour smoking restrictions over completely smoke-free places.[1,3,5–7]

Support for smoke-free indoor places is strongest for those that are defined as workplaces. In the 2004 ASH/MORI poll, when asked whether they agree that all employees should have a right to work in a smoke-free environment, almost 9 out of 10 (89%) respondents either strongly agreed or tended to agree; only 1 in 20 (5%) expressed disagreement (Fig 9.3).[5] Polls show greater support for smoke-free public places when the questions highlight that public places are also workplaces, demonstrated by the comparison between the ASH/Mori poll and the Mintel/BMRB poll which showed support of 52% and 73% respectively.[5,6] This support is only slightly lower when it is made clear that pubs and bars are

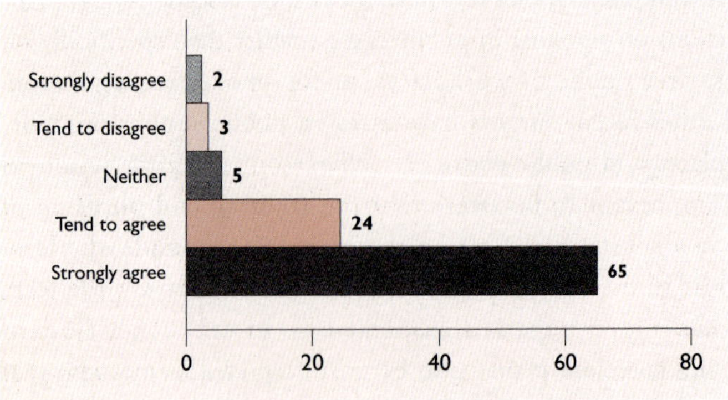

Fig 9.3 Agreement with the statement: 'All employees have the right to work in a smoke-free environment' (ASH/MORI 2004).[5]

included as workplaces. For example, both the ASH/Mori poll and the BBC Healthy Britain poll refer to public places being workplaces but only the BBC poll refers to pubs and bars, with support of 73% and 67% respectively.[5,7]

Support for smoke-free policies at work appears to be high amongst employers, according to a survey by the law firm Peninsula which found that over 90% would encourage a law banning smoking in the workplace.[8]

Support for smoke-free restaurants is also high. In the ONS survey, 86% supported smoking restrictions in restaurants,[1] while the ASH/MORI poll found that 79% of respondents would support a law to make restaurants completely smoke-free.[5] However, while public support for smoke-free workplaces – including smoke-free restaurants – is strong, the evidence suggests that the public do not always recognise bars, pubs and clubs as workplaces. Thus, in the ONS survey, whilst over 80% supported restrictions on smoking at work, only 56% of respondents supported restrictions on smoking in bars.[1] In the ASH/MORI poll, just under half (49%) of respondents supported a law to make pubs and bars smoke-free.[5] However, in the same survey, when reminded that most enclosed public places are also workplaces, almost three-quarters (73%) of respondents said they would support a law making all public places and workplaces smoke-free; just 15% of those questioned would oppose such a law.[5]

9.4 Public attitudes to government action to protect health

Some commentators portray public health policies such as smoke-free legislation as excessive interference by the 'nanny state'. However, the evidence shows that the British public mostly sees a legitimate role for the government in helping people to live healthy lives. A King's Fund/Health Development Agency (HDA) poll found that 75% of those questioned thought the government should actively discourage people from doing things that put their health at risk.[9] Government action to help smokers give up also enjoys strong support. In the BBC/ICM poll, 67% of respondents thought that the government should help people to change their smoking behaviour.[7] Public support for action to protect others' health is also strong: 77% of respondents thought that the government should prevent people from doing things that might harm other people's health.[7]

There is also substantial public recognition that smoke-free laws are an effective health measure. In the King's Fund/HDA poll,[9] 68% of those questioned agreed that a ban on smoking in workplaces, including pubs, bars and restaurants, would be an effective way to reduce the health risks of smoking. A majority also wanted to see action by national government to provide protection against ETS. Among the large majority of people who supported some smoking restrictions, the preference is for central government legislation. In the ASH/MORI poll,[5] almost two-thirds (64%) of respondents thought that smoking restrictions should be introduced at national level, with only 21% preferring action by local councils. There is also substantial support for action to introduce legislation on smoke-free public places based on successful laws in other countries. For example, 79% of respondents to the ASH/MORI poll responded with support to the following question:

> *Ireland, Canada, Norway and New Zealand have each passed laws to ensure all enclosed workplaces are smoke-free. How strongly, if at all, would you support or oppose a proposal to bring in a similar law in this country?*[5]

9.5 Public support for smoke-free laws in other countries

The experience of smoke-free laws in other countries has been one of widespread public support, and that this support typically increases during the build-up to implementation, and increases still further after introduction. In California, support for a law to make bars smoke-free jumped from 68% before its introduction in 2000 to 75% afterwards.[10] In Connecticut, a survey of public attitudes to a law making all workplaces smoke-free, including bars and restaurants, found that 85% of those surveyed supported the law.[11] Support for the Maine smoke-free Act grew from 77% when it was introduced in December 2003 to 88% one year later; among smokers, support rose from 40% to 54% over that period.[12] In New York, there was a steady increase in support for the Clean Indoor Air Act (CIAA) under which indoor workplaces – including bars, pubs and clubs – became completely smoke-free. The levels of support for the Act among smokers, ex-smokers and never-smokers, before and after it came into force on 24 July 2003, is shown in Fig 9.4.[13] While support for the Act dipped slightly immediately after its introduction, it climbed steadily thereafter; one year later, support had risen 10 percentage points higher among both smokers and ex-smokers, to around 74%.[14] Compliance with the Act (another measure of support for the legislation) is high, with some 94% of premises being smoke-free.[14]

The smoke-free workplace law introduced in Ireland in March 2004 has also been well received. In a survey of public attitudes carried out among a representative sample of adults one year after implementation, there was almost universal agreement (98%) that workplaces are healthier since the introduction of the law (Fig 9.5). The vast majority (96%) believe that the law is successful, including almost 9 out of 10 (89%) smokers. Likewise, the majority (93%) think the introduction of the law was a good idea, including 80% of smokers. Public

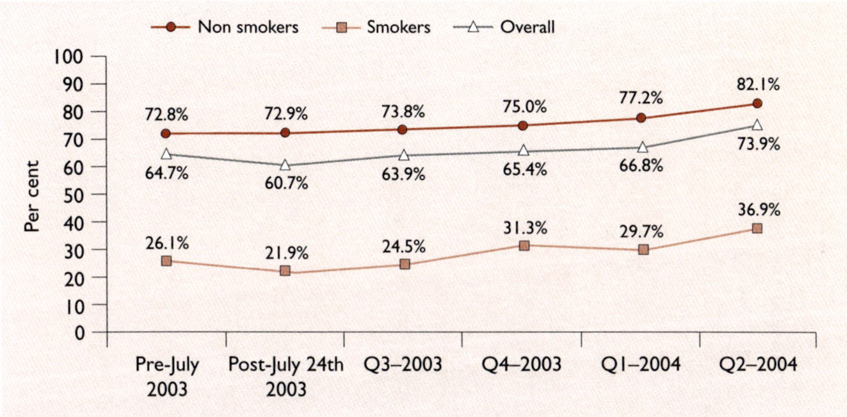

Fig 9.4 Percentage of adults, smokers and non-smokers who support the New York Clean Indoor Air Act (CIAA) before and after implementation in July 2003.[13]

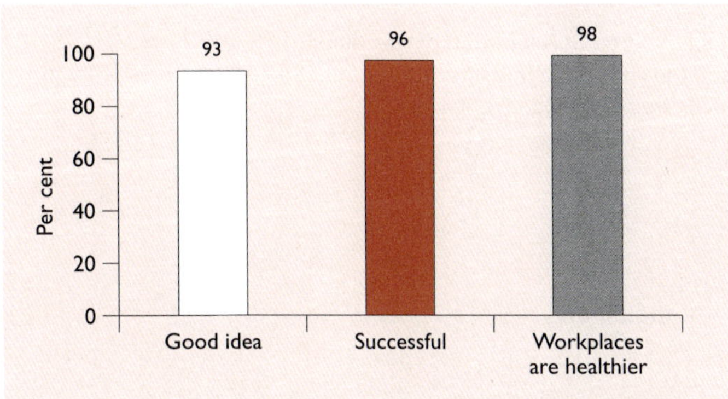

Fig 9.5 Public attitudes to Irish smoke-free legislation one year after implementation.[15]

support for the Irish law increased steadily, from 67% before its implementation to 82% five months after implementation, and 93% after one year.[15] The law has also achieved high levels of compliance, which indicates that it is generally respected. Nine months after its introduction, compiled inspection data showed overall compliance was 94%, with 99% compliance in restaurants, 93% in hotels and 90% in licensed premises. The increased popularity of smoke-free laws in Ireland is also evident among smokers (see Chapter 15 for further detail). Figs 9.6 to 9.8 demonstrate the changes in attitudes to smoke-free policy in workplaces, restaurants, pubs and bars among smokers in Ireland before and after the smoke-free legislation was introduced.[16] Support for smoke-free policy increased in Ireland by more than in the UK, where no legislation was introduced.

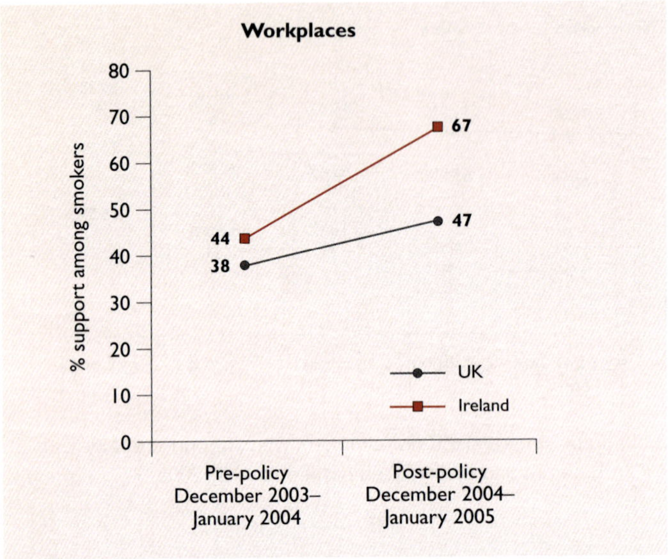

Fig 9.6 Support for smoke-free policy in workplaces among smokers in Ireland and the UK before and after the introduction of smoke-free legislation in Ireland in March 2004.[16]

Fig 9.7 Support for smoke-free policy in restaurants among smokers in Ireland and the UK before and after the introduction of smoke-free legislation in Ireland in March 2004.[16]

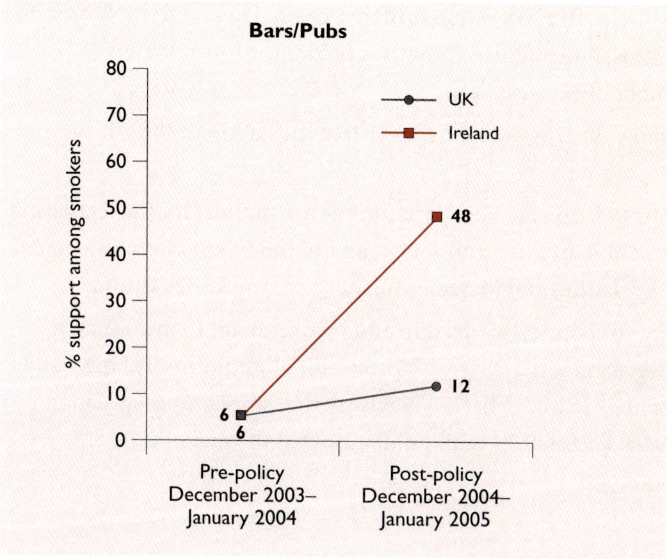

Fig 9.8 Support for smoke-free policy in bars and pubs among smokers in Ireland and the UK before and after the introduction of smoke-free legislation in Ireland in March 2004.[16]

9.6 Is the UK ready for comprehensive smoke-free legislation?

The key to successful smoke-free policy is a high level of public awareness of the health risks of passive smoking, and strong support for smoke-free laws. The Scottish Parliament has already judged that the time has come for smoke-free legislation, and has determined that Scotland will go smoke-free in 2006. Some have argued that public support for smoke-free places in England has not yet reached the critical level that would allow its successful introduction and implementation, but the data from representative surveys, including those reviewed in this chapter (and indeed the Scottish decision), suggest otherwise. Moreover, some have argued that smoke-free laws can only be successfully enacted when adult smoking prevalence falls below a certain level, but smoking prevalence in the UK is now lower than it was in Ireland before their smoke-free law was introduced. Therefore, there seems to be no basis to expect that support and compliance for a smoke-free law in England would not reach the same high levels seen elsewhere.

9.7 Summary

- There is majority support in the UK for all public places and workplaces to go smoke-free.

- Support for smoke-free legislation is higher in England, and smoking prevalence is lower, than it was in Ireland before the introduction of successful smoke-free legislation.
- The trends show that support for smoke-free legislation in the UK is increasing.
- Evidence from Ireland and New York shows that support for the legislation grows in the period after the announcement of the intention to implement smoke-free legislation, and increases further after implementation.
- A combination of political leadership and commitment to introducing smoke-free legislation, together with provision of public information and encouragement of public debate, will ensure that smoke-free legislation can be implemented successfully with public support throughout the UK.

References

1 Lader D, Goddard L. *Smoking-related behaviour and attitudes, 2003.* London: Office for National Statistics, 2004.

2 MORI/Cancer Research UK. *Workplace smoking causes concern*, January 2003. www.mori.com/polls/2002/cancerresearchuk.shtml

3 ICM Research. *BBC smoking poll*, July 2004. www.icmresearch.co.uk/reviews/2004/BBC-Breakfast News-Smoking July04/BBC Breakfast Smoking July04.asp

4 Philip Morris International. *How today's smokers and non-smokers in Europe feel about smoking issues*, October 1989. Bates number 2500147468. www.pmdocs.com

5 MORI. *Overwhelming support for workplace smoking ban*, June 2004. www.mori.com/polls/2004/ash.shtml

6 Mintel British Market Research Bureau. *Majority of public favour smoking ban*, May 2004. www.news.bbc.co.uk/1/hi/health/3728511.stm

7 ICM Research. *BBC healthy Britain poll*, September 2004. www.news.bbc.co.uk/1/hi/health/3633018.stm

8 Peninsula. Majority of employers support workplace smoking ban. *Personnel Today*, July 2004. www.personneltoday.com/pt_news/news_daily_det.asp?feed=rss&liArticleID=24628

9 King's Fund/Health Development Agency; Opinion Leader Research. *Public attitudes to public health policy*, June 2004. www.kingsfund.org.uk/pdf/publichealthattitudes summary.pdf

10 Weber MD, Bagwell DA, Fielding JE, Glantz SA. Long-term compliance with California's Smoke-Free Workplace Law among bars and restaurants in Los Angeles County. *Tob Control* 2003;**12**:269–73.

11 Global Strategy Group. *Connecticut statewide survey*, August 2004. www.matchcoalition.com/SB_report/Chart.pdf

12 A snapshot of perspectives on second-hand smoke in the workplace (Maine). *Critical Insights*, September 2004.

13 RTI International; New York State Department of Health. *First annual independent evaluation of New York's tobacco control program*, November 2004. www.health.state.ny.us/nysdoh/tobacco/reports/docs/nytcp_eval_report_final_11-19-04.pdf.

14 RTI International, New York State Department of Health *First annual independent evaluation of New York's tobacco control program.* November 2004. p.6–36, exhibit 6–18. www.health.state.ny.us/nysdoh/tobacco/reports/docs/nytcp_eval_report_final_11-19-04.pdf

15 Office of Tobacco Control, Ireland. *Smoke-free workplaces in Ireland: a one-year review.* Clane, Ireland: Office of Tobacco Control, 2005. www.otc.ie/article.asp?article=271

16 Fong GT *et al. Initial evaluation of the comprehensive smoke-free workplace legislation in the Republic of Ireland: Findings from the ITC–Ireland/UK Survey.* Presentation at the meeting of the Society for Research on Nicotine and Tobacco, Prague, March 22, 2005.

10 Legislating to prevent exposure to environmental tobacco smoke in public places and workplaces: ethical and civil liberties arguments

> *Acts of whatever kind, which, without justifiable cause, do harm to others, may be, and in the more important cases absolutely require to be, controlled by the unfavourable sentiments, and, when needful, by the active interference of mankind. The liberty of the individual must be thus far limited; he must not make himself a nuisance to other people.*
>
> John Stuart Mill, On Liberty, 1859.[1]

10.1 Introduction

This chapter discusses the ethical case for and against smoke-free legislation for workplaces and other public places. The issue of restrictions on smoking in the home is also explored briefly.

Laws are social rules that are backed by the threat and possibility of coercion.[2] Most modern scholars agree that laws normally require some sort of ethical basis to be justifiable, and that there are ethical constraints on the sorts of laws that can be promulgated, the type and degree of coercion that can be justified in enforcing the laws, and the way in which a law may be selectively or universally enforced depending on circumstances. Punishments under a criminal law should also be proportionate to the type and severity of the offence committed. For a law to be ethically justified it must be established that the intention is ethically justified, that the penalty is proportionate and fairly targeted, and that the implementation policy is fair.

Commentators in law and ethical and social philosophy generally agree that it is the legitimate business of law and public regulation to be concerned with protecting third parties from harms caused by the activities of others; with protecting parties who are unable or incapable of looking after their own interests effectively; and with regulating certain kinds of public nuisance.[1,3–9] In relation to ETS exposure, these considerations all appear to lend strong support to a policy of making public places smoke-free, and may support measures to discourage smoking in the home or while pregnant. However, there are also many who dispute the value and legitimacy of what they consider an unreasonable ban on smoking in defined places. This chapter addresses these issues.

10.2 The ethical arguments for smoke-free public places

The main arguments which can be used to construct the case for smoke-free public places are as follows:

- The harm to health argument (which includes the harm to the unborn and harm to children of smokers arguments)
- The general harm by example argument
- The harm to ex-smokers argument
- The health promotion argument
- The nuisance argument.

The harm to health argument

Exposure to ETS is established as a significant cause of illness, disease, and death (see Chapters 1 and 2). The burden of that morbidity and mortality falls to varying degrees on unborn children exposed in utero, children and adults exposed to ETS at home, workers in smoky environments, and members of the general public who are exposed in the course of their business, leisure or other activities.

Direct health effects apply to both short- and long-term exposure to ETS. In the short term, direct exposure to smoke, although perhaps no more than irritating to most people, can be harmful to those with asthma, other respiratory disease, and those with ischaemic heart disease. In the longer term, passive smoking is harmful in that it causes a substantial number of serious diseases and deaths every year (see Chapter 4).

These classes of harm are different. The short-term harm affects some at-risk groups in particular, whereas the long-term harm potentially affects everyone. The short-term harm can be linked directly to a particular act of smoking, or a concentrated set of acts of smoking, while the long-term harm is the aggregate result of lots of distinct acts of smoking, often by a large number of identifiable and unidentifiable individuals. The short-term harm is related to what most people would identify as a significant, proximate risk, whereas the long-term harm is related to a long series of exposures, each of which may arguably be insignificant in terms of risk, but which become significant when aggregated. An important exception to this model of aggregated, short-term harms is the more immediate impact of maternal smoking on the fetus.

The risk to non-smokers, especially those who cannot choose to avoid smoking environments easily, is far and away the most compelling argument for smoke-free policy, due to the involuntary nature of the assumption of risk, and the magnitude of that risk.

The general harm by example argument

Indirect effects of allowing smoking in public places include the effect that exposure to smoking has on the uptake of smoking by others. Allowing smoking to continue in public places sends a powerful message that smoking is somehow acceptable, and has general institutional and social approval. This message may be particularly powerful in the eyes of children and adolescents, who, for a variety of reasons, are more susceptible to the attractions of taking up smoking, and less aware of or less concerned by the health effects of smoking and the difficulties of giving up smoking.

This type of harm by example presents itself in two ways. Firstly, there is what could be called a 'background' risk: children and other vulnerable groups (for example, patients in inpatient psychiatric facilities, prisoners in jail or on remand, military personnel, employees in environments where smoking is habitual or taken for granted) who are exposed continually to smoke may think of it as normal, or come to think that since they are exposed to smoke all the time, there is no additional risk to smoking itself ('I might as well smoke'). Second, there is what could be called a 'cultural' risk: if smoking in public places is sanctioned then the complex of cultural signals around smoking (for instance, that smoking is 'cool', that it is a sign of transition to adulthood, a mark of independence of thought, or of rebellion) may be enhanced. This cultural risk can be considered a harm as it undermines the ability to make autonomous decisions by strong signals which are substantially false (in particular, that smoking is no more harmful than exposure to passive smoking).

The harm to ex-smokers argument

Given the powerfully addictive nature of tobacco smoking, it can be argued that, in addition to the general harm by example outlined above, ex-smokers may find that being exposed to smoke is a powerful and seductive reminder of their addiction, which may seriously weaken their resolve not to smoke.[10] This is a kind of ethical harm, in that it attacks the ethical personality by assisting in the persuasion of an addict to give in to his or her addiction.[11] This kind of weakening of resolve comes about through a combination of susceptibility to cravings, the desire to smoke, and easy availability of tobacco through proximity to smokers and the social norm among smokers of sharing tobacco products.

The health promotion argument

There is evidence that making workplaces (and hence most public places) smoke-free has a significant impact on the prevalence and incidence of smoking,[2] presumably by making smoking more difficult and less attractive, and hence encouraging smokers to give up. It can be argued, therefore, that preventing smoking in public places is an effective health promotion strategy.

While promoting health in a population is a legitimate public interest, it is difficult to justify restricting where people can smoke purely on this basis. Such a justification could be regarded as paternalistic, since it promotes behaviour change without paying any attention to whether or not the smoker him or herself wants to give up. However, smoke-free policies can be fully justified by the harm-to-others principle,[4–6,12,13] so the potential of smoke-free policies to promote cessation is only a side-effect, rather than the ethical justification for the policy. The health promotion argument, properly understood, therefore figures only as a side issue in the general ethical justification of smoke-free policies.

The nuisance argument

It is widely recognised and accepted that many people find being in a smoky environment unpleasant, due to the direct irritant effects of ETS and the odour of stale tobacco smoke that persists on clothing, hair and skin after exposure.[14] Second-hand tobacco smoke is a nuisance which, given a choice, many people would want to avoid (see Chapter 9).

However, the nuisance argument is a weak basis for legal controls. Law very rarely intervenes to prohibit something merely on the grounds that it is a private or public nuisance, although it does construct grounds for redress between parties, one of whom is causing a nuisance to the other, on the grounds of the loss of amenity that may be involved. For a legal prohibition of a public nuisance, there would need to be a general public nuisance which interfered with the amenity of a public place to all, or made it inaccessible to some section of the public with a legitimate claim on using it and free access to it.

For some people who are asthmatic, suffer from eye problems, or ischaemic heart disease, it might be claimed that there is a nuisance involved in involuntary exposure to smoke. It is an open question just how many such people there need to be for the private nuisance to become a general public nuisance. However, these considerations are largely irrelevant in such cases as a smoke-free policy can be justified not on the nuisance grounds, but on the grounds of harm. It is arguably only those who do not suffer from such problems who could conceive the impact of smoke as merely a nuisance.

What can be salvaged from the nuisance argument is a stronger argument about the preservation of public goods. That argument is considered later.

10.3 Preventing personal harms as a basis for smoke-free policies

Common to the first three arguments above is the harm principle as stated by Mill in the epigraph to this chapter.[1] Of the three arguments, the first is by far the most powerful and clearest on the basis of the harm principle, although the other two arguments do contribute to the ethical case for smoke-free legislation.

All of these three arguments depend on two different types of consideration: a consequence-based consideration and a rights-based consideration. These considerations are independent, and either on its own might be sufficient to establish that a law would be justified in the absence of any powerful counter-arguments.

Consequence-based arguments

The consequence-based argument for preventing the harms imposed by smoking in public places is based upon the principle that a smoke-free policy is a highly effective measure for saving lives that would otherwise be lost, and preserving quality of life that would otherwise be damaged, by exposure to second-hand smoke.

The burden of morbidity and mortality from both active and passive smoking is not generally experienced as merely a slight foreshortening of life expectancy, with the burden falling at the end of a 'natural' lifespan of, say, 75 years.[12,13] Rather, smoking-related diseases reduce both quality of life and length of life in a very large number of cases, with the burden of disease falling at *any* point within the 'natural' lifespan. So the issue is not 'health professionals trying to make us live longer, with fewer pleasures', but instead 'health professionals trying to save us from preventable serious illness, disability, and death at an age well before anyone would want to die'. Moreover, while some smokers, and some non-smokers who support the liberty to smoke, may be persuaded that the pleasure of smoking can be offset against a risk of early loss of life or serious disease, surely no advocate of smoking could support the infliction of these harms on third parties.

An argument made by supporters of smoking in public places is that making public places smoke-free would only save 'statistical' lives, rather than the lives of actual people.[13] It is true that in many cases deaths caused by passive smoking are deaths of people who live with smokers (see Chapter 4). These lives would not be saved by a ban on smoking in public places alone. Since, arguably, these people consent to the smoking behaviour of the person they share accommodation with (at least in private homes), these deaths might not be thought to contribute to the case for bans in public places, which are the concern here. However, the evidence shows that exposure to ETS in the workplace is injurious to health (Chapter 2) and that many deaths attributable to passive smoking are caused by exposure to smoke in workplaces and other public places (Chapter 4).

Most deaths attributed to ETS exposure in public places occur among individuals who have encountered ETS in many different places. These deaths are not attributable to a specific environment or to a specific sequence of exposures to smoking, and thus seem to many people to be 'merely' statistical, rather than as a result of specific harms done at specific times through specific acts, or through immersion in a specific risk environment. Yet deaths attributable to ETS exposure they are, and they are preventable, even if they are the aggregate consequence of multiple small exposures. The importance of reducing the exposure is not diluted. The mistake in considering 'statistical' lives different from 'real' ones arises from the desire to identify specific people or situations as to blame – rather than whole series or contexts of events and impacts. Smoke-free policy is not a blame-based policy, but a harm-based policy.[14]

The 'statistical lives' argument does, however, lead to a very powerful argument in favour of smoke-free policy; that is, one identifiable group does have a specific exposure to a smoking risk environment. This is the group of employees in public places – particularly employees in the hospitality industry in which ETS exposure levels are high (see Chapter 3). Although many people who work in places where smoking is permitted may be free and able to seek alternative employment in smoke-free workplaces, or able to encourage voluntary smoke-free policies, probably the greatest proportion of staff exposed habitually to smoke are in low pay, low status work where they have little say in their working conditions and

122

relatively few options for alternative employment. Most trades u. Health and Safety Executive recognise exposure to workplace smoke a. to health, and support voluntary or legislative bans on smoking at wor. result.[15–17]

A consequence-based argument will only be compelling on its own merits if it involves an assessment of all the consequences of imposing smoke-free policies. So it is important to be sure that these consequences (a) will not include unintended consequences which would undermine the value of the policy, and (b) will be fairer than alternative policies (including the status quo).

Most of the consequences of smoke-free policy, other than a reduction in passive-smoking-related illness, are of no particular ethical importance. For example, arguments about whether takings in bars or restaurants will fall if a ban is introduced certainly have a pragmatic importance, and no one wants to deprive restaurateurs or licensees or their employees of their livelihood.[18–20] However, most impartial judges would trade a small decline in profitability for a significant decline in death and serious illness. Saving lives has an ethical importance, whereas changes in bar takings do not.

Some consequences may have ethical importance. For example, if smoking bans stigmatise smokers this would undoubtedly be a harm and, moreover, a proximate and non-trivial one which they would notice and suffer. Nevertheless, the category of harm (social or psychological) and the degree to which it would impair the welfare of the smoker are hardly comparable to the category of harm and the degree of impairment associated with passive-smoking-related illness and mortality.

A different problem attends the consequences of smoke-free policies for smokers themselves. In most cases, smoke-free policies lead to no more than a certain degree of inconvenience (needing to go outside to smoke, for example). Smokers are already used to this in many contexts, since many workplaces and public places in the UK are already smoke-free. In some situations (such as long-haul flights), smokers can find this onerous. In the typical situation where a smoker is unable to smoke for an extended period, this is justified by considerations of immediate safety and the excess hazard to the small number of people affected seriously by exposure to smoke (asthma sufferers, for example). Smokers typically accept this as reasonable, even if difficult, and can take steps to ameliorate the inconvenience – for example, by using nicotine replacement products. The smokers likely to be affected most seriously by a ban on smoking in public places (including workplaces) are those who, for some reason, are not permitted to leave the environment they are working or living in, such as prisoners or patients in inpatient psychiatric facilities (see Chapter 14).

Fairness arguments

The structure of the argument here is about whether the benefits and burdens of smoke-free policy are distributed fairly. Fairness arguments involve both rights- and consequence-based reasoning, and in some sense cut across both. Forbidding someone to smoke in a place when they cannot go elsewhere, and when their addiction to smoking is such that not smoking causes them actual pain or suffering, would be cruel, and hence can be argued as not fair. Where the burden of compliance with a ban is trivial, however, there is no unfairness in requiring compliance. One way in which the burdens of compliance could become non-trivial would be if the definition of 'public' was so broad as to make finding a non-public place difficult, if not impossible, within a reasonable time. However, this is not the generally the case with smoke-free legislation as smoking can usually occur outside of the enclosed workplace or public place.

Another fairness consideration sometimes invoked is that a ban would be unfair if there was some other, less restrictive approach which would achieve the same ends. For example, if ventilation systems were able to keep the air clear of ETS then fitting public places with such systems might be fairer to smokers than requiring them not to smoke or to go outside. But quite apart from the expense of such ventilation systems, there is no scientific evidence that they are effective at protecting non-smokers from the harm caused by ETS exposure (see Chapter 5), the primary ethical justification for smoke-free public places.

Another approach might be to allow smoking in places that are licensed for the purpose of smoking. For example, on the face of it, private clubs might be considered exempt from being considered 'public places'. This is incorrect, however, since employees of such clubs would still be covered by employment law, and such premises would still be covered by health and safety law.[16,17,21,22] So, while the members of such a club might want to contract privately among themselves to permit smoking and waive any claim against each other for smoking-related harm, any employee of the club could still argue that they were exposed to a workplace health hazard. An open question is whether employees could sign away their rights to claim damages for smoking-related injury, or that signing away such rights could be a condition of employment. This sort of binding contract seems defective, since an employee's right to change his or her mind would seem as important as any right to make employment contracts.[23,24]

Public interest arguments

Over and above these questions of fairness to individuals there is also the question of whether there is a general public interest, such that forbidding private contracts between employee and employer of the type just described can be justified. Public interest arguments are a kind of collective or aggregate interest-based argument and, as with personal interest arguments, may be construed either in consequence-based or in rights-based terms. Arguably, the entire history of legal regulation of workplace safety turns on this question, and the precedents are clear that such a public interest in workplace safety does exist.[23] Recently, scholars have begun to discuss whether this argument can be generalised. The approach taken is a 'public goods' approach.[8,9,21,25,26]

A 'public good' is a good which is 'non-excludable' and 'non-rival' in consumption.[25] For example, street-lighting is non-excludable, since anyone using the street benefits from the lighting, and cannot be prevented from doing so. It is also non-rival in consumption, since one person's benefit does not diminish the quantity of light available to anyone else. Similarly, clean air is a public good. Breathing clean air in an open space neither diminishes the quantity or quality of air available to others, nor prevents others from enjoying the same benefit, and hence is also non-excludable and non-rival.

A central difficulty in preserving a public good is that while everyone would agree that it should exist, it may be in no one's interest to pay for it, and possibly in someone's interest that it be diminished. How far is a smoke-free atmosphere in a closed public place a public good? Clearly it is non-rival and non-excludable in consumption. It is easily damaged or diminished, for instance by smoking. On the other hand, advocates of tobacco sometimes claim that tobacco creates a particular kind of public good, in the form of facilitating sociable interaction, conviviality and easing social awkwardness. However, there is nothing intrinsic to tobacco smoking that is not substitutable by other activities equally effective and valuable in promoting social interaction, while also being less harmful to the smoker or those around him or her. Moreover, the sociability of smoking can be transferred to the gatherings of smokers outside smoke-free places, as seems to have happened since pubs and bars became smoke-free in Ireland. The 'culture' around smoking is regarded by some as valuable in itself, and it would be paternalistic to say that participants in that culture can simply find another outlet so they should do so. However, asking such people to enjoy smoking culture outside, where it does not harm others who are exposed to it involuntarily, does not significantly damage that culture, although it does dilute it. The dilution is justified on consequence-based grounds of preventing harm to others, as in the consequence-based arguments above.

More nebulous claims about public good associated more loosely with smoking are also advanced. For example, some commentators argue that promoting smoke-free public places is damaging to the collective welfare by promoting risk aversion, or by paternalistically prioritising health interests over other interests that people legitimately have, or by illegitimately forcing a majority view on a minority.[12,13,27,28] Each of these arguments can be dealt with easily.

The risk aversion claim can be tested empirically, and there is no evidence that it is true.[29,30] Further, it should be taken as a claim about irrational risk aversion (over-cautiousness, perhaps). Yet the evidence presented in this report shows that aversion to the risks posed by second-hand smoke is well founded and proportionate. A more indirect claim is that, even if the aversion to smoking-related risk is rational, addressing such risk makes us more risk-averse generally, even where other risks are feared with less reason. Again, this is an empirically testable claim, which lacks much evidential support. Moreover, each risk should rationally be considered on its merits.[29] Addressing smoking-related risks is rational; other risks can and should be considered separately.

The argument that smoke-free legislation represents the over-prioritisation of health-related interests over other, equally legitimate, interests is important in the smoking debate generally. But this argument cuts both ways. The concern here is whether smoke-free policies protect the interests of people who don't want to be exposed to second-hand smoke. The function of a smoke-free policy is to prevent harm, not to focus attention on health at the expense of other interests. It is not focused on the health-related behaviour of smokers as such.

The argument that smoke-free policies tyrannously enforce the desires of the many on the few is also important.[1,12,13,27,28] However, if smoke-free policies are brought about through the legislative process, it is as a consequence of rational argument and persuasion, not by whim or force. Legislation may be a form of legitimate coercion, but it is a form of coercion which must both be intellectually coherent and on the basis of reasons, and be passed in an accountable (and revisable) way.[31] Moreover, since the burden on smokers is trivial, whereas the burden of ill-health on non-smokers involuntarily exposed to smoke is not, again, it is arguable that the argument runs the other way, and that allowing smoking in public imposes an unfair burden by the minority on the many. More troubling may be the suggestion that banning a common behaviour like smoking in public places undermines the civic virtue of tolerance of diverse behaviour, and frays the border between behaviour which is annoying but should be tolerated and behaviour which is not tolerated. Yet, again, the contrary argument that allowing smokers to smoke around others encourages an antisocial or thoughtless disregard for the welfare of others and the harmful consequences of one's own behaviour, seems just as strong.

The toleration issue is important, since it can be argued that a climate of tolerance is unequivocally an ethical public good. But it is far from proven that smoke-free legislation would dilute this good. What is important is to maintain a clear focus on the objective of the legislation, which is not to regulate a nuisance, or to stop smokers smoking on paternalistic grounds, but to limit a harm to third parties. Unwanted harms to others are not something usually regarded as a proper object of toleration.[32]

Having canvassed all the public good arguments, are there any other public interest arguments? Clearly there is a public interest in reducing the burden of smoking-related illness and mortality. Much of the burden of what this interest might mandate falls on smokers' behaviour in connection with their own health, and is controversial. For present purposes, the focus on the protection of the health of third parties required by this public interest is covered by the consequence-based arguments above.

Rights-based arguments

For many people, all this talk of consequences misses the point. That most would be better off if smoking were banned in public places does not matter, because a ban violates the rights of smokers.[4,6,12,13,27] Discussion of the nature and extent of rights is enormously complex but, for present purposes, the sort of rights considered are manifestations of two kinds of right to continue life without improper interference from others: the right to smoke without interference from others, and the right to conduct life without unfair exposure to health hazards caused by others.

The central points of this argument are quite simple. First of all, in a focus purely on rights it looks like a simple stand off. In their shared public space the smokers want to smoke; the non-smokers want them not to. Secondly, just that one person has a certain right does not mean that person is ethically permitted to exercise it whenever and wherever he or she wants to. For instance, as a smoker, an individual has the right to smoke next to an open can of petrol, but if this were to start a fire and damage property or others this would clearly be the smoker's responsibility, right or no right.

This sort of consideration has led to a proposal that the best approach to ETS exposure is a combination of appeal to smokers' etiquette (placing the responsibility on the smoker not to smoke without the permission of others) and voluntary restrictions. Where a restriction is voluntarily assumed, so the argument goes, the smoker's rights are not infringed, since he or she consents to not smoking.

Of course, voluntary measures are to be encouraged for all sorts of reasons. But are they enough? The more important point is that reliance on good manners and voluntary restrictions does not respect the non-smoker's right not to be harmed (which is a limitation on an individual's exercise of rights to do what suits them).

Furthermore, the incentive for a smoker to smoke (to ease a craving) may well be stronger than the disincentive attached to smoking in an area with voluntary restrictions where penalties other than ethical pressure are absent. Moreover, the degree of voluntariness is questionable, as in most voluntary restrictions. Smokers have relatively little bargaining power over the terms of the restrictions, and relatively little incentive to respect them. In sum, then, effective voluntary restrictions are no less coercive than formal legal policies, and ineffective voluntary restrictions are hardly worth having. Voluntary restrictions are thus less effective, and no better ethically, than formal smoke-free policies.

10.4 Conclusion

All the various ethical considerations reviewed above on the limited question of the legal justification for making public places smoke-free support the view that such a policy is fair, enforceable and effective. Detailed arguments about the type of penalties and enforcement practices that would be required to bring a ban into effect have not been set out, but the principles are similar to those underlying the ban itself.

The crucial argument for compulsorily smoke-free public places is that the harms caused to third parties both in the immediate present and in the long term are serious, and warrant preventing smoking in public places to avert these harms. Hence, smoke-free policies for public places are ethically justified.

The various other arguments in favour of such policies (helping ex-smokers avoid relapse, discouraging others from taking up smoking, health promotion, nuisance and public goods arguments) all carry some weight. However, they are insufficient on their own to justify a smoke-free policy. Yet in combination with the harm to others arguments they ground a persuasive case for smoke-free public places.

Second-hand smoke is harmful. A simple policy is available to greatly reduce it. The costs of the policy are small, the impact on smokers similarly small, and the ethical justification is compelling. The ethical case for smoke-free public places is conclusive.

10.5 Summary

- The ethical justification for smoke-free public places and workplaces rests primarily on the harm caused by second-hand smoke to third parties.
- Other arguments, such as that smoke-free policies protect ex-smokers from relapse, protect children and other vulnerable groups from starting to

smoke, reduce smoking prevalence in the population, and protect against the nuisance of ETS exposure, give secondary support to the main ethical justification.

- Smoke-free public places do not represent an unfair imposition on smokers.
- Appeals to smokers' rights and to the values of sociability and tolerance systematically mislead as to the true nature of rights, sociability and tolerance.
- Smoke-free public places protect the most vulnerable in society from harms caused wittingly or unwittingly by smokers.
- Making all public places smoke-free is, therefore, ethically justified.

References

1 Mill JS. On Liberty. In: AD Lindsay, intro., *Utilitarianism, liberty, representative government.* London: Dent, 1910. Citation from p.114.

2 Feinberg J. *The moral limits of the criminal law* 4 vols. Oxford: Oxford University Press, 1984–1988.

3 Feinberg J. Review essay: no smoking – the ethical issues by Robet J Goodin. *Bioethics* 1991;5(2):150–157.

4 Goodin RJ *No smoking: the ethical issues.* Chicago: University of Chicago Press, 1989.

5 Husak DN. *Drugs and rights.* Cambridge: Cambridge University Press, 1992.

6 Pope TM. Balancing public health against individual liberty: The ethics of smoking regulations. *University of Pittsburgh Law Review* 2000;**61**:19–498.

7 Verweij M. *Tobacco discouragement and the values of public health.* Unpublished manuscript, 2004.

8 Verweij M. *Paternalism and tobacco discouragement.* Unpublished seminar paper, 2004.

9 Coleman J, Shapiro S (eds.) *The Oxford handbook of jurisprudence & philosophy of law.* Oxford: Oxford University Press, 2002.

10 Royal College of Physicians. *Nicotine addiction in Britain.* London: Royal College of Physicians, 2001.

11 Frankfurt H. Freedom of the will and the concept of a person. In: Frankfurt H, *The importance of what we care about and other essays.* Cambridge: Cambridge University Press, 1988.

12 Scruton R. *WHO, what and why?* London: Institute of Economic Affairs, 2000.

13 Skrbanek P. *The death of human medicine and the rise of coercive healthism.* London: Social Affairs Unit, 1994.

14 Lader D, Meltzer H. *Smoking-related behaviour and attitudes, 2002.* London: Office for National Statistics, 2003.

15 Hope RA (Tony). Rationing and life-saving treatments: should identifiable patients have higher priority? *J Med Ethics* 2001;**27**:179–185.

16 Trades Union Congress. *Passive smoking at work: the global pressure mounts.* London: TUC, 2003.

17 Health and Safety Executive. *Proposal for an approved code of practice on passive smoking at work.* London: HSE, 1999.

18 Health and Safety Executive. *Passive smoking at work.* London: HSE, 2002.

19 Chief Medical Officer. Going smoke-free: the economic case. *Health Check* 2003:20–25.

20 Bosanquet N, Trigg A. *A smoke-free Europe in the year 2000: wishful thinking or realistic strategy?* Chichester: Carden Publications, 1991.

21 World Bank. *Smoke-free workplaces.* Washington, DC: The World Bank, 2002.

22 World Health Organization. *Tobacco control legislation: an introductory guide.* Geneva: WHO, 2004.

23 Pan American Health Organization. *Developing legislation for tobacco control: template and guidelines.* Washington, DC: PAHO, 2002.

24 Atiyah PS. *The rise and fall of freedom of contract.* Oxford: Oxford University Press, 1979.

25 Draper E. *Risky business: genetic testing and exclusionary practices in the hazardous workplace.* Cambridge: Cambridge University Press, 1991.

26 Smith R, Beaglehole R, Woodward D, Drager N (eds). *Global public goods for health: health economic and public health perspectives.* Oxford: Oxford University Press, 2003.

27 Boyle P, Gray N, Henningfield J, Seffrin J, Zatonski (eds). *Tobacco: science, policy and public health.* Oxford: Oxford University Press, 2004.

28 Curran J. The libertarian non-smoker's defence of smoking. Book review. *Lancet* 1998;352:745.

29 Tocqueville, A de. *Democracy in America.* London: Everyman's Library, 1994.

30 Slovic P (ed). *Smoking: risk, perception and policy.* Thousand Oaks, CA: SAGE Publications, 2001.

31 Elster J, Skog O-J (eds). *Getting hooked: rationality and addiction.* Cambridge: Cambridge University Press, 1999.

32 Raz J. *The morality of freedom.* Oxford: Oxford University Press, 1988.

11 Economics of smoke-free policies

11.1 Introduction

As with many other areas of tobacco policy, powerful myths have built up about the potential economic impacts of policies for restricting smoking in public places on different interests and groups within the population. An evidence-based policy approach requires that both the costs and benefits of different smoke-free policy options are assessed. Such economic analyses attempt to identify, measure and then value all the impacts, good and bad, on all groups of the population. The costs concern the use of scarce resources of labour (and leisure time), raw materials, land and capital. These are the resources that could be used for other goods and services to improve the overall welfare of the population. Such economic cost-benefit studies often focus on the distribution of benefits and harms among different groups, for example, smokers and non-smokers, taxpayers and non-taxpayers, the hospitality industry and other industries. The change in total level of welfare in the whole population is rarely considered. Thus, it is often the issue of who gains and who loses that tends to be emphasised by opponents of smoke-free policies, rather than the question of whether there is a net gain to society in choosing one policy over another.

In this chapter, the available economic evidence is reviewed and related to the potential costs and benefits of establishing smoke-free policies within the UK. The chapter draws upon several empirical studies conducted recently on the economic impact of workplace smoke-free policy in various parts of the UK. These include research by the Health and Safety Executive,[1] the Economics and Operational Research Division of the Department of Health,[2] the extensive review and modelling work by the University of Aberdeen for the Scottish Executive,[3] and new estimates undertaken for this report. The specific impacts within the hospitality sector are considered separately in the following chapter.

11.2 What are the costs of passive smoking and the benefits of reducing it?

Environmental tobacco smoke has a range of direct health effects, as outlined earlier in this report. The economic impact and cost of these health effects arise from the value of the health loss in terms of quantity and quality of life. One of the major difficulties in estimating the economic impact of any policy involves estimating the number of premature deaths, and valuing these deaths. Of particular concern is whether these deaths, caused by others smoking, should be valued at a higher rate than those of active smokers. Treating the health problems related to passive smoking involves consumption of healthcare resources which, in the absence or reduction of passive smoking, could be used for other health issues.

While there are a number of methods for valuing loss of life and reduced quality of life, it is much more difficult to estimate the nuisance and irritation costs of ETS. Whether public places and leisure venues are smoke-filled or smoke-free may influence consumer behaviour, and contribute to the economic effects of policy change. This evidence of how different smoking restrictions may affect trade levels and profits in the hospitality sector is considered in Chapter 12. In some venues, and particularly in the workplace, individuals may not have the choice of avoiding ETS exposure. Even smokers often find some smoke-filled venues unattractive. No monetary estimate of this lack of amenity for smokers or non-smokers was found in the literature, though it is perhaps partially reflected in public opinion about different smoke-free policies.

If workplace ETS exposure causes illness or discomfort this may reduce workers' productivity. This is generally valued by some estimate of the lost time valued by earnings.

11.3 The costs of different smoke-free policies

The most popular policy for encouraging smoke-free environments has been legislation or regulations to make public places, especially enclosed spaces, smoke-free. In some countries this has been extended from enclosed places to include restrictions on smoking in selected outdoor public places and even to the home, especially where there are children or other households in close proximity. Clearly, the wider the coverage of the smoke-free policy, the greater the number of beneficiaries and the size of the benefits. The policy costs are not zero as they typically include the preparation and consultation involved in changing laws and regulations, and some enforcement and monitoring costs. The experience in Ireland (see Chapter 15) also suggests that engaging in extensive publicity and other preparatory activities before the legislation is enacted helps gain acceptance and public support. Overall, however, legislation has relatively low set-up costs.

In contrast, the Health and Safety Executive (HSE) estimate of the costs of a policy of improved ventilation and more segregation of smokers and non-smokers is considerable.[1] Modern ventilation systems are expensive to install and to maintain. Also, the evidence suggests that such systems have limited ability to reduce the adverse health impact of passive smoking, particularly for hospitality workers (see Chapter 5). In 1999, the HSE estimated that the initial installation costs of ventilation equipment in all organisations not currently separating smokers and non-smokers would be between £580 million and £2,400 million, with an annual maintenance cost of about 10% of the initial outlay. The HSE estimated that the total cost of a voluntary scheme for all workplaces to have either smoking rooms or mechanical ventilation would consist of 'one-off' costs of between £1,259 million and £3,167 million in 1998/99 prices and recurring costs over ten years of £1,889 million to £5,694 million.

A third approach to achieving smoke-free public and workplaces is to use mass media advertising to change opinion and promote voluntary change. Advertising and other promotion costs involved in this strategy would be very high, the process would be slow, and its effectiveness unproven. In considering different options, the HSE concluded that there was little scope for a specific campaign to add to the campaigns on passive smoking already being undertaken in different parts of the UK at the time.[1] However, no evidence was presented in support of this statement. It is, therefore, difficult to give a comparative estimate of the costs of this approach compared to the familiarisation that would make a legislative approach more acceptable to the population, as was the case in Ireland. As discussed in the next chapter, there are other problems with voluntary approaches, especially in the hospitality industry.

However, it is not these specific costs of policies that cause the most controversy in economic appraisals of smoke-free policies. Rather, questions have been raised as to the costs to smokers, employers and the wider economy. If smoke-free polices are introduced then there is some loss of choice and amenity to smokers. Economists generally value the loss of such benefits to consumers by considering the maximum that consumers would be willing to pay for the consumption opportunity. This approach, measuring the consumer surplus, is based on the assumption that consumers are well informed and economically rational.[4] However, many smokers want to give up and may value smoke-free policies either at work or in leisure venues to help them quit. The consumer surplus approach could, therefore, overestimate considerably the amenity loss to smokers from smoke-free legislation.

For employers, the potential impact on productivity of different policies is more complex to estimate. If smokers can take smoking breaks, smoke-free policies could increase their time away from their work. However, this may depend on the attractiveness of the facilities available for smoking. For example, the provision of smokers' rooms may encourage more breaks than in totally smoke-free workplaces where smoking must occur outside. However, the time taken to have a smoking break outside the workplace may be longer than for one in a smoking room.[5]

Finally, a reduction in smoking has economic impacts on employment and government revenue. A loss of revenue may be seen as a reason why governments are reluctant to introduce effective tobacco control measures. In reality, governments have many sources of revenue, and a change in yield from one area of taxation can generally be recouped easily from other areas. The most likely outcome of policies like smoke-free public places, which result in a reduction in smoking, is a fairer distribution of tax payments across different taxpayers. Taking account of changes in tax revenue sources, Buck *et al*[6] demonstrated that a reduction in smoking in the UK would lead to an increase in overall employment – a result also found in other countries.[7]

11.4 Estimating the benefits of smoke-free policies

The benefits of smoke-free policies accrue in four areas. First, there are the positive health effects of the reduction in ETS levels. Second is the effect of such policies on reducing active smoking. Third, are other benefits of smoke-free environments, including reductions in cleaning, and in fire and accident risks. Finally, policies on smoking at work influence productivity by affecting the amount of work-time used by smokers for smoking breaks. This, as well as changes in adverse health impacts of active and passive smoking, could lead to changes in smokers' productivity.

The magnitude of the benefits due to reduced ETS levels resulting from smoke-free policies depends on the effectiveness of the policy. Effectiveness depends on acceptability, enforcement and compliance, and extent of exemptions. Experience to date suggests that compliance with smoke-free policies is high. Therefore, in estimating reductions of ETS exposure achieved, it can be assumed that future extensions of smoke-free policies will achieve high levels of compliance.

Estimating the effectiveness of other policies, such as a voluntary approach, is more difficult. Reductions in ETS exposure in the workplace to date have been due partly to reduced prevalence of active smoking and partly to changes in workplace smoking policies. Official UK figures[8] suggest that in 2003, 50% of workers were employed in smoke-free workplaces, 38% where smoking was only allowed in designated areas, 8% where there were no restrictions on smoking at all, and the remaining 4% of workers did not work with others. The percentage of workers covered by smoking restrictions has increased since 1996 when only 40% were in smoke-free workplaces, 42% in workplaces with designated smoking areas, and 13% in workplaces with no smoking restrictions. However, the reasons for these changes over time are unclear, and it is difficult to ascertain how much has been achieved by the voluntary approach and how much by other smoking policies.

Estimating the various impacts from reduced exposure to ETS also presents a number of methodological challenges. The issues involved in estimating the number of deaths related to different exposures of ETS are discussed in Chapter 4, and centre on separating out workplace, leisure and home exposure. For economic studies, the other issue is how to value this gain in life-years. Different approaches have been taken: some studies put a higher value on any loss of life associated with ETS compared to active smoking, while others have valued all gain in life equally. Data are also required to estimate the reduction in healthcare costs related to passive smoking and productivity gains from reduced ETS exposure.

Smoke-free policies also have an impact on mortality and morbidity through reducing the overall prevalence of smoking (see Chapter 7). In 1999, the HSE considered that smoke-free workplaces would result in 15–20% of smokers quitting (that is, about a four or five percentage point fall in overall prevalence).[1] The Department of Health estimates[2] used the figures from a review of the impact of smoke-free workplaces on smoking prevalence from well-designed studies.[9] This review, also used in the Scottish study,[3] concluded that smoke-free workplaces decrease smoking prevalence in the workplace by 3.8%.

The Department of Health and Scottish studies both used conservative estimates of the impact of introducing smoke-free workplaces on population smoking prevalence. The Scottish study[3] assumed that 2% of smokers at work would quit with comprehensive smoke-free legislation, but conducted sensitivity estimates of between 1% and 3%. In the Department of Health study[2] it was assumed that only half of smokers in workplaces with no restrictions on smoking would be affected by smoke-free policies and, of these, only 12% would then stop smoking. The estimates were difficult to follow but it seems that the Department of Health calculated that an additional 180,000 smokers currently working where there are designated smoking rooms would quit. Although the Department of Health study used a very conservative estimate of the reduction in active smoking as a result of introducing comprehensive smoke-free policies, the study also estimated that such policies would prevent 5,000 young people between the ages of 16 and 24 starting smoking each year.[2]

The additional ex-smokers generated by smoke-free policies would not only reduce the number of premature deaths caused by smoking but would also reduce morbidity and lead to reduced sickness absences, thereby saving NHS resources and productivity losses for employers. It is argued sometimes that there is no gain from reducing deaths among smokers, since they will ultimately consume NHS resources as a result of developing other illnesses. This argument is hard to sustain as there is clearly a gain from people living longer and in better health, for the individuals, their partners and dependants, and the wider society. Indeed, regulatory agencies and governments recognise this. Not only does the Department of Transport have a value for a life, but the National Institute for Health and Clinical Excellence supports additional spending by the NHS of between £20,000 and £30,000 for every quality-adjusted life year saved for a range of healthcare interventions, and this is used independent of individuals' ages or health-related behaviours, such as smoking.

11.5 Smoke-free public places: the economic evidence for the UK

Findings from previous studies

Figures prepared for the Chief Medical Officer from the Economics and Operational Research Division of the Department of Health are reproduced in Table 11.1.[2] The main conclusion drawn from this study is that there would be an annual net benefit of £2,300 million to £2,700 million from making all workplaces smoke-free.

A number of important points can be made about the detail of these estimates. First, the report uses an estimate of 107 deaths averted each year related to passive smoking. The value given to these deaths is much lower than other studies. The HSE estimate suggests that deaths caused by passive smoking should be valued at a higher rate than other deaths caused by ill-health or accidents;[1] they suggest using double the rate of value used by the Department of Transport.[10] The Department of Health estimates[2] were based on valuing the estimated 7.5 life years gained for a 35-year-old victim at £210,000 and the one to two life years gained for 55- to 64-year-olds at £40,000. They argued that deaths in active smokers occur at a later age than the average road traffic accident and, therefore, have a lower value. However, the original estimate for the Department

Table 11.1. Estimated annual costs and benefits of smoke-free workplaces. Department of Health, 2003.[2]

Items	Monetary estimate (£ million, 2002 prices)
Benefits	
From reduction in passive smoking	
Productivity gains from reduced sickness absences	70–140
Reductions in NHS costs from reduced sickness	4
Value of reduced deaths from passive smoking	21
From reductions in smoking	
Value of reduced deaths from reduced uptake	550
Value of reduced deaths from smokers quitting	1,600
Smoke-free workplaces	
Reduced fire damage, deaths and injuries	57
Reduced cost to fire services	0.2
Reduced administrative costs associated with fewer fires	6.3
Reduced cleaning and refurbishment costs	100
Productivity gains[1]	340–680
Total Benefits	2,700–3,100
Costs	
Production losses[1]	430
Losses of consumption benefits of continuing smokers and quitters[2]	(655)
Losses to the Exechequer[2]	(1,145)
Annual net benefits	2,300–2,700

Notes:
1 The estimates of direct productivity changes arising from a smoke-free workplace policy follows the HSE report on the impact of introducing more ventilation. It was expected that better ventilation and air quality for non-smokers currently exposed to ETS would have a 1% gain in productivity. No account was made in this report of the impact of abolishing smoking rooms within the workplace. It was expected, therefore, that smokers (who did not quit when a smoke-free policy was introduced) would continue to consume five cigarettes on average with a 3% productivity loss.
2 The table gives estimates for two effects that were not included in the estimated annual net benefits. Losses to the Exchequer are in the nature of a transfer. The loss of benefits to smokers who have to reduce or quit smoking in the workplace is also questionable, and the study makes no attempt to calculate the amenity benefits gained by non-smokers from smoke-free workplaces.

of Transport was taken from a review that considered the value put on any loss of life and the conclusions were not drawn from age-specific sources.[11]

In the Department of Health estimate there was no attempt to measure the benefits to non-smokers of a reduction in the nuisance of smoking in the workplace, or the potential reduction in NHS expenditure from smokers quitting as a result of introducing a smoke-free policy. A number of costs were estimated but not included in the total. For example, a maximum estimate of the value of smokers' loss of amenity for those who continued to smoke was estimated at £155 million. Even if included in the economic assessment, the conclusion would still be that there were major social benefits of smoke-free workplaces. More puzzling is the suggestion that those smokers who choose to quit would also lose some satisfaction and incur costs. This is difficult to justify as most smokers express the wish to stop smoking, and many smokers support further workplace restrictions and may welcome smoke-free workplaces. However, even if this larger sum of £550 million was included, the conclusion is the same that there are major net benefits from a smoke-free policy.

The more recent study undertaken for the Scottish Executive[3] used a different model but came to a similar conclusion that the annual net benefit to Scotland from making public places totally smoke-free would be £124 million, with a low estimate of £8 million and a high estimate of £205 million. This study calculated the potential gains over a 30-year period. These figures are in net present value terms, discounting the amounts that would occur in future years at 3.5%. The results, expressed as total (undiscounted) value across the 30-year period, are given in Table 11.2 to provide a comparison of the breakdown of the benefits of the policy across the different areas described in the previous section. The total figure of £316 million excludes the estimated positive impact on hospitality industry revenues (reviewed in Chapter 12).

A number of the estimates used in this study differ from those of the Department of Health shown in Table 11.1. First, the model was constructed over a 30-year period. An estimated 120 deaths per year in Scotland were attributed to non-domestic exposure to ETS. Without changes in policy, it was expected that exposure would rise, as would the annual death toll. The central estimate used in the model was 219 deaths, with a low estimate of 186 and a high estimate of 406 deaths. These are much higher than the Department of Health estimated for the UK as a whole. The central value used for a loss of life was £417,000, which, although adjusted for the potentially fewer life years gained, is also higher than that used in the Department of Health's study.

In estimating the NHS savings, the Scottish study estimated the potential impact of lower CHD and lung cancer prevalence if there was no ETS exposure in the workplace. However, very low figures for smoking-related health service expenditure were assumed. This study also placed a human cost on the ill health related to passive smoking, based on the Department of Transport estimates for road accidents. Productivity gains from a reduction in smoking breaks were based

Table 11.2. Estimates of 30-year cumulative undiscounted gains for Scotland from making public places smoke-free.[3]

	£ million (2003 prices)
From reduction in passive smoking:	
Productivity gains from reduced sickness absences	4.1
Reductions in NHS costs from reduced sickness	5.3
Value of reduced deaths from passive smoking	91.4
Value of reduced ill-health from passive smoking	12.8
From reduction in active smoking:	112.1
From smoke-free workplaces:	
Reduced fire damage, deaths and injuries, fire services and administration	5.0
Reduced cleaning and refurbishment costs	11.7
Net productivity gains:	73.7
Total	316

on an earlier study.[5] The figures given in Table 11.2 are the net productivity gains. Similar estimates were taken for costs from fires and for cleaning based upon the HSE study. [1]

Some new estimates

It is worth combining the best evidence from the Department of Health and the Scottish Executive studies and the previous HSE study to provide some new UK estimates. These new estimates are based on an estimate of potential annual cost savings in 2003/04 prices. As with the other models, the figures for benefits of smoke-free policy are divided into four areas: the health-related benefits from the reduction in ETS exposure; the benefits from the reduction in active smoking; the environmental benefits from creating smoke-free workplaces (reductions in cleaning, and in fire and accident risks); and the net effects on workplace productivity due to effects on the behaviour of smokers in smoke-free workplaces.

In 2002, there were 29,847,000 people in the UK workforce (15,936,000 men and 13,911,000 women), of whom 25,975,000 were employees (13,122,000 men and 12,853,000 women).[12] From the General Household Survey it is estimated that 28% of those in employment were smokers in 2002 (29% men and 28% women).[13] The employee figures suggest there are some 3,805,000 male smokers and 3,599,000 female smokers in work in the UK.

The benefits of a reduction in ETS exposure include the value of reduced mortality and morbidity from passive smoking, increased productivity from a reduction in illness caused by passive smoking, and savings to the NHS from treating these illnesses. As with other studies, no value has been give to the amenity benefits attributable to both non-smokers and smokers from a smoke-free workplace.

Benefits from a reduction in ETS exposure. New estimates of the number of deaths attributable to ETS exposure are presented in this report (see Chapter 4). In the UK, an estimated 500 deaths per year, including about 50 in hospitality industry staff, are attributable to passive smoking in the workplace.

The three existing studies have used different estimates for the value of these deaths. While there seems to be no reason to value such deaths at twice the rate given by the Department of Transport for accidents, there is also no reason to value such deaths at such a low rate as given by the Department of Health. The willingness-to-pay estimates used by the Department of Transport were based on a review of all available estimates of the population values of any loss of life, and it is this figure which seems the sensible estimate to use for those deaths attributed to other people's smoking. Using a figure of £1,312,260 per death,[8] the total value of preventing 497 deaths per year (see Chapter 4) is £652 million in 2003/04 prices.

The HSE provided some estimates of sickness absence which could be attributable to asthma or chronic bronchitis arising from ETS exposure in the workplace.[1] They estimated some 90,000 people are likely to be at risk from asthma and 50,000 from bronchitis. There are fewer workplaces that allow unrestricted smoking in 2002 than in 1998 (8% compared to 13%). However, this suggests that there are still between 2.4 million workers likely to be affected by ETS exposure. Using the same methodology as the HSE (assuming 140,000 workers with one week additional sickness absence and 140,000 with two weeks) but with updated figures on earnings[14] yields an estimated potential gain in productivity valued at £249 million.

For the additional health costs associated with sickness it was assumed that each bronchitis patient had one additional GP visit per year. The cost of such a visit with a prescription is estimated at £51.52 in 2003/04 prices.[15] This gives a total estimated cost of £2,576,000 per year. For asthma sufferers, the HSE assumed that 98% of asthmatics would also have one additional GP visit, 1.4% would have an inpatient episode and 0.3% would receive treatment as an outpatient. Using the National Reference Costs[16] unit cost estimates of £858 for a minor asthma inpatient episode and £123 for an outpatient episode, this gives a total of £5,658,400 cost to the NHS of asthma episodes associated with ETS exposure in the workplace. These figures are a clear underestimate as they exclude any impact for heart disease, stroke or cancer related to exposure to ETS in the workplace, and do not assign costs for additional inpatient or outpatient treatments for bronchitis patients.

Taking the value of reduced deaths, productivity gains and reduction in NHS costs together yields an annual cost of passive smoking in the workplace of £909 million in 2003/04 terms. All these costs would be saved if smoke-free workplaces were implemented, and savings would be recurred year by year. This total underestimates the likely true saving because it does not include healthcare cost savings for several common diseases caused by smoking and, unlike the Scottish estimates,[3] does not include any value for the human cost of ill health.

Benefits from the reduction in active smoking. The second area of benefits from a smoke-free policy would arise from a successful reduction in the number of people who smoked actively. Currently, 46% of smokers in employment would be faced with further restrictions on smoking in the workplace. The evidence for reductions in smoking prevalence is reviewed in Chapter 7, and the conservative estimate of a 1% reduction in population prevalence is used in the estimates below. This is lower than the figure of 2% used in the Scottish study.[3] What is less clear is how far reductions in smoking prevalence would continue year by year after implementation of the smoke-free policy. As the Department of Health study[2] suggested, restriction on smoking would continue to be a deterrent, particularly for young people joining the workforce. It is, therefore, not unreasonable to suggest that such a policy would have a continuous impact, although there is some uncertainty around the size of this impact. The impact of reductions in active smoking has been estimated with caution.

The benefits from lower levels of smoking would be a reduction in the number of deaths, a reduction in NHS costs, and an increase in productivity because of less smoking-related illness. A cautious approach would suggest that the reduction in smoking in the workplace would impact initially on deaths among those aged under 65; in the longer term the reductions would occur across the age ranges. Estimates suggest that there are currently at least 10,099 smoking-related deaths among those aged under 65 in the UK each year,[17] so a 1% reduction would prevent about 101 deaths per year. Considering only deaths under 65 years takes some account of the age at death of smokers and, therefore, it seems sensible to value these deaths at the full rate. There are no credible arguments to suggest that a different value should be given to the health of a smoker than any other member of society. This would yield a total value of £133 million. Those that quit smoking as a result of the smoke-free workplace policy would also save NHS costs. Figures taken from Godfrey *et al* of discounted NHS costs averted of £520 per 12-month quitter in 2003/04 prices,[18] and 1% of employed smokers quitting per year because of the smoke-free policy, suggest a saving to the NHS of £39 million.

Finally, for those who quit following the introduction of smoke-free policies, there will also be reductions in smoking-related absences, and gains in productivity. Following Parrott *et al*,[5] it is assumed that smokers have an additional 7.5 hours (one day) smoking-related sickness absence in any year. From the estimated 74,040 quitters per year, this would yield productivity savings of £9 million in 2003/04 prices.

Other benefits from creating smoke-free workplaces. It has been estimated that smoking-related fires caused £53.3 million pounds of damage, two deaths and 125 injuries in 1998 in the UK.[1] Updating for 2003/04 prices gives a damage value of £63 million. Following the same methodology as the HSE, 25% of the injuries are estimated to be serious and 75% minor. Updating the accident costs yields a total estimate of £8.3 million. It is assumed that 75% of the costs from fires would be saved by introducing smoke-free workplaces – a saving of £53 million per year.

From the HSE report it was calculated that for each smoker in places where there are unrestricted policies there are some £210 additional cleaning costs per year.[1] If 8% of workers are in workplaces with unrestricted smoking, this yields an estimate of 518,100 smokers. However, this is likely to be a severe underestimate. It is estimated that in 2002 there were 1,471,000 smokers working in hotels, restaurants, pubs and clubs alone.[19] Updating the cost to 2003/04 values (£247), and using just the costs in unrestricted workplaces, yields cleaning cost of £128 million per year; costs which would be saved by a smoke-free policy.

Effects of the behaviour of smokers in smoke-free workplaces on productivity. Following Parrott *et al*,[5] different types of smoking policies were assumed to have different impacts on the amount of time smokers take breaks from work compared to their non-smoking colleagues. Those allowed to smoke in the workplace are assumed to take five minutes per day in lighting cigarettes, disposing of butts etc. Those with designated smoking rooms are assumed to take 30 minutes each day in smoking breaks, and those with smoke-free buildings are assumed to be more likely to reduce their smoking and would take 10 minutes in smoking breaks per day.

A smoke-free workplace policy would mean the removal of designated smoking rooms, affecting 38% of smokers in 2003. This would bring a gain in productivity if these smokers reduced the overall time taken smoking from 30 minutes to 10 minutes. However, those 8% of smokers who currently have no restrictions would spend more time in breaks (10 minutes on average) than time currently taken (five minutes on average).

The changes in productivity that arise from changing work patterns of existing smokers will continue year on year. However, there will be a reduction in the number of smokers each year after the smoke-free policy is introduced. There is a net gain in productivity for each quitter, whatever their current workplace policy. Overall, these productivity gains would tend to increase year by year. Ideally, a model across 30 years would be constructed, as in the Scottish study. However, for this exercise the figure is calculated for the first year following introduction of the smoke-free policy to give a reasonable estimate of annual savings.

It can be assumed that those quitting would be concentrated among smokers currently working where there are no restrictions or where there is a designated smoking room. An estimate of 4% quitting among these workers (to give the overall estimate of a 1% quit rate across all smokers in the workplace) implies the following productivity changes:

- 2,486,700 extra minutes lost per working day among the 497,340 smokers who were working previously in workplaces with no restrictions and continue to smoke (due to increase in the average time for smoking breaks).
- 47,247,590 minutes saved per working day for the 2,363,380 continuing smokers who previously had access to a designated room at work.

The net gain in productivity valued by average wages is £12 million per day – some £2,596 million per year. No attempt is made to estimate any health benefits that occur from the likely reduction in the number of cigarettes smoked among continuing smokers.

The available estimates are summarised in Table 11.3. These estimates suggest that making a workplace totally smoke-free in the UK may yield total savings of some £4 billion a year. A substantial proportion of this is due to shorter smoking breaks. However, even if this is excluded, the savings are over £1.3 billion a year. Gains would be distributed across non-smokers, smokers, employers and the NHS. These estimates confirm previous studies and suggest there would be real economic welfare gains from introducing smoke-free workplaces.

What remains to investigate is whether such a policy would have a disproportionate effect on profits and trade in the hospitality sector. This is explored in the next chapter.

Table 11.3. Summary of revised estimates of the annual potential benefit of making UK workplaces smoke-free, at 2003/04 prices.

	£ million (2003/04 prices)
From reduction in passive smoking:	
Value of reduced deaths from passive smoking	652
Productivity gains from reduced sickness absences	249
Reductions in NHS costs from reduced sickness	8
From reduction in active smoking:	
Reduction in number of smoking related deaths among those aged under 65	133
Reductions in NHS costs from quitters	39
Productive gains from reductions in smoking absences among current smokers.	9
From smoke-free workplaces:	
Reduced fire damage, deaths and injuries, fire services and administration	53
Reduced cleaning and refurbishment costs	128
From productivity gains arising from changes in working patterns	2,596
Total	3,867

11.6 Summary

- The most cost-effective and quickest means of reducing ETS exposure is to legislate to make all public places smoke-free.
- Making all workplaces in the UK smoke-free would realise substantial economic benefits, of approximately :
  - at least £832 million from prevention of death and disease
  - £181 million from prevention of fires and reduced cleaning costs
  - £2,854 million from improved productivity.
- The likely total economic benefit to society of implementing comprehensive smoke-free policies would be, therefore, of the order of £4,000 million per annum at current prices.

References

1 Health and Safety Executive (HSE). *Draft regulatory impact assessment for an approved code of practice on passive smoking at work.* London: Health and Safety Executive, 1999.

2 Department of Health. *Smoke-free workplaces and public places: economic analysis.* London: Economics and Operational Research Division, Department of Health, 2003.

3 Ludbrook A, Bird S, can Teijlingen E. *International review of the health and economic impact of the regulation of smoking in public places.* Edinburgh: National Health Service Health Scotland, 2004.

4 Buck D, Godfrey C, Sutton M. Economic and other views of addiction: implications for the choice of alcohol, tobacco and drug policies. *Drug and Alcohol Review* 1996;**15**:357–368.

5 Parrott S, Godfrey C, Raw M. Cost of employee smoking in the workplace in Scotland. *Tob Control* 2000;**9**:187–192.

6 Buck D, Godfrey C, Raw M , Sutton M. *Tobacco and jobs: the impact of reducing consumption on employment in the UK.* York: Society for the study of addiction, Centre for Health Economics, 1995.

7 Jacobs R, Gale F, Capehart T, Zhanf P, Jha P. The supply-side effects of tobacco-control policies. In: Jha P, Chaloupka F (eds), *Tobacco control in developing countries.* Oxford: Oxford University Press, 2000.

8 Lader D, Goddard E. *Smoking-related behaviour and attitudes, 2003.* London: Office for National Statistics, 2004.

9 Fichtenberg C, Glantz S. Effects of smoke-free workplaces on smoking behaviour: systematic review. *BMJ* 2002;**325**:188.

10 Department of Transport. *Highways Economic Note No 1 2003 Valuation of the benefits of prevention of road accidents and casualties.* London: Department of Transport, 2004.

11 Hopkin JM, Simpson H. *Valuation of road accidents.* TRL Research Report 163. Crowthorne: Transport Research Laboratory, 1995.

12 Office for National Statistics (2003a). *The official yearbook.* London: The Stationery Office, 2004.

13 Rickards L, Fox K, Roberts C, Fletcher L, Goddard E. *Living in Britain: results from the 2002 General Household Survey.* London: The Stationery Office, 2004.

14 National Statistics. *Annual survey of hours and earnings: analysis by all employees 2004.* www.statistics.gov.uk

15 Curtis L, Netten A. *Unit costs of health and social care 2004.* Canterbury: PSSRU, University of Kent, 2004.

16 Department of Health. *National Reference Cost 2003 and National Tariff 2004.* London: Department of Health, 2004.

17 Twigg L, Moon G, Walker S. *The smoking epidemic in England.* London: Health Development Agency, 2004.

18 Godfrey C, Parrott S, Coleman T, Pound E. Cost effectiveness of English smoking cessation services: evidence from practice. *Addiction* 2005;**100** (Supp 2):70–83.

19 Tighe A. *Statistical handbook 2004.* London: Brewing Publications Limited, 2004.

12 Economics of smoke-free policies and the hospitality industry

12.1 Introduction

The evidence presented in earlier chapters demonstrates that smoke-free policies in public places in the UK would generate large improvements in public health, and substantial overall economic benefits. However, there are concerns that smoke-free policies may adversely affect one particular sector of the economy: the hospitality industry. This chapter reviews the economic evidence for the potential effects on the hospitality industry of different smoke-free policies.

12.2 What are the economic impacts on the hospitality industry of smoke-free policies?

The hospitality industry provides a workplace for 1.5 million workers in the UK.[1] Most of these workers currently have little effective protection from ETS exposure. The conclusions of this report (see Chapter 5) and others[2] are that there are few benefits to these workers from any policy other than going completely smoke-free. Concerns have been expressed about the effects of comprehensive smoke-free policies on the level of sales and profitability of the hospitality industry. However, such critical assessments of the economic impact of smoke-free policies generally do not evaluate the overall costs and benefits, ignoring, for example, the protection from harm that ETS-exposed workers will gain.

Clearly, the introduction of smoking restrictions in pubs, restaurants and other public venues will impact directly on those current customers who smoke. They will have costs imposed either in forgoing smoking or having to go outside to smoke. This may deter some customers, or mean they spend less time in such venues, resulting in loss of trade for the venue. Conversely, some smokers may prefer smoke-free atmospheres and, as in non-hospitality workplaces, welcome the restrictions and be more likely to use smoke-free venues, thereby increasing trade. This is most often the case if the smoker is attempting, or considering an attempt, to quit. In relation to non-smokers, smoke-free venues may attract new customers, or cause existing clients to visit more often or stay longer at each visit.

Since there are many more non-smokers than smokers in the UK it is perhaps surprising that more hospitality venues are not currently smoke-free. There has been an increase in the number of restaurants that have become completely smoke-free in the UK, but far fewer pubs have taken this step. This may be because of two factors – real or perceived. First, heavy drinkers are more likely to be smokers than light drinkers. Second, mixed groups of smokers and non-smokers may be less likely to use smoke-free venues if alternative venues that permit smoking are easily available. It is difficult in a highly competitive market for one particular venue to impose different conditions to those in close proximity. The potential dilemma was demonstrated by Shiell and Chapman,[3] who showed that, even in the face of potential compensation claims from workers, no one owner of a restaurant, bar or public house would go smoke-free because they could not be certain that other owners would do the same. This may be the main reason why some representatives of the hospitality trade have been vocal in a demand for a 'level playing field'.[4]

The full impact of a comprehensive smoke-free policy on the hospitality industry is difficult to predict. There may be a change in the customer base, with the attraction of some new customers and the loss of some established ones. Existing customers may change spending behaviour. The hospitality trade is large and varied, encompassing many different types of business. For example, in some venues such as city centre 'vertical drinking' establishments, the profits achieved are driven by large volume drink sales. Other establishments, such as 'gastro' pubs or themed venues, offering food and other value-added services may rely less on high volume, low cost alcohol sales. The economic impact of smoke-free policy depends not just on the overall volume of expenditure but also the profit margin on different goods. This will vary between times and locations.

It is even more difficult to estimate the impact of partial restrictions. In highly competitive market conditions it may be difficult for owners and managers to decide how to position their particular venue. As suggested in Chapter 11, providing ventilation is expensive and, in common with provision of designated smoking areas, does not provide adequate protection to workers (see Chapter 5).

12.3 International evidence for the economic impact on the hospitality sector of smoke-free regulations

There are a number of difficulties in attempting to assess the impact of any change in smoking regulations. The first is determining the appropriate outcome measure. Change in an objective measure provides better evidence than subjective evidence, such as the opinion of owners, managers or customers. The most likely evidence available would be in the form of the total value of sales. However, as suggested above, sales figures may not correlate well with profit levels. Changes in employment in the sector may be another useful indicator.

Most studies have examined outcomes before and after a change in smoking restrictions. However, changes over time are also influenced by underlying trends and general economic conditions. This can make it difficult to determine the independent impact of the change in smoking restrictions. A major systematic review of the literature on the economic impact of smoking restrictions on the hospitality sector has recently been undertaken.[5–7] The reviewed studies were considered further in the later work conducted for the Office of Tobacco Control in the Republic of Ireland[8] and the Scottish Executive.[2] The overall conclusions of these reviews are unanimous. The 21 studies of reasonable methodological quality show that smoking restrictions have no impact or a slight positive impact when objective data such as tax revenue, sales data or employment levels are considered. The American Lung Association[9] highlighted that these studies have been conducted in a range of different jurisdictions, and across urban, suburban and rural environments; therefore, the results typically showing small positive or no impacts on business apply widely.

The Scottish review[2] usefully divided the available good quality studies into three groups: those concerned with impact on restaurants, those examining bars, and those concerned with hotels and the tourist trade. Studies on the impact of partial and full smoke-free policies have been conducted in the United States and Australia. Wakefield *et al* analysed restaurant sales data, comparing the figures in South Australia where a smoke-free restaurant policy had been imposed with figures from the rest of Australia.[10] The trends in these sales data are shown in Fig 12.1. The analysis, using interrupted time series methods, found no significant change as a result of the smoke-free policy. A study by Bartosch and Pope explored the impact of highly restrictive smoking policies in Massachusetts, and had the benefit of a relatively large number of observations and a longer

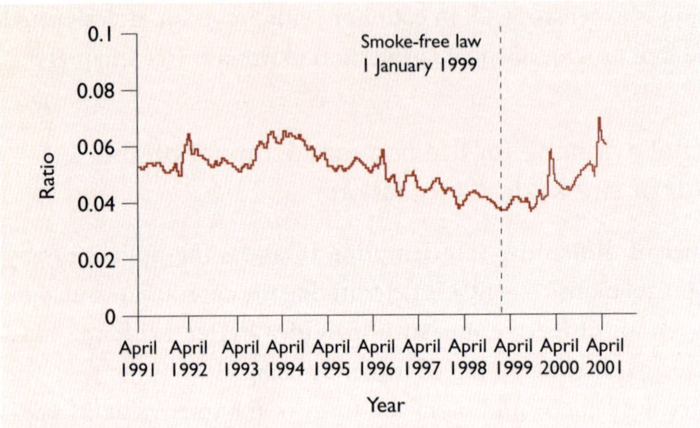

Fig 12.1 Effect of smoke-free policy on restaurant sales (as a ratio of retail sales) in South Australia.[10]

follow-up than many other studies.[11] This study suggested an overall positive but small impact of the restrictions on restaurant sales of +0.25% (95% confidence interval (CI) –1.32 to +1.81).

The Massachusetts study was used in the Scottish model[2] of the impact of a smoke-free workplace policy in Scotland, along with two other American studies, one examining the impact on bar revenues[12] and the other on hotel room revenues.[13] Glanz and Charlesworth[13] examined the impact of ordinances for smoke-free restaurants on hotel room revenues as a fraction of retail sales and found an average effect (using the corrected figures as given in the Scottish study[2]) of –0.054 (95% CI –0.128 to +0.020) from a mean value of 2.43. Only one good quality study that had examined the impact of smoke-free restrictions on bar revenues for California was found;[12] this study showed an effect on bar sales as a fraction of retail sales of +0.5 (95% CI –0.284 to 1.284) from a mean value of 7.1.

The confidence intervals for the estimates of the effects of smoke-free policy in these three examples all include zero, and are therefore consistent with no effect. Their range also indicates the extent of the uncertainty about the true magnitude of the effect of smoke-free policies, and that the net effect could be positive or negative. However, the magnitude of the potential negative impacts, if there are any, is also shown to be very small in these three and, indeed, in all other good quality studies.

Two studies using objective outcome measures, and controlling for trends in economic conditions and other factors, published since the above reviews were completed confirm these findings. The first explored profitability rather than revenue in the restaurant businesses in the United States, and found that restaurants in a smoke-free location had a 16% premium in price when the venue was being sold compared to others with the same level of sales in areas where there were no smoke-free ordinances.[14] The authors concluded, as outlined in the previous chapter, that workplace restrictions bring benefits to employers and, therefore, could reduce costs and increase profitability. Another recent study explored the impact of smoke-free laws on the gaming industry in Delaware in the US.[15] In this study, economic activity and seasonal effects were modelled using regression methods. It was found that the smoke-free law enacted in this area of the US did not have any effect on total revenue or average revenue per gaming machine. Further work in Massachusetts' bars and restaurants,[16] although preliminary, has since suggested that the numbers of customers using bars and restaurants increased slightly (by three persons per venue on the occasions visited), and tax collection for meals increased as a result of a smoke-free policy, while those for alcoholic drinks remained steady. None of these changes was statistically significant. Air quality was vastly improved, however, with a decrease of 93% in levels of respirable suspended particles (RSPs) less than 2.5 microns in diameter.[16]

Another important observation from the literature reviews is the difference in both the quality of the studies and the 'findings' reported, depending on the source of funding. Tobacco company-financed studies tend to use subjective reports of perceived impact rather than objective data, and some only report views of the likely impact of smoke-free policies before rather than after implementation. Scollo and Lal report that all of the studies linked to the tobacco industry have found negative effects on the hospitality industry, and that very few of these have been published in peer-reviewed journals.[7]

The overall conclusion from this international literature is that hospitality sector revenue and profits are likely to remain the same or even increase as a consequence of comprehensive smoke-free policy. Recent work in Massachusetts suggests there may be changes in the mix of business, but also that owners may be able to use these changes to increase profits.[17]

12.4 Potential impact of smoke-free policies on the UK hospitality industry

The experience from other countries introducing smoke-free regulations indicates that there is much misinformation about the likely impact on the hospitality industry. However, the hospitality industry is large and varied, and it is important to consider whether there may be differential impacts across the sector. The international evidence is strong in suggesting the economic impact will be slight and probably positive in the restaurant or hotel sector, but there is less evidence to predict the impact on public houses.

In a number of countries, including the UK and Ireland, there has been an underlying secular trend in alcohol consumption by sector, with drinking in pubs falling relative to consumption within the home. The trends in alcohol expenditure for the UK between 1980 and 2003 demonstrate a progressive longer-term decline or, at best, a plateau of alcohol sales through the on-trade (that is, sales of alcohol for consumption on the premises, as in bars, hotels and restaurants) in the UK (Fig 12.2). During this period, alcohol bought through the off-trade (such as supermarkets) increased from £6.7 million to £12 million in constant 2000 prices, while the amount of alcohol bought in pubs, hotels and restaurants was at a similar level of £24 billion in both years.[1] Beer sales, particularly important for pubs, show a similar trend. In 1980, 88% of beer sales took place in the on-trade, but this figure had fallen to 61% by 2003.[1] This trend towards increasing alcohol sales through off-licensed premises has been particularly acute in the last ten years, such that the overall trend in alcohol sales has been driven by the off-trade while the on-trade has had static expenditure at a time of increasing economic prosperity. Any assessment of the impact of smoke-free policies, therefore, needs to take account of these trends in consumption. These figures also illustrate the considerable commercial pressure that currently exists, in particular in the public house sector.

Evidence from Ireland is especially important in assessing any impact of smoke-free policies on the pub and bar sector. Early evaluation suggests that the

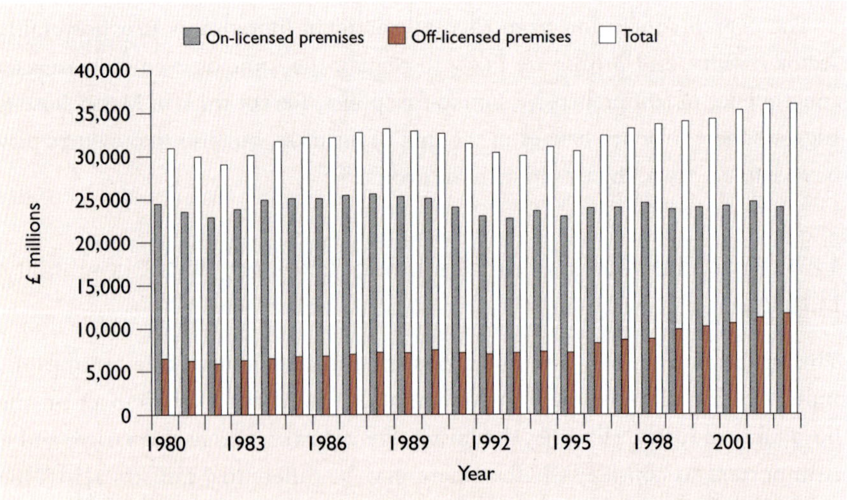

Fig 12.2 Trends in UK household expenditure on alcohol (in £millions) at year 2000 equivalent prices from on- and off-licensed premises, 1980–2003.[1] (On-trade includes pubs, hotels and restaurants.)

implementation of comprehensive smoke-free policy in March 2004 had little impact on trade in pubs and bars over and above the background of progressive decline; bar sales declined by 4.4% in 2004 compared to 4.2% in 2003.[18] The sales data, adjusted for seasonal differences and expressed as an index, are shown in Fig 12.3.[19] While there is a need for further analysis that fully adjusts for the long-running decline in sales and other factors such as increased alcohol prices, the unadjusted official objective data confirm that any impact on pub profits attributable solely to the smoke-free legislation was very small.

Ludbrook *et al*[2] used the three studies described earlier to estimate the likely range of impacts of a smoke-free policy on the Scottish hospitality and tourist industry. They estimate that the annual impact on sales would lie somewhere between a reduction of £104 million to a gain of £299 million, the central estimate being a gain of £97 million. As they suggest, however, it is not clear that any change in revenue from one sector to another has an overall impact on economic or social welfare. If revenues in the hospitality industry change either positively or negatively, there may be offsetting changes in revenues for other industries as people's spending patterns change. However, all the estimates of changes in hospitality revenue are very small in relation to the other economic benefits of smoke-free workplaces (see Chapter 11). These economic benefits will also accrue to the hospitality industry, and potentially improve profitability, whatever shorter-term small changes in revenue occur in some parts of the sector.

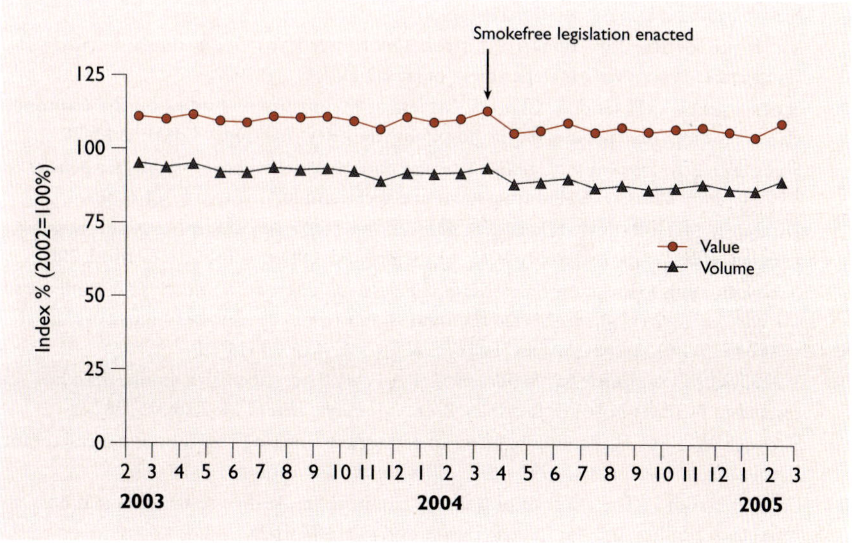

Fig 12.3 Seasonally adjusted sales from pubs and bars in Ireland before and after the introduction of smoke-free legislation in March 2004.[19]

12.5 Summary

- Evidence from high quality studies carried out around the world suggests that implementing comprehensive smoke-free policies in the hospitality industry is likely to have a small positive impact on overall revenues from the sector.
- There is little evidence to predict the impact of more partial regulations.
- The evidence from Ireland suggests that alcohol sales in public houses declined minimally immediately after the introduction of smoke-free workplaces by approximately 0.2%.
- In the longer term, smoke-free policies improve the health of workers, so costs to employers are likely to fall. Therefore, profits are likely to increase in the hospitality sector as well as other sectors of the economy.

References

1 Tighe A. *Statistical handbook 2004.* London: Brewing Publications Ltd, 2004.

2 Ludbrook A, Bird S, can Teijlingen E. *International review of the health and economic impact of the regulation of smoking in public places.* Edinburgh: National Health Service Health Scotland, 2004.

3 Shiell A, Chapman S. The inertia of self-regulation: a game-theoretic approach to reducing smoking in restaurants. *Soc Sci Med* 2000;**51**:1111–1119.

4 British Beer and Pub Association. *Submission by the British Beer and Pub Association to the House of Commons Health Committee: Inquiry into the Public Health White Paper.* London: British Beer and Pub Association, 2005.

5 VicHealth Centre for Tobacco Control. *Environmental tobacco smoke in Australia.* Canberra: Commonwealth Department of Health and Aging, 2002.

6 Scollo M, Lal A, Hyland A, Glanz S. Review of the quality of studies on the economic effects of smoke-free policies on the hospitality industry. *Tob Control* 2003;**12**:13–20.

7 Scollo L, Lal A. *Summary of studies assessing the economic impact of smoke-free policies in the hospitality industry.* Melbourne, Australia: VicHealth for Tobacco Control, 2004.

8 Durkan J, McDowall M. *Smoke-free policies: market research and literature review on economic effects of the hospitality sector.* Clane, Ireland: Office of Tobacco Control, 2004.

9 American Lung Association Fuzzy Math. *How the tobacco industry distorts the truth about the economic effects of smoke-free restaurants and bars*, 2004. www.lungusa.org/atf/cf/-(7A8D42C2-FCCA-4604-SADE-7Fd5E762256)-/FUZZYMATH.PDF

10 Wakefield,M, Siahpush M, Scollo M, Lal A *et al.* The effect of a smoke-free law on restaurant business in South Australia. *Aust NZ J Public Health* 2002;**26**:375–382.

11 Bartosch W, Pope G. Economic effect of restaurant smoking restrictions on restaurant business in Massachusetts, 1992–1998. *Tob Control* 2002;**11**(Suppl 2):38–42.

12 Glanz S, Smith L. The effect of ordinances requiring smoke-free restaurants and bars on revenues – a follow-up. *Am J Public Health* 1997;**87**:1687–1693.

13 Glanz S, Charlesworth A. Tourism and hotel revenues before and after passage of smoke-free ordinances. *JAMA* 1999;**281**:1911–1918.

14 Alamar B, Glantz S. Smoke-free ordinances increase restaurant profit and value. *Contemp Econ Policy* 2004;**22**:520–525.

15 Mandel L, Alamar B, Glantz S. Smoke-free law did not affect revenue from gaming in Delaware. *Tob Control* 2005;**14**:10–12.

16 Connelly G, Carpebterm C, Alpert H, Skeer M, Travers, M. *Evaluation of the Massachusetts Smoke-free Workplace Law: A preliminary report.* Cambridge, Mass: Harvard School of Public Health, Tobacco Control Working Group, 2005.

17 Bartosch W, Pope G. The economic effect of restaurant smoking restrictions on restaurant business in Massachusetts, 1992 to 1998. *Tob Control* 2002;**11**(Supp 2):38–42.

18 Office of Tobacco Control. *Smoke-free workplaces in Ireland: A one-year review.* Clane, Ireland: Office of Tobacco Control, 2005.

19 Central Statistical Office, Ireland. *Retail sales index, seasonally adjusted value and volume series, 2000=100,* January 2005. www.cso.ie

13 Tobacco industry responses and approaches to smoke-free policy

13.1 Early recognition of ETS effects as a threat

The 1962 Royal College of Physicians report entitled *Smoking and health* called for 'wider restriction of smoking in public places' as one of its seven key recommendations for government action.[1] However, while some action was taken on several of these original recommendations, relatively little was done to promote smoke-free environments for a further twenty or more years. This was not only a failure of government, but also of mainstream health agencies which, for many years, failed to recognise the importance of the passive smoking issue.

The tobacco industry was, however, quick to recognise the threat posed to its business by the designation of smoke-free public places and workplaces. Although highly competitive over market share, the trans-national tobacco corporations collaborate closely by sharing information and jointly funding a wide range of initiatives to combat any measures that might reduce overall tobacco consumption. With the emergence of once-secret internal tobacco industry documents, first through whistleblowers[2] and then, principally in the US, through litigation in the 1990s, details of the strategies employed to protect and grow the global tobacco business are now in the public domain.

13.2 Early tobacco industry activity

Tobacco industry scientists were investigating the problem of the irritation caused by sidestream smoke as early as 1970. A meeting of the British American Tobacco (BAT) Biological Testing Committee held in Southampton in 1970 noted:

> *Dr. Green drew attention to the additional point... that the operators of the smoking machines at Battelle have complained about the odour/irritating nature of the sidestream smoke from the cigarette containing 100% I-308* [a BAT term for a type of tobacco].[2]

A 1973 document from Brown & Williamson [a USA subsidiary of BAT] summarises the results of an internal review on issues related to smoking and health.[2] It notes that passive smoking is a growing issue of concern to the industry because of the negative impact of increased regulation on the social acceptability of smoking:

> *Increasing emphasis is being given to the smoking habits of employees and the whole question of occupational exposure. One anticipated result can be the increased attention of government and organized labor to the personal smoking habits of employees.*
>
> *The popular claims that heart and lung disease are closely associated with community air pollution are being extended to include passive smoking.... In many instances, cigarette smoking is taking the rap for environmental pollution.*
>
> *More and more, smoking is being pictured as socially unacceptable. The goal seems to be the involvement of others – non-smokers, children, etc – in addition to health and government organizations. The main thrust of these zealots seems to be that 'smoking is not a personal right because it hurts others; that smoking harms non-smoking adults, children, and even the yet unborn.'*[2]

The first peer-reviewed paper drawing attention to the health impact of passive smoking was published in *The Lancet* the following year.[3] At a BAT research conference held in Merano, Italy in April 1975, BAT scientists discussed passive smoking at length. The minutes of the conference note:

> *Passive smoking was discussed and reviewed in detail. It is considered that this is an important area and interest in it is unlikely to recede … It is desirable to be in a position to anticipate the identification of new sidestream constituents which may be considered harmful to non smokers.*[2]

In 1978, the Roper Organization conducted a confidential study for the US Tobacco Institute on the attitudes of the public toward smoking.[4] This report, which was obtained by the Federal Trade Commission and subsequently made public, stated:

> *The original Surgeon General's report, followed by the first 'hazard' warning on cigarette packages, the subsequent 'danger' warning on cigarette packages, the removal of cigarette advertising from television and the inclusion of the danger warning in cigarette advertising, were all 'blows' of sorts for the tobacco industry. They were, however, blows that the cigarette industry could successfully weather because they were all directed against the smoker himself. The anti-smoking forces' latest tack, however – on the passive smoking issue – is another matter. What the smoker does to himself may be his business, but what the smoker does to the non-smoker is quite a different matter. ... six out of ten believe that smoking is hazardous to the nonsmoker's health, up sharply over the last four years. More than two-thirds of non-smokers believe it; nearly half of all smokers believe it. This we see as* ***the most dangerous development yet to the viability of the tobacco industry that has yet occurred.***[4] [Emphasis added.]

The Roper report was prescient, since passive smoking was about to become a much more prominent issue with the publication and ensuing publicity in 1981 of several further papers on passive smoking and lung cancer.[5–7]

13.3 The tobacco industry's assessment of the threat to its profits

The threat to the industry posed by smoke-free environments manifests itself in a number of ways. The first and overriding concern of tobacco companies is the impact on sales and profits, explained succinctly in this extract from an internal Philip Morris presentation:

> *... if our consumers have fewer opportunities to enjoy our products, they will use them less frequently and the result will be an adverse impact on our bottom line.*[8]

Voluntary restrictions on smoking in some workplaces and public places during the 1970s had the companies calculating their losses. In 1978, the *Financial Times* reported the concerns of William Hobbs, a president of the US-based tobacco company, R.J. Reynolds, on the topic of restrictions on smoking:

> *If they caused every smoker to smoke just one less cigarette a day, our company would stand to lose $92 million in sales annually. I assure you we don't intend to let that happen without a fight.*[9]

It is not surprising that the industry was concerned. Social attitudes towards smoking had shifted markedly during the 1970s and then, as now, people were responding positively to the provision of smoke-free facilities. In 1971, London Transport banned smoking on single-deck buses and Rank Leisure introduced smoke-free seating in most of its cinemas. In 1976, a Department of Health and Social Security survey conducted by NOP showed that 70% of the population – a majority of smokers and non-smokers – favoured further restrictions on smoking in all public places.[10] The industry foresaw that the successful introduction of smoke-free policies would encourage their further extension. The industry will also have been aware of the longer-term threat to business arising from the effect of smoke-free policies in de-normalising smoking in society, and the role smoke-free environments play in reducing the number of exemplar occasions and individuals that help to recruit young people to take up smoking.

13.4 The industry response – a coalition of the obedient

The industry responded by building a broader coalition against measures to restrict smoking in public – both as individual companies and collectively through national trade bodies such as the Tobacco Advisory Council in the UK and the Tobacco Institute in the US. This involved establishing strategic relationships with other industries potentially affected by the introduction of restrictions on smoking, such as the hospitality, ventilation and, more recently, the gambling industries. The tobacco industry also funded apparently independent bodies and individuals who would take direction from industry executives, and argue for outcomes favourable to the industry.

One of the earliest examples of this 'third party' tactic was the formation and maintenance of smokers' rights groups, often at arm's length through a public relations company. Some groups have been created solely to campaign against a particular piece of legislation. For example, Californians For Common Sense was formed by Brown and Williamson in 1978[2] to help defeat Proposition 5, the California Clean Air Act. In the UK, FOREST – the Freedom Organisation for the Right to Enjoy Smoking Tobacco – was launched in 1979 with the motto 'Tolerance, courtesy and common sense'. While portraying itself as a membership organisation of disgruntled smokers, FOREST acknowledges that it receives around 95% of its income from tobacco companies.[11] Although particularly active in resisting the restriction of smoking in public places and workplaces, FOREST has also used the guise of representing smokers' rights to act as an advocate for many other aspects of tobacco company business.

13.5 Tobacco industry goals – buy time and maintain the status quo

In the face of rising public approval for smoke-free environments, the tobacco industry's main objective has been to preserve the status quo as to where smoking is allowed, and resist any policy, voluntary or statutory, designed to increase smoke-free provision. This is not to say the industry has opposed literally all smoking restrictions. In a 1987 Philip Morris strategy-planning session, for example, it was agreed to, 'Focus on costless areas of compromise, eg we will accept a no-smoking "policy" bill for elevators if you need to pass something.'[12]

However, the same meeting of senior executives also mapped out a very wide-ranging, multi-pronged strategy to deal with 'The problem: how to alter public perception of ETS in terms of perceived risk and annoyance.'[12]

The strategy was dubbed 'The Big Chill' because its expected outcome was to 'chill anti-smoking rhetoric', and it included all of the tactics outlined below. There is little doubt that Philip Morris was leading the industry in the response to the passive smoking issue. It determined at the same meeting in 1987 to seek the participation of other companies in this global strategy: 'Offer them... opportunity to join us, but tell them diplomatically that we are going ahead with our program, regardless of their decision.'[12]

In February 1988, Philip Morris executives laid their plans before British-based companies, including BAT, at a meeting in London:

> *Philip Morris presented to the UK industry their global strategy on environmental tobacco smoke. In every major international area ... they are proposing, in key countries, to set up a team of scientists organised by one national co-ordinating scientist and American lawyers, to review scientific literature or carry out work on ETS to keep the controversy alive. They are spending vast sums of money to do so.*[13]

The UK companies met again in June 1988 and this time presented their own agreed industry-wide strategy:

> *Andrew Nelmes [from Gallaher] outlined the UK strategy on ETS. That strategy is made of three components: (1) challenging unfounded reports linking ETS and human disease, (2) placing ETS in the proper perspective with regard to overall air quality, and (3) disassociating the public's annoyance with ETS from alleged health effects. By this strategy, TAC* hopes to (1) create 'marketable' science, (2) to deflect criticism of ETS, and (3) to place the industry in the most favorable position possible.*[14]

---

*TAC is the Tobacco Advisory Council, now known as the Tobacco Manufacturers Association.

13.6 The strategy

The tobacco industry response arising from this process included the following strategic components:

- Dispute the science – argue that the problem of ETS is one of annoyance not real harm.
- Advance 'courtesy' and 'accommodation' – find a social solution to the problem by promoting schemes where smokers and non-smokers can co-exist in the same environment.
- Champion ventilation – offer a technical solution to the problem.
- Warn of dire economic consequences of smoke-free solutions – suggest that this is the real problem.
- Portray champions of smoke-free solutions as extremists and smoke-free solutions as coercive.
- Argue that enforcement of smoke-free solutions will be difficult – thus suggesting they will never work.

Dispute the science

In 1978, the Roper report recommended that the industry engage in research to discredit the evidence that passive smoking is dangerous to non-smokers:

> *The strategic and long run antidote to the passive smoking issue is, as we see it, developing and widely publicizing clear-cut, credible, medical evidence that passive smoking is not harmful to the non-smoker's health.*[4]

Disputing the science on passive smoking has been a major plank of the global strategy, and has been pursued in spite of the companies' own scientists and consultants advising that the science was sound. A 1981 Brown & Williamson memo notes that consultants were engaged by the US Tobacco Institute to find fault with the Hirayama[5] study, but they concluded: '...[we] believe Hirayama is a good scientist and that his nonsmoking wives publication was correct'.[2]

The routine denunciation of studies such as Hirayama's was concurrent with the companies' own research into the 'biological activity' of sidestream smoke.[15]

Disputing the science can be seen as an umbrella term for a myriad of activities, some overt and some covert, which have now been traced back to the industry through investigation and analysis of internal documents. These activities include:

- commissioning research specifically to refute findings of independent studies, and promoting it through apparently independent scientific consultants[16–21]

- creating apparently independent agencies to conduct and publicise research on indoor air pollution[22–24]
- attempting to subvert the International Agency for Research on Cancer (IARC) study on passive smoking and cancer[25]
- attempting to derail the 1993 US Environmental Protection Agency risk assessment on ETS[26–28]
- attempting to derail the 1997 Australian National Health and Medical Research Council report on passive smoking[29]
- promoting the label 'junk science' to discredit the evidence that second-hand smoke causes disease[30]
- developing the concept of 'sound science' and 'good epidemiology' to question any methodology which produces results unfavourable to the industry[31]
- creating and maintaining the illusion of scientific controversy over the health effects of ETS through industry-sponsored symposia, and commissioning scientists to write favourable reviews of the evidence and critiques of ETS studies.

Attempts to discredit the emerging evidence on passive smoking have also been mounted by the industry using direct advertising. In 1986, when the Tobacco Institute of Australia ran advertisements stating that 'there is little evidence and nothing which proves scientifically that cigarette smoking causes disease in non-smokers', the top consumer organisation in Australia successfully sued, alleging misleading and deceptive trade practices.[32] In 1996, when Philip Morris ran a Europe-wide advertising campaign trivialising the risks of ETS by suggesting passive smoking was no more likely to cause cancer than eating biscuits or drinking milk, the UK Advertising Standards Authority upheld complaints and deemed the advertisements misleading.[33]

Both cases hinged on the industry's attempt to shape the scientific debate on the statistical interpretation of passive smoking. Industry copywriters turned 'not statistically significant' into 'insignificant' or 'very little, if any' or 'no meaningful increase in risk'. This is a tactic the industry continues to use. Addressing the Greater London Assembly's 2001 Inquiry into Smoking in Public Places, BAT's Head of Science and Regulation, Chris Proctor, expressed the opinion that the link between chronic disease and ETS was 'too small to measure with any confidence.'[34]

During the 1990s, the industry used more covert tactics to dispute the science. Perhaps the most comprehensive campaign was that spearheaded by Philip Morris to undermine a study on passive smoking undertaken by IARC. Since it feared that the study would lead to increased restrictions on passive smoking in Europe, Philip

Morris developed an inter-industry, three-pronged strategy to subvert IARC's work. Its scientific strategy attempted to undercut IARC's research and to develop industry-directed research to counter the anticipated findings. Its communications strategy planned to shape opinion by manipulating the media. Its government strategy sought to prevent increased smoking restrictions by lobbying politicians. Philip Morris organised the industry worldwide:

> *PM initiated and chairs an industry-wide task force to manage both the IARC monitoring and scientific intelligence gathering process and the development of a global communications/government relations plan to address [the] impact of the [IARC] study.*[25]

The task force was known as the International ETS Management Committee (IEMC) and its objective was to, '… coordinate plans and resources among the companies and in conjunction with National Manufacturers Associations.'[25]

The explicit aims of the campaign were to:

- *Delay the progress and/or release of the study.*
- *Affect the wording of its conclusions and official statement of results.*
- *Neutralize possible negative results of the study, particularly as a regulatory tool.*
- *Counteract the potential impact of the study on governmental policy, public opinion, and actions by private employers and proprietors.*[35]

The industry prepared a coordinated response to the publication of the IARC report with the help of public relations firm, Burston Marstellar.[25] Philip Morris management also held 'IARC simulation' response exercises.

In the end, BAT influenced the timing of global media coverage of the IARC study by briefing *The Sunday Telegraph.*[25] A front page article entitled 'Passive smoking doesn't cause cancer – official' with an accompanying editorial entitled 'A setback for nanny' ran on 8 March 1998. Journalists around the world were provided with a comprehensive press package which included a pre-recorded interview with a BAT spokesperson, background material on IARC, and statistical results of second-hand smoke studies and surveys of irritating behaviours. *The Sunday Telegraph* story preceded by three days the release of the UK's Scientific Committee on Tobacco and Health report on passive smoking on No Smoking Day, 11 March 1998, and generated worldwide coverage.

Another strategy used by the industry is to organise and promote high profile symposia on ETS, sometimes held in the premises of reputable scientific organisations, at which the health effects of ETS are debated and an illusion of controversy about proven and well accepted health effects is created. A recent example in the UK was the November 2004 seminar 'The science of environmental tobacco smoke' at the Royal Institution, sponsored by the Tobacco Manufacturers Association (TMA).[36]

The industry has also been developing the 'sound science' theme. Philip Morris sees it as a 'good offensive strategy' for its consultants to be 'out there trying to fix epidemiology instead of being critical all the time'.[25]

Advance 'courtesy' and 'accommodation' whilst describing opponents as extremists

While continuing to deny that passive smoking is a health problem, the industry also realised early on that opposing any and all restrictions on smoking was likely to be politically untenable. If smoking was going to be allowed to continue in workplaces and public places, non-smokers would need to be 'accommodated'. Hence the industry developed and promoted 'accommodation programmes' around the world.

In contrast to health agencies' talk of 'bans' and 'restrictions', the industry has used more positive language for its public relations and lobbying strategies. By advancing 'courtesy' as a social solution to the problem of passive smoking, tobacco companies have been successful in positioning themselves as polite and obliging, as distinct from the 'zealots' and 'health fascists' who will restrict freedoms by arguing for controls on how people choose to live their lives.

An early example of this, and one which continues to this day especially in developing countries, is the 'Courtesy of Choice' campaign. While funded by the tobacco industry, the campaign was run through the International Hotel & Restaurant Association (IH–RA) until 2002 when it handed over responsibility for the campaign to its national association members.[37]

The Yin Yang symbol used in Courtesy of Choice has been appropriated by the industry for other campaigns, including the original Philip Morris 'Accommodation Program', which places the lit cigarette in the green half of the image, and AIR in the UK.[38]

While the Courtesy of Choice front has been used extensively in campaigns to defeat proposals for smoke free environments,[39] the extent to which it has actually been adopted by hotels and restaurants varies from country to country.

Champion ventilation

Similar in many ways to the strategy to dispute the science, the ventilation strategy is complex and still evolving.[40] Just as the industry has created a network of scientists and third parties ready to discredit the evidence on health effects of passive smoking, so it has created a network of 'ventilation experts' and worked through intermediary organisations to argue that smoke-free environments are simply not necessary.

One such intermediary is Healthy Buildings International (HBI) which operates in the UK, Ireland, US and Australia. HBI and its predecessor company, ACVA Atlantic (Air Conditioning & Ventilation Analysis), were financed by the industry to promote the message that tobacco smoke was not the problem, but rather 'sick building syndrome' and poor indoor air quality in general. With industry backing, HBI company representatives sought to influence the setting of standards to measure indoor air quality and to have authorities set them at a level which would not preclude tobacco smoke.[41] This is another industry strategy which has been well documented.[42]

In early 1997, the TMA in the UK engaged Corporate Responsibility Consulting (CRC) to create the AIR initiative (Atmosphere Improves Results) 'to identify and promote practical techniques to resolve the public smoking issue'. In July 1997, the newly-elected Labour Government hosted the Anti-Smoking Summit and canvassed the proposal of 'no smoking in public places'.[43] A wide-ranging White Paper on smoking was promised by the end of 1997, and was finally published in December 1998. In the meantime, CRC, operating as AIR, had:

- *worked with key groups to identify voluntary standards and targets with the Government: the Public Places Charter on Smoking*
- *built a network of partners – trade associations, health professionals, local councils, pub and restaurant groups and training companies – to promote best practice to end-users.*[44]

The result was to persuade the Government to adopt a voluntary self-regulation approach. The Public Places Charter on Smoking was highly desirable to the industry, since the Charter promotes ventilation as a solution and provides venue operators with a range of options, including 'smoking allowed throughout'. Thus, by simply displaying appropriate signage, a venue can achieve full compliance with voluntary self-regulation while continuing to permit unrestricted smoking.

An added bonus for the tobacco industry of persuading publicans and restaurateurs to install ventilation systems is that these businesses can become advocates for maintaining indoor smoking to justify the significant sums they have expended on costly equipment (see Chapters 11 and 12).

Warn of dire economic consequences of smoke-free legislation

The main reason why whole sections of the hospitality industry have been such willing, if at times unwitting, partners of the tobacco industry in the campaign to maintain indoor smoking is that they have been convinced that smoke-free policies would have catastrophic consequences for their business. This is understandable considering the lengths to which the tobacco industry has gone to convince them that this would be the case.[38,45]

The accommodation and ventilation strategies outlined above were conceived and developed to accommodate non-smokers (who might find smoke 'irritating') in venues where smoking has been the norm. Faced with the prospect of totally smoke-free venues, the industry has re-framed the issue to be less about the smoke itself than about smokers as customers. By extension, their campaigns aimed at the hospitality trade often imply that smokers (and their friends and families) will just stop using venues that are declared smoke-free altogether, rather than simply not smoke while in those venues.

The industry has commissioned and promoted studies claiming that smoke-free environments cause serious financial hardship,[46,47] even when internally they have acknowledged that this is far from true. As long ago as 1994, a director of marketing and sales for Philip Morris said:

> *... economic arguments often used by the industry to scare off smoking ban activity were no longer working, if indeed they ever did. These arguments simply had no credibility with the public, which isn't surprising when you consider our dire predictions in the past rarely came true.*[8]

Scollo *et al* analysed more than 130 studies of the economic impact of smoke-free policies in the hospitality industry.[47] They concluded that those studies that report a negative impact share characteristics, in that they:

- *predominantly based their findings on outcomes predicted before introduction of policies, or on subjective impressions or estimates of changes rather than actual, objective, verified or audited data*
- *were funded predominantly by the tobacco industry or organisations allied with the tobacco industry*
- *were almost never published in peer-reviewed journals.*[47]

For understandable reasons, these scaremongering studies and their attendant publicity have alarmed hospitality business owners, especially when they are disseminated by trade organisations which purportedly exist to look after the interests of the hospitality trade. The chief executive of the Association of Licensed Multiple Retailers and chairman of the Charter Group, Nick Bish, is on record as saying that only a 'major stock market crash or terrorist attack' could possibly have a more profound effect than smoke-free legislation.[48]

The *Publican* newspaper ran a campaign in early 2005 against proposed smoke-free legislation in Wales, in which it urged publicans to lobby Members of Parliament with the following information:

> *The economic effects of a ban on pubs in Wales are huge, and recent research from the Licensed Victuallers (Wales) suggests that as many as 25 per cent of pubs will go out of business if a blanket ban is introduced.*[49]

In fact, in its submission to the Welsh Assembly's Committee on Smoking in Public Places,[50] the Licensed Victuallers (Wales) speculates on the impact on pubs 'assuming a 15% reduction in turnover', but does not actually explain why a 15% reduction would be likely to occur.

Another means of arguing that business would be badly hit is to claim that public opinion is not in favour of smoke-free environments. In the preface to its own research on public attitudes, the TMA asserts that, 'There have been conflicting claims about what people really want. Some of these claims seem to be based on 'research' that is, frankly, poorly conducted and unreliable.'[51]

However, in reporting its own results, the TMA does not provide its survey questions. Box 13.1 illustrates how a question can be framed to ensure a low response.[52] The TMA's results[51] are at variance with the data from a range of representative population surveys (see Chapter 9).

Box 13.1.

Thinking of the quality of life in your area, which of the following would you MOST like the local Government (or your local Council) to concentrate resources on?

Controlling yobbish behaviour	37%
Increasing CCTV (security) camera surveillance	19%
Maintaining parks and open spaces	18%
Prohibiting litter and graffiti	12%
Banning smoking in public places	9%
Banning cars in city centres	3%
Don't know	1%
None of these	2%

Source: Tobacco Manufacturers Association [52]

Argue that enforcement will be difficult

As cities, states and countries have enacted legislation requiring smoke-free workplaces and public places, the industry and its allies have argued that mass disobedience will ensue, and that police and other enforcement agency resources will be diverted unnecessarily. For example, when a nightclub bouncer was stabbed to death two weeks after New York bars went smoke-free, the new law was reported to be the cause of the crime.[53]

In reality, compliance with smoke-free legislation is generally high and public support has been overwhelming in Ireland and elsewhere (see Chapter 9).

13.7 Still looking for the 'safer cigarette'

While conducting this multi-faceted strategy against smoke-free policies, tobacco companies have not stopped trying to develop products they could promote as not only 'safer' for the active smoker but also for the passive smoker. A 1984 summary of BAT's research activities confirmed that:

> *Strategic objectives* [of sidestream smoke research] *remain as follows:*
> 1 *Develop cigarettes with reduced sidestream yields and/or reduced odour and irritation.*
> 2 *Conduct research to anticipate and refute claims about the health effects of passive smoking.*[2]

Company scientists investigated techniques for achieving these goals, including the use of additives to reduce or mask the aroma, visibility and irritation of sidestream smoke, and also to lower actual smoke emissions.[54] In 1998, Philip Morris started to test-market the Accord Lighter Kit, a product that only burns tobacco on inhalation. The promotional slogans for Accord addressed smokers' concerns about the impact of their smoking on those around them:

> *Accord makes you feel right at home smoking at home.*
> *Less smoke around you. Virtually no lingering odor. No ashes.*

R.J. Reynolds sells Eclipse, a product that primarily heats rather than burns nicotine, and which it claims reduces second-hand smoke by 82% to 87%.[55]

13.8 Present and future industry priorities and strategies

While the UK is still to enact smoke-free legislation, the industry is concentrating its efforts on ensuring that such legislation is delayed and as weak as possible.

However, in other jurisdictions where legislation has been in place for some time, the same companies are working to undermine it. In several Australian states, governments have come under immense pressure from hospitality industry bodies with close ties to the tobacco industry to regulate to allow smoking in semi-enclosed environments, for example bars which have doors on to terraces or balconies.[56] This has resulted in proposals in the Australian Capital Territory for smoking to be allowed in areas which are 75% enclosed by walls and a roof or ceiling. In other Australian jurisdictions, similar negotiations are under way.[57] If these regulations are approved, the owners of bars, hotels and casinos are likely to invest considerable sums of money in alterations to their buildings which will make overturning such regulations in the future all the more difficult.

Another issue on the horizon for the UK is the liberalisation of gambling, and whether the new gambling venues will allow smoking. The relationship between smoking and gambling is well understood by the gambling industry.

'Smoking is a powerful re-inforcement for the trance-inducing rituals associated with gambling.'[58] This quote is from a confidential report for a major Australian gambling company, commissioned in the wake of legislation in the state of Victoria in 2002 requiring all gambling venues to be smoke-free. The research identified that players were still attending gambling venues and were just as likely to play electronic gaming machines; however, smokers were spending less time and less money on the machines:

> *The reduction in spend rate and duration appears linked to smokers playing less time per hour to take smoking breaks and reduced duration due to smokers leaving the venue earlier.*[58]

The report states that the smoke-free laws were breaking the gambling routine of smokers, and that cigarette cravings were breaking player concentration. Further, when smokers did take a cigarette break they were reviewing their gambling expenditure and, in some cases, this prompted them to consider that their gambling was 'a waste of money', or tempted them to 'go home rather than play on'.[58]

Taxes from gambling are a significant source of income for some state governments in Australia. In state cabinets, the ministers responsible for finance and gaming are finding themselves at odds with their colleagues responsible for public health and workplace safety. The tobacco industry and its allies will have prepared the ground in the UK for persuading politicians that smoke-free gambling could result in significantly less revenue to government coffers, and to place more importance on this than on the health of workers or patrons in gambling venues.

13.9 Summary

- The tobacco industry has recognised for many years the significance of the passive smoking issue and the enormous threat it poses to its short-term profits and long-term viability.
- Internal documents demonstrate that the industry's strategy on the passive smoking issue is sophisticated and subversive, with the overall goal to maintain sales and profits by preventing the introduction of smoke-free legislation.
- The key strands of the industry strategy are to dispute the science, advance courtesy as a social solution, portray opponents as extremists, champion ventilation as a technical solution, warn of dire economic consequences of restrictions and argue that enforcement will be difficult.
- The industry engages in these tactics directly but also covertly through the funding of third party 'arms length' organisations that appear independent of the tobacco industry.
- The industry has been successful in influencing scientists and policy makers and subverting normal decision-making processes.
- The industry is seeking to market products which reduce the impact of tobacco smoke on non-smokers.
- Any and all of the above tactics and strategies are likely to be in use now, or used in the future, to counter the introduction of smoke-free policies.

References

1 Royal College of Physicians. *Smoking and health.* Pitman Medical Publishing Co Ltd, London, 1962.

2 Glantz SA, Slade J, Bero LA, Hanauer P, Barnes DE. *The cigarette papers.* Berkeley: University of California Press, 1996.

3 Colley JR, Holland WW, Corkhill RT. Influence of passive smoking and parental phlegm on pneumonia and bronchitis in early childhood. *Lancet* 1974;2:1031–4.

4 The Roper Organization. *A study of public attitudes towards cigarette smoking and the tobacco industry in 1978*, Vol. 1, 1978. Bates No. TIMN0048149 at 0048152.

5 Hirayama T. Non-smoking wives of heavy smokers have a higher risk of lung cancer: a study from Japan. *BMJ* 1981;**282**(6259):183–5.

6 Trichopoulos D, Kalandidi A, Sparros L, MacMahon B. Lung cancer and passive smoking. *Int J Cancer* 1981;27(1):1–4.

7 Garfinkel L. Time trends in lung cancer mortality among nonsmokers and a note on passive smoking. *J Natl Cancer Inst* 1981;**66**(6):1061–6.

8 Walls T. CAC presentation number 4, 8 July 1994. Bates Number 2041183751-90. www.legacy.library.ucsf.edu/tid/vnf77e00

9 *Financial Times*, 27 September 1978, cited in Chapman S, Woodward S. Australian court rules that passive smoking causes lung cancer, asthma attacks and respiratory disease. *BMJ* 1991;**302**:943–945.

10 Department of Health and Social Security survey, NOP, 1976.

11 Personal communication with Simon Clark, Director of FOREST, 22 March 2005.

12 Philip Morris, 24 June 1987. www.tobaccodocuments.org/landman/139657.html

13 Boyse S. *Note on a special meeting of the UK industry on environmental tobacco smoke London*, February 1988. Bates Number 2063791181-87. www.tobaccodocuments.org/landman/182219.html

14 Hoel D. *Joint meeting on ETS – London, England.* Privileged and confidential memo to FS Newman. Philip Morris, 18 June 1988. Bates Number 2021548222-35. www.tobaccodocuments.org/landman/23706.html

15 Barnes DE, Hanauer P, Slade J, Bero LA, Glantz SA. Environmental tobacco smoke. The Brown and Williamson documents. *JAMA* 1995;**274**(3):248–53.

16 Bero L, Galbraith A, Rennie D. Sponsored symposia on environmental tobacco smoke. *JAMA* 1994;**271**:612–17.

17 Barnes D, Bero L. Scientific quality of original research articles on environmental tobacco smoke. *Tob Control* 1997;**6**:19–26.

18 Barnes D, Bero L. Why review articles on the health effects of passive smoking reach different conclusions. *JAMA* 1998;**279**:1566–70.

19 Drope J, Chapman S. Tobacco industry efforts at discrediting scientific knowledge of environmental tobacco smoke: a review of internal industry documents. *J Epidemiol Community Health* 2001;**55**(8):588–94.

20 Hong MK, Bero LA. How the tobacco industry responded to an influential study of the health effects of secondhand smoke. *BMJ* 2002;**325**(7377):1413–16.

21 Muggli ME, Hurt RD, Blanke DD. Science for hire: a tobacco industry strategy to influence public opinion on secondhand smoke. *Nicotine Tob Res* 2003;5(3):303–14.

22 Barnes DE, Bero LA. Industry-funded research and conflict of interest: an analysis of research sponsored by the tobacco industry through the Center for Indoor Air Research. *J Health Polit Policy Law.* 1996;**21**(3):515–42.

23 Hirschhorn N, Bialous SA, Shatenstein S. Philip Morris' new scientific initiative: an analysis. *Tob Control* 2001;**10**(3):247–52.

24 Muggli ME, Forster JL, Hurt RD, Repace JL. The smoke you don't see: uncovering tobacco industry scientific strategies aimed against environmental tobacco smoke policies. *Am J Public Health* 2001;**91**(9):1419–23.

25 Ong EK, Glantz SA. Tobacco industry efforts subverting International Agency for Research on Cancer's second-hand smoke study. *Lancet* 2000;**355**(9211):1253–9.

26 Bero LA, Glantz SA. Tobacco industry response to a risk assessment of environmental tobacco smoke. *Tob Control* 1993;**2**:103–113.

27 Muggli ME, Hurt RD, Becker LB. Turning free speech into corporate speech: Philip Morris' efforts to influence U.S. and European journalists regarding the U.S. EPA report on secondhand smoke. *Prev Med* 2004;**39**(3):568–80.

28 Muggli ME, Hurt RD, Repace J. The tobacco industry's political efforts to derail the EPA report on ETS. *Am J Prev Med* 2004;**26**(2):167–77.

29 Trotter L, Chapman S. 'Conclusions about exposure to ETS and health that will be unhelpful to us': how the tobacco industry attempted to delay and discredit the 1997 Australian National Health and Medical Research Council report on passive smoking. *Tob Control* 2003;**12**(Suppl 3):iii102–6.

30 Samet JM, Burke TA. Turning science into junk: the tobacco industry and passive smoking. *Am J Public Health* 2001;**91**(11):1742–4.

31 Ong EK, Glantz SA. Constructing 'sound science'and 'good epidemiology': tobacco, lawyers, and public relations firms. *Am J Public Health* 2001;**91**(11):1749–57.

32 Everingham R, Woodward S (eds). *Tobacco litigation. The case against passive smoking. AFCO v TIA. An historic Australian judgement.* Sydney: Legal Books, 1991.

33 Department of Health. *Report of the Scientific Committee on Tobacco and Health,* March 1998. www.archive.official-documents.co.uk/document/doh/tobacco/part-2.htm#2.31

34 Greater London Assembly. *Smoking in Public Places Investigative Committee,* March 2002. www.london.gov.uk/assembly/reports/health/smoking_report.pdf

35 Greenberg DI. International Agency for Research on Cancer study, 15 September 1993. Bates Number 2501341817-23. www.legacy.library.ucsf.edu/tid/frq39e00%20

36 *The Times.* Scientists clash over tobacco talks, 11 October 2004, www.timesonline.co.uk/article/0,,2-1304209,00.html

37 Personal communication with International Hotel & Restaurant Association, 10 June 2005

38 Dearlove JV, Bialous SA, Glantz SA. Tobacco industry manipulation of the hospitality industry to maintain smoking in public places. *Tob Control* 2002;**11**(2):94–104.

39 Essential Action. *Challenging smoke-free policies worldwide: tobacco industry programs and front groups.* Accessed 1 June 2005. www.essentialaction.org/tobacco/qofm/0110a.html

40 Drope J, Bialous SA, Glantz SA. Tobacco industry efforts to present ventilation as an alternative to smoke-free environments in North America. *Tob Control* 2004;**13** (Suppl 1):i41–7.

41 Chapman S, Penman A. 'Can't stop the boy': Philip Morris'use of Healthy Buildings International to prevent workplace smoking bans in Australia. *Tob Control* 2003;**12** (Suppl 3):iii107–12.

42 Bialous SA, Glantz SA. ASHRAE Standard 62: tobacco industry's influence over national ventilation standards. *Tob Control* 2002;**11**(4):315–28.

43 Warden J. Smoking crackdown by UK government. *BMJ* 1997;**315**:143–148.

44 Corporate Responsibility Consulting. www.crconsulting.co.uk/casestudies.html?cs1

45 Ritch WA, Begay ME. Strange bedfellows: the history of collaboration between the Massachusetts Restaurant Association and the tobacco industry. *Am J Public Health* 2001;**91**(4):598–603.

46 Scollo M, Lal A. *Summary of studies assessing the impact of smoking restrictions on the hospitality industry.* VicHealth Centre for Tobaco Control. www.vctc.org.au/tc-res/Hospitalitysummary.pdf

47 Scollo M *et al.* Review of the quality of studies on the economic effects of smoke-free policies on the hospitality industry. *Tob Control* 2003;**12**:13–20.

48 *BBC Online magazine.* The hunt for the pro smokers, 10 March 2004. news.bbc.co.uk/1/hi/magazine/3497170.stm

49 The *Publican.* Butt out campaign. www.thepublican.com/butt_out_letter.doc

50 National Assembly for Wales. Committee on Smoking in Public Places. www.wales.gov.uk/keypubassemsmoking/content/0205-paper6-e.htm

51 The Tobacco Manufacturers Association. *What people really think about public smoking.* www.publicsmoking.the-tma.org.uk/files/Public_Place.pdf

52 Tobacco Manufacturers Association; British Market Research Bureau International, September 2003.

53 *The New York Post.* Cig ban killed him, 14 April 2003. www.data-yard.net/10c1/bouncer.htm

54 Connolly GN, Wayne GD, Lymperis D, Doherty MC. How cigarette additives are used to mask environmental tobacco smoke. *Tob Control* 2000;**9**(3):283–91.

55 R.J. Reynolds Tobacco Company. *Eclipse, a cigarette that primarily heats, rather than burns, tobacco.* Summary of scientific tests, April 2000. www.eclipsescience.com/results/default.html

56 Action on Smoking and Health Australia. *Partly enclosed rooms defeat the purpose.* www.ashaust.org.au/SF'03/partly.htm

57 Action on Smoking and Health Australia. *Smoke-free laws in Australian states.* www.ashaust.org.au/SF'03/law.htm

58 Harper T. Smoking and gambling: a trance inducing ritual. *Tob Control* 2003;**12**:231–233.

14 Special cases: smoke-free policies in long-stay institutions

14.1 Introduction

This chapter considers some of the special cases arising from implementing smoke-free policies in long-stay institutions such as nursing or residential homes, psychiatric hospitals and prisons. The conflict of interest presented by these and other similar institutions is that they are both workplaces and residences. As workplaces, long-stay institutions are obliged to protect staff and visitors from all ETS exposure. As residences, they have an obligation to afford the same protection to non-smoking residents. However, resident smokers may wish to smoke, as indeed they could if they were living in their own home. Furthermore, whilst voluntary long-stay institutions such as residential homes may be able to deal with this issue by make non-smoking an agreed condition of residence, this is not a practically workable option for institutions such as prisons. Therefore, long-stay institutions have to find pragmatic ways of resolving these conflicts.

In some countries, Ireland for example,[1] long-stay institutions have been exempted from smoke-free legislation. It is argued in this chapter that this is not an appropriate solution, as the health of non-smokers working and living in these institutions needs to be protected to the same extent as in any other environment. Experience has demonstrated that smoke-free policies can be implemented successfully in long-stay institutions, but that for pragmatic and ethical reasons they need to be supported actively by much greater access to advice and support for stopping smoking. In addition, some flexibility needs to be retained when implementing smoke-free policies in these circumstances, and particularly when residency is involuntary, as discussed further below.

14.2 UK Government policy on smoking in long-stay institutions

The Government White Paper *Choosing Health* published in November 2004, made the commitments that by the end of 2006 the NHS would be smoke-free, and by the end of 2008 all enclosed public places and workplaces would be smoke-free, except for those specifically exempted.[2] Exemptions were proposed for pubs not serving food and for private members' clubs. The White Paper also highlighted the difficulties that might be faced by long-stay institutions, for example:

> *We will use the intervening period of time to consult widely in the process of drawing up the detailed legislation, including on the special arrangements needed for regulating smoking in certain establishments – such as hospices, prisons and long stay residential care* (Chapter 4, p.99).[2]

On smoke-free policies in psychiatric institutions in the NHS, the White Paper commented:

> *NHS organisations should take action to eliminate secondhand smoke from all their buildings and provide comprehensive support for smokers who want to give up. We recognise that in some cases, such as mental hospitals where for some patients the hospital may be their main place of residence and therefore their home, this may not be achievable* (Chapter 7, p.167).[2]

The White Paper noted that the Health Development Agency (HDA) would be publicising guidance for NHS organisations on the provision of smoke-free buildings, which would provide practical advice for a wide range of settings.[3] This is discussed further below.

14.3 Smoking in psychiatric institutions

Smoking is common in most psychiatric institutions. A study of smoking among over 1,200 patients living in a range of psychiatric institutions, including lodgings, group homes, hostels, residential care homes and hospitals, in 1996 found that the majority of psychiatric patients were smokers, and that smoking was especially common (at over 70%) in those with the most severe mental health diseases (see Fig 14.1).[4] In addition, smokers in psychiatric institutions tended to smoke more, and to show greater levels of dependence on smoking, than smokers in the general population. The consequence of these high smoking levels in patients with severe mental health problems is a substantially higher risk of premature death from smoking-related diseases than the general population.[5]

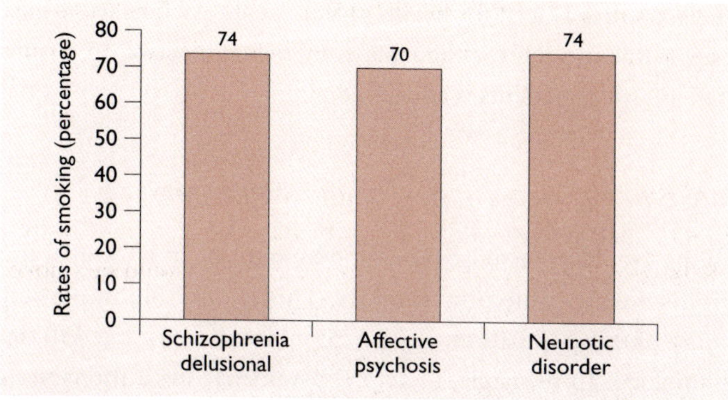

Fig 14.1 Smoking rates for people with psychiatric illnesses living in institutions.[4]

It is not yet fully understood why people with mental health problems are more likely to be smokers, and to be heavy smokers, than healthy reference populations, but it is likely that a number of factors are involved.[6] For example, there is a suggestion that smoking in pregnancy causes a higher risk of some mental health illnesses later in life.[7] It is also possible that nicotine obtained from smoking is used as self-medication to control some of the symptoms of the illness or the side effects of the antipsychotic medication. However, there is also evidence that lax smoking policies in psychiatric institutions and hospitals help to perpetuate these high levels of smoking. A recent study of staff working in a large psychiatric hospital in England found that 60% of those who responded (476 nurses, 19 psychiatrists and 104 from other clinical professions) believed that staff should be allowed to smoke with patients; 54% believed that staff smoking with patients was of value in creating therapeutic relationships; and 22% that cigarettes should be given out to patients to achieve therapeutic goals.[8] Smokers living in such institutions also report that boredom is a key factor in their heavy smoking.[5] Finally, patients report that they are rarely advised of the dangers of smoking or the need to stop, and very little support is offered to assist with quit attempts, despite a small majority of such patients reporting that they want to stop smoking.[5] In the hospital study reported above,[8] only 85% of the staff who responded believed that patients who smoked should be encouraged to stop or cut back. Concerns have been expressed that stopping patients smoking might result in an exacerbation of mental health problems; 93% of staff in the hospital study cited above believed that patients would become 'less calm' or 'mentally deteriorate' if they could not have cigarettes.[8]

Although there are no recent national surveys of smoking among staff working in psychiatric institutions, concerns have been expressed about the high levels of smoking among psychiatric nursing staff.[2] In psychiatric institutions, as in other NHS settings, there is a need for health professionals, particularly whilst on duty, to be positive role models for their patients. It is important to ensure that smoking by staff as well as patients is addressed.

The need for smoke-free policies in psychiatric institutions

Psychiatric institutions should not expose resident non-smokers to ETS or, at the extreme, induce non-smokers to become smokers. This is critically important given the vulnerability of this population. Neither should staff be exposed to the dangers of passive smoking. In principle, therefore, psychiatric institutions need to implement smoke-free policies to prevent exposure of staff and patients, but, in pragmatic terms, also need to ensure that those patients who cannot or will not quit smoking can smoke without causing harm to others.

Experience in the US and in England has shown that this can be achieved. A recent review of smoking bans in mental health and addiction settings in the US indicated that total or partial smoking bans resulted in 'no major long-standing untoward effects in terms of behavioural indicators of unrest or compliance.'[9] Another study indicated that the apprehensions of staff and patients dissipated with time after the smoking ban was implemented.[10] In England, the Norfolk and Waveney Mental Health Partnership Trust implemented a smoke-free policy in buildings and grounds in December 2003, and greatly increased accessibility to treatment for stopping smoking. At the time of writing, the success of this initiative has not been fully evaluated, but anecdotal reports suggest that substantial reductions in smoking have occurred throughout the trust, both among staff and patients.

How should smoke-free policies be implemented in psychiatric institutions?

The recently published HDA guidance for smoke-free hospital trusts sets out the steps necessary for all trust buildings to become smoke-free,[3] including the additional steps needed to achieve the 'gold standard' of smoke-free grounds as well as buildings. The rationale for such comprehensive smoke-free policies includes the strong message that they communicate about the dangers of smoking and the need for a supportive environment for those trying to quit.

The HDA guidance and the White Paper both highlight the importance of supplementing smoke-free policies with appropriate support for those who want to stop smoking.[2] Thus, those introducing smoke-free policies should ensure that stop smoking advice and pharmacological support is fully accessible to all smokers. At the very least this can be achieved by establishing strong links with NHS stop smoking services, which are now available throughout England.

The HDA guidance also discussed the specific issues facing psychiatric institutions when implementing smoke-free policies. It states that in certain cases, such as a patient with mental health problems in an acute psychiatric state, or when a smoker's stay in an institution is involuntary, the nurse or doctor in charge of the ward should be able to make an exception where this has been agreed within the patient's care plan.[3] The guidance stressed that:

> *For all exceptions there should be demonstrable evidence that smoking cessation has been fully considered as part of the patient pathway. For example, over time all patients* [who are smokers] *in long-stay institutions should be offered an appointment with a specialist stop-smoking adviser who can offer support for stopping or advice on how to manage withdrawal symptoms when abstaining.*[3]

In addition, the guidance stresses the importance of ensuring that all proven smoking cessation treatments are widely accessible by making them available on hospital formularies.

The difficulty with allowing exceptions is the resultant exposure of others to passive smoking. It is important, therefore, that in NHS institutions where stay is involuntary, smoking is restricted to outdoor places out of sight of other patients, staff and visitors, and that there is an agreed protocol for risk management. For patients sectioned under the Mental Health Act, a secure outdoor courtyard would be appropriate or, where there is no suitable secure outdoor area, a smoking room may need to be retained. However, these rooms should be unattractive, restricted to a maximum of two patients at any time, with basic seating, no television, radio or other form of entertainment. All exceptions should be reviewed regularly by a senior member of staff. Staff should not be permitted to smoke in these facilities under any circumstances.

Nicotine replacement therapies (NRT) can be used to help manage withdrawal symptoms in patients who do not want to stop but are unable to smoke due to smoke-free policies.[3] NRT should be made available as stock items on wards for use by both patients and staff.

14.4 Smoking in prisons

Approximately 150,000 prisoners pass through the UK prison system each year.[11] Surveys have indicated that smoking rates in prisons are very high, at over 80%.[12] To a large extent, such a high rate of smoking reflects the socio-demographic profile of prisoners, the majority of whom come from low income groups. In addition, a recent survey showed that over 90% of prisoners entering prison had a mental health or substance misuse problem.[13] Smoking is, however, widely perceived as the norm in such settings and cigarettes help to punctuate mundane daily routines.[14]

The need for smoke-free policies in prisons

A key aim of a recently published strategy on prison health is to promote health and reduce inequalities:

> *Promoting the health of prisoners is a core activity for both the Prison Service and the NHS, and this strategy sets the agenda for future developmental work in this area. For the Prison Service it forms part of the process of rehabilitation and resettlement, and for the NHS it gives access to a population it would normally be hard to reach, offering a unique opportunity to tackle issues of social exclusion and inequalities in health.*[12]

A survey in 2003 identified that although most prisons had smoking policies, nearly all of these permitted smoking in cells, and indeed in many other areas.[14] Since tobacco smoke toxins drift relatively freely within the indoor environment, this policy is likely to result in significant ETS exposure to prisoners and staff alike.

In addition, permitting smoking in cells creates problems as many prisoners share their accommodation. This is reflected in the current Prison Service information book, which states:

> *If you don't smoke, and want to share a cell with other non-smokers, ask your personal/wing officer or apply to see the Governor. There is no guarantee that you will be able to share with a non-smoker or have your own cell.*[15]

Such a statement is at odds with the Government's objective of 'providing safe and well-ordered establishments in which we treat prisoners humanely, decently and lawfully',[16] and with its commitment to promote prison health, as described above, which includes aims such as, 'Help prevent the deterioration of prisoners' health during or because of custody, especially by building on the concept of decency in our prisons'.[17]

The strategy on prison health cited above highlights the need for serious consideration to be given to smoke-free policies and smoking cessation support for prisoners. Governors and directors of prisons, working in partnership with primary care trusts (PCTs), were asked to ensure that smoking is addressed explicitly within local planning mechanisms by December 2003.[17] In a pilot project by the Department of Health which offered smoking cessation treatment in five prisons, it was found that a significant proportion of prisoners wanted to stop smoking and there was a considerable demand for stop smoking services.[18] With well planned projects, many prisoners were helped to stop smoking. A toolkit, which includes advice on stop smoking medications (gums and nasal sprays are not permitted in prisons for security reasons), has been produced to help prisons set up stop smoking services.[19]

As stated above, exposure of prison staff to ETS is a significant problem. There are around 44,000 prison staff in England. Although there has been no national survey of smoking among prison staff, the strategy on prison health identified respiratory disease as one of the key health issues in this group, and emphasised the importance of prisons facilitating support for staff wishing to stop smoking.[12]

Experience shows that smoke-free policies can be implemented successfully in prisons. Following a successful pilot in 2002, California passed a law in 2004 to make all 33 prisons in the state completely smoke- and tobacco-free by 1 July 2005. Several prisons went smoke-free in advance of this date and few problems have been reported. Withdrawal symptoms have been reported to be minimal after a few weeks due to the lack of tobacco cues in the surrounding environment. While no NRT or other stop smoking medications were permitted in these prisons [Hanson S, personal communication], the prison process in the UK is very different from that in California and it is recommended that both behavioural and pharmacological cessation support are offered in prisons in the UK. In the UK, HMP Stafford successfully introduced a non-smoking policy following the provision of NRT and smoking cessation training. Two young offender institutions in the UK, Ashfield and Wetherby, have also successfully implemented smoke-free policies in which no smoking is allowed within the perimeters of the prisons.

How should smoke-free policies be implemented in prisons?

We recommend that prisons implement comprehensive smoke-free policies and, specifically, that smoking should not be allowed inside prison buildings. Although some prisons may want to extend smoke-free policies to grounds, this may be difficult in closed or high security prisons. Smoking could be permitted in outside recreation areas, but some smoke-free outdoor areas should be provided so that people not wishing to smoke can avoid the triggers that may cause them to smoke or relapse to smoking. In addition, entrances to buildings should be kept smoke-free to avoid smoke drifting in through doors and windows, thereby continuing to be a hazard to health.

Smoke-free policies can be, and are being, implemented in a stepped approach, beginning with smoke-free prison wings, and being extended until the whole prison is smoke-free. Flexibility may be needed in prisons with a high preponderance of category A prisoners but, as with psychiatric institutions, where there are exceptions every attempt must be made to minimise staff and non-smokers' exposure to passive smoking. Again, smoking rooms should be unattractive and restricted to a maximum of two prisoners at any time. Smoking must never be permitted in a cell shared by non-smokers.

As discussed above, smoke-free policies should be introduced alongside the provision of accessible support and advice to help prisoners stop smoking. The success of the pilot projects described above illustrates that many prisoners can be helped to stop smoking in this way. In addition, the provision of NRT can help prisoners gain control over their smoking, and act as a stepping-stone towards quit attempts. By 2006, all PCTs will be responsible for commissioning health services within their prisons. As PCTs are also responsible for NHS stop smoking services in their area this will facilitate the provision of smoking cessation support in prisons.

14.5 Nursing homes, hospices and other long-stay institutions

The issues faced in many nursing homes and hospices are similar to those discussed above. The main difference is that, for many residents, stay in such an institution is voluntary. Therefore, adherence to the smoke-free policy can be made a condition of stay and part of the contract between the individual and the institution. As with the settings discussed above, it is recommended that smoke-free policies be introduced alongside much greater accessibility to treatment, and with flexibility where necessary so that smokers are not deterred from moving into a long-stay institution when it is in their interests to do so. Flexibility may also be needed in hospices, although the limited experience thus far of introducing smoke-free policies in such institutions has shown that very few exceptions need to be made. For example, Priscilla Bacon Lodge, an NHS palliative care unit provided by Norwich Primary Care Trust and serving the whole of Norfolk, implemented a comprehensive smoke-free policy in 2003. A small conservatory area was designated for those patients wishing to smoke and for whom exceptions were to be made. Patients were notified in advance of the policy. Serious anxieties were raised on behalf of patients and carers in advance of going smoke-free but, in the event, the implementation has been successful and compliance by patients and staff has been high.

14.6 Hotels

Hotels encounter conflicts of interest when implementing smoke-free policies, but for different reasons. Hotels are workplaces offering residency but usually on a temporary short-term basis. Proprietors have stated that it will be unworkable for them to enforce a ban in hotel bedrooms as any random checks by enforcement officers would interfere with privacy and require a warrant. Designated hotel bedrooms have been made exempt from the Irish smoke-free legislation[1] and the proposed Scottish regulations,[20] but the remainder of the hotel facilities are covered by the legislation. Hotels can choose to become totally smoke-free and many do so for economic reasons (the costs of cleaning and refurbishment are higher when smoking is allowed) and to reduce fire risks.

14.7 Domiciliary visits

Many community-based staff, such as midwives, community nurses and social workers spend much of their working time visiting patients in their homes. Concerns have been raised about their exposure to ETS during these domiciliary visits. A small-scale survey among health professionals working in the community in the Bury and Rochdale area revealed very high levels of reported exposure to ETS and resultant physical effects such as coughing, watery eyes, runny nose and dry throat.[21] This is a complex issue: employers have a duty of care to protect their employees from the health hazard that ETS represents, but patients cannot be prevented from smoking in their own homes. Furthermore, staff who refuse to visit homes where ETS exposure occurs might compromise their duty of care to vulnerable people such as children at risk.

There is little guidance in this area. The Department of Health in New South Wales, Australia,[22] has developed a policy to reduce second-hand smoke exposure of its community health employees. This states that information on the smoke-free policy and the dangers of ETS must be distributed to patients prior to the first home visit, and that staff can request patients to refrain from smoking whilst they are receiving treatment. If patients do not refrain when requested then treatment can be suspended until the patient complies with the request. In such cases the manager of the service can contact patients to reiterate the reasons behind the policy.

In England, this is an evolving area of policy, and similar strategies are being developed and implemented locally. For example, in some areas patients are requested not to smoke in the 30 minutes to one hour prior to their appointment with a community health professional. Evidence from these localities indicates that most patients comply with the policy.[23]

14.8 Summary

- Very high levels of smoking are observed in some categories of long-stay institutions such as psychiatric institutions and prisons.
- Smoking is often condoned by staff, and is the accepted norm in such settings. Exposure to ETS can be very high.
- Experience shows that comprehensive smoke-free policies can be implemented successfully in these settings, but they should be flexible and pragmatic, and supported by greatly increased accessibility to advice and support in stopping smoking.
- No blanket exemptions should be made to exclude long-stay institutions from implementing smoke-free policies. Whilst exceptions can be made on a case-by-case basis, these should be reviewed regularly and every effort must be made to minimise exposure of non-smokers to tobacco smoke.

References

1 *The Public Health (Tobacco) Acts 2002* and *2004*. Dublin: Stationery Office, 2004.

2 Department of Health. *Choosing health: making healthier choices easier.* London: Stationery Office, 2004.

3 McNeill A, Owen L. *Guidance for smoke-free hospital trusts.* London: Health Development Agency, 2005.

4 Meltzer H, Gill B, Petticrew M *et al. Economic activity and social functioning of residents with psychiatric disorders.* OPCS surveys of psychiatric morbidity in Great Britain Report No. 6. London: Stationery Office, 1996.

5 McNeill A. *Smoking and patients with mental health problems.* London: Health Development Agency, 2004.

6 McNeill A; NHS Smokefree London; ASH. *Smoking and mental health – a review of the literature*, 2001. www.ash.org.uk/html/policy/menlitrev.html

7 Milberger S, Biederman J, Faraone SV, Jones J. Further evidence of an association between maternal smoking during pregnancy and attention deficit hyperactivity disorder: findings from a high-risk sample of siblings. *J Clin Child Psychol* 1998;**27**:352–8.

8 Stubbs J, Haw C, Garner L. Survey of staff attitudes to smoking in a large psychiatric hospital. *Psychiatr Bull* 2004;**28**:204–7.

9 el-Guebaly N, Cathcart J, Currie S *et al.* Public health and therapeutic aspects of smoking bans in mental health and addiction settings. *Psychiatric Serv* 2002;**53**:1617–22. psychservices.psychiatryonline.org

10 Hempel AG, Kownacki R, Malin DH *et al.* Effect of a total smoking ban in a maximum security psychiatric hospital. *Behav Sci Law* 2002;**20**:507–22.

11 Prison Health. *Prison health handbook*, 2003. www.dh.gov.uk/assetRoot/04/06/56/82/04065682.pdf

12 Department of Health. *Health promoting prisons: a shared approach – a strategy for promoting health in prisons in England and Wales, 2002.* www.doh.gov.uk/prisonhealth

13 Singleton N, Farrell M, Meltzer H. Substance misuse among prisoners in England and Wales. *Int Rev Psychiatry* 2003;**15**:150–2.

14 MacAskill S, Eadie DR. *Tobacco-related work in prisons: survey of activity in England and Wales.* Glasgow: University of Strathclyde, Centre for Social Marketing, 2003.

15 HM Prison Service/Prison Reform Trust. *Prisoners' information book: male prisoners and young offenders.* London: HM Prison Service/Prison Reform Trust, 2002. Page 47.

16 HM Prison Service. *Statement of purpose.* www.hmprisonservice.gov.uk/abouttheservice/statementofpurpose/

17 HM Prison Service. *Prison Service Order. Order 3200. Health Promotion,* October 2003. pso.hmprisonservice.gov.uk/PSO%203200%20-%20Health%20Promotion.htm

18 MacAskill S, Eadie DR. *Evaluation of a pilot project on smoking cessation in prisons.* Glasgow: University of Strathclyde, Centre for Social Marketing, 2002. www.marketing.strath.ac.uk/ctcr/publications/prison-cessation-rept.pdf

19 Department of Health. *Acquitted: best practice guidance for developing smoking cessation services in prisons.* London: DH/MH Prison Service, 2003. www.doh.gov.uk/tobacco/pdfs/acquitted.pdf

20 Scottish Executive. *Health Committee Sixth Report,* 2005. www.scottish.parliament.uk/business/committees/health/reports-05/her05-06-vol01-02.htm#Part1

21 de Cruz T, Davies C, Edwards R; members of working group. *Report on community staff exposure to second hand smoke during domiciliary visits,* 2004 (Unpublished report.)

22 New South Wales Department of Health. *Smoke-free workplace policy circular 99/76* p.11, 1999. www.health.nsw.gov.au/archive/cib/circulars/1999/cir99-76.pdf

23 Royal College of Nursing. *Working can damage your health,* Congress 2005. www.rcn.org.uk/news/congress2005/display.php?ID=1479

15 Smoke-free public places in Ireland: how was it achieved and what has been learnt?

15.1 Introduction

On 29 March 2004, Ireland became the first country in the world to introduce comprehensive legislation making all enclosed workplaces, including bars and restaurants, smoke-free.[1,2] Implementation has proved to be extremely popular and successful.[3] In a one-year review of the legislation, 96% of all indoor workers reported that they now worked in smoke-free areas.[4] Whilst other countries, including Norway and Italy, have now also introduced smoke-free legislation successfully, the Irish experience provides particularly clear guidance on how to prepare to go smoke-free, the problems that arise, and the effects. This chapter addresses these issues in three distinct time periods:

1. The period before the public announcement of the legislation on 30 January 2003
2. The period between the announcement of the legislation and its implementation on 29 March 2004
3. The period after the legislation came into effect, from 29 March 2004 to date.

15.2 The period before the public announcement of the legislation on 30 January 2003

It is important to recognise that legislation to create smoke-free workplaces in Ireland did not emerge overnight, or in isolation. Rather, it arose in a context of sustained support and advocacy by a range of groups and organisations campaigning for comprehensive tobacco control policies to include protection from the harmful effects of ETS. Towards the end of the 1980s, as evidence first began to emerge on the harmful effects of ETS,[5] Irish politicians were persuaded that there was a need to legislate to protect people from ETS exposure in certain public places such as government public offices, cinemas, theatres and schools.[6,7] However, this first attempt at protective legislation had no direct application in the workplace.

In the early 1990s, the growing evidence on ETS health effects, and research that found high levels of concern among workers about these effects,[8] led to an agreement between the Irish Government, employers, and trade unions for a voluntary code of practice on smoking in the workplace.[9,10] This voluntary code offered little protection for those exposed to ETS at work, however, and nothing for those working in the hospitality sector. Further lobbying led to the enactment of legislation in 1995 to extend the range of public places in which smoking was prohibited. This legislation included the requirement that 50% of seating in restaurants should be smoke-free.[11]

Sustained advocacy for stronger smoke-free legislation ensured that politicians, public servants and trade unions were continually made aware of the need to protect workers from ETS. International research on the health effects of passive smoking, and developments in the United States,[12] helped to keep tobacco control issues firmly on the agenda of policymakers in all sectors, and to draw attention to the simple health and safety issue that all workers, including those in the hospitality sector, are entitled to protection.

The importance of tobacco control was highlighted in a health strategy document by the Department of Health and Children.[13] In addition, a blueprint document for creating a tobacco-free society was published by senior health officials in 2000 and was adopted by Government.[14] The political system responded; the influential all-party Oireachtas (Parliament) Joint Committee on Health and Children examined the issue of smoking and health, taking advice from a wide range of groups, including the tobacco industry. The industry insisted that there was insufficient evidence to link passive smoking to any illness in non-smokers, but the Committee, made up of politicians from across the political spectrum, rejected this argument and unanimously recommended a new national anti-smoking strategy to restrict smoking in workplaces, including bars.[15] Tobacco industry representatives subsequently refused to come before another meeting of the committee – a decision that undermined their efforts to lobby politicians once the legislation was published.[16]

In a further key development, the Irish Government established the Office of Tobacco Control (OTC) (www.otc.ie) to build capacity for tobacco control measures. The OTC drew on international expertise in identifying the best means of dealing with the issue of passive smoking, and to advance knowledge and understanding of the problems among politicians, policymakers, the media, and trade unions representing hospitality workers. Of particular importance was an independent report which estimated that up to 150 Irish bar workers could be dying each year as a result of their exposure to ETS.[17]

A new tobacco bill published in 2001 gave the Minister for Health and Children the power to create smoke-free workplaces.[1] It was supported by the opposition parties and signed into law in 2002. Further discussions continued on how widely restrictions on smoking in the workplace should extend. To help that debate, the OTC and the Health and Safety Authority commissioned independent scientists to review the evidence on workplace passive smoking. They concluded that ETS was harmful, that employees needed to be protected in the workplace, and that legislative measures were needed.[18] At the launch of this report on 30 January 2003, the Minister for Health and Children, Micheál Martin TD, announced that he would make the necessary orders to ensure that all enclosed workplaces, including bars, would become smoke-free on 1 January 2004. In the event, various technical issues delayed the implementation of the legislation until March 2004.

15.3 The period between the announcement of the legislation and its implementation on 29 March 2004

Although the legislation was to apply to all indoor workplaces, it was the hospitality industry, and most notably bar owners and their representatives (the Vintners' Federation of Ireland (VFI) and the Licensed Vintners Association (LVA)), that objected most vociferously to the legislation. A flavour of their objections can be gleaned from their many press releases and public statements throughout the subsequent 14 months.[19,20] In addition to these well established representative bodies, a new organisation, Irish Hospitality Industry Alliance (IHIA), emerged and engaged in opposition to the proposed legislation. This organisation claimed to have widespread membership amongst the hospitality sector and appeared to have significant financial and public relations support at its disposal, the source of which remains uncertain. Since the successful introduction of the legislation, IHIA has disappeared without further comment. It is not clear whether this was an example of a tobacco-industry funded third party organisation (see Chapter 13).[21]

Throughout this 14-month period, the hospitality industry lobby argued that a complete ban on smoking in their venues was unnecessary, unworkable and unenforceable. Whilst they accepted that smoking was harmful, they continually disputed the findings of the commissioned report.[18] They argued that further research was needed, and cited the findings of one new and controversial study of passive smoking which found no evidence of adverse effects (see Chapter 2 for context).[22] They claimed that ventilation and the provision of separate no-smoking areas – policies they had supported for some time – offered a better way to address the health issue while accommodating smokers.[23] They predicted that a ban on smoking in bars would have serious negative economic consequences for themselves and for the country as a whole, with massive job losses and a stem in the flow of tourists coming to Ireland.[24] They suggested that there would be significant public order problems as a result of the ban, and cited the experience in New York where a bouncer was killed sometime after a similar ban was enforced.[25] They used connections with the political system to try and get the legislation diluted, overturned or postponed. They suggested alternatives to the ban by way of 'customer choice and common sense'. They threatened to withhold VAT payments to Government if the legislation went ahead. They also threatened to run candidates against the Government parties in the local elections, and to challenge the legislation in Irish and European courts. None of these threats was actually carried out.

There were others who also questioned the need to bring in smoke-free legislation. The Irish Cigarette Machine Operators Association, which supplies cigarette vending machines to bars, campaigned vigorously against the legislation, raising concerns about a possible decline in their business should the legislation come into being. The Irish Business and Employers Confederation (IBEC), one of the country's most powerful lobby groups representing 7,000 top businesses, said more research should be conducted before implementing the ban, and supported the retention of designated smoking rooms in the workplace. The tobacco industry contributed to the debate by arguing that the science underpinning the legislation was flawed, and that ventilation and designated smoking areas were the way forward.[26]

During this period, three distinct groups of governmental and non-governmental organisations (NGOs) were prominent in their support for the legislation: the Minister for Health and Children and other politicians; the public service sector including the OTC, the Department of Health and Children, the Health and Safety Authority and the Regional Health Authorities; and the NGOs, most notably Action on Smoking and Health (ASH) Ireland, the Irish Cancer Society, the Irish Heart Foundation and the MANDATE trade union, which represents hospitality workers. Together with others, these groups played different but significant roles in promoting consistent lines of argument:

- Passive smoking is a significant health and safety issue.
- Passive smoking is a serious cause of ill health.
- All workers, including hospitality workers, deserve protection.
- Ventilation will not remove the harmful constituents of passive smoke.
- Separate smoking areas do not work – smoke cannot read.
- Smokers are reasonable people and most want to quit.
- Assistance should be readily available to help smokers quit if they wish to.

In addition, all parties were clear that the primary objective of the legislation was to protect workers from the harmful effects of ETS. The smoke-free legislation was not presented as a means of protecting the public, or encouraging smokers to quit smoking or reduce tobacco use. Thus, it was held that if the public – patrons of a hospitality venue, for instance – benefit from smoke-free workplaces, or if smokers cut down or quit smoking as a result of the ban, these would be welcome consequences but not central objectives of the legislation.

The Minister for Health and Children took a leading role in defence of the legislation and explained how it would be implemented. Whilst he had the support of most of his colleagues in Government, he also had the backing of the opposition parties who had declared their support previously via the Joint Committees on Health and Children. During the course of the debate in the lead up to implementation of the law, some senior and junior ministers did respond to the hospitality lobby and called for the Minister for Health and Children to modify his proposals. However, the Taoiseach (prime minister) continued to support the Minister for Health and Children and the proposed legislation throughout.

Various NGOs played an important role. In particular, ASH Ireland, the Irish Cancer Society and the Irish Heart Foundation combined resources to mount a public health media advocacy campaign in favour of the smoke-free initiative, and to provide leadership and support for other NGOs wishing to be involved. In addition, many healthcare professional organisations such as the Irish College of General Practitioners and the Environmental Health Officers' Association, and support NGOs such as the Asthma Society, supported and contributed to the media campaign. The trade unions ensured support for the legislation during the debate: those representing the hospitality sector played a crucial role, and those representing the medical and nursing professions provided support at key times.

The OTC played a key role, not only in advocating the smoke-free initiative, but also in running a campaign to build public compliance with the smoke-free workplace legislation. They ensured that the experiences of those charged with enforcing similar legislation elsewhere, especially New York and Boston, were brought to the attention of all concerned in Ireland. They were also responsible, in association with the Health and Safety Authority, for ensuring that all the necessary information and signage was available to those who were expected to enforce the legislation when it came to be implemented.[27]

From the Department of Health and Children, the Chief Medical Officer issued an unambiguous view of the potential health impact of the legislation, which was reported widely in the media.[28] The Department also ran a multi-media campaign entitled 'Every cigarette is doing you damage' to highlight the harmful effects of smoking on the individual, and they ensured that adequate support was made available in advance of the legislation for those who wished to quit smoking. Additional smoking cessation staff and an enhanced national telephone 'quitline' with back-up support were provided in association with the Irish Cancer Society and local health authorities. A dedicated website was launched to deal with all aspects of the legislation and to provide the public with clear answers to their many questions concerning its implementation.[29]

The legislation was scheduled initially to come into force on 1 January 2004, and to include all indoor workplaces, but problems arose regarding the constitutional ramifications of a workplace that was also a home. As a result of legal advice, some exemptions were eventually allowed for places that could be legally regarded as a person's temporary home, such as hotel bedrooms and prison cells. The ban was postponed, partly because of the debate over exemptions but also because of the legal requirement to provide a minimum period of notice to the European Union. Once these difficulties had been resolved, the Minister for Health and Children announced on 18 February 2004 that the legislation would take effect from 29 March 2004. A short time before the implementation date, the hospitality industry called off their proposed legal challenges to the legislation and asked the public to help them in their efforts to be compliant with the law.

Under the smoke-free legislation, a person who smokes in a designated smoke-free area and the owner, manager or person in charge of the area are both guilty of an offence, punishable by fines of up to €3,000 if so convicted in a court of law.[1] To assist with the implementation of the smoke-free legislation, and to maximise compliance with the law, the OTC launched a television and radio advertising campaign to raise awareness about the introduction of smoke-free workplaces. The campaign included repeated broadcasts of two 20-second television advertisements and a 20-second radio advertisment, plus print advertisments in various trade publications.[30] Phase one of the campaign was launched at the beginning of March and focused on announcing the commencement of smoke-free workplaces on 29 March. Phase two, launched on 29 March, focused on building compliance with the new legislation, and provided details of a 'lo-call' telephone number for reporting episodes of non-compliance.

To support and, where necessary, enforce compliance, the OTC[31] and the Health and Safety Authority[32] prepared detailed guidance notes and signage for employers.[33]

Guidance for members of the public who encounter someone smoking in a prohibited workplace, such as a pub or restaurant, is to approach the manager or other person responsible in that place to register their complaint. If they do not receive a satisfactory response they should then call the lo-call compliance line to register their complaint. The details of their complaint are then passed on to the relevant Health Service Executive area or the Health and Safety Authority, whose officers are tasked with enforcing the legislation. All complaints are prioritised by the enforcement agencies and dealt with accordingly. If, following an inspection, an enforcement officer finds evidence of a breach of the law he or she can decide to issue a warning to, or initiate proceedings against, either the smoker or the owner or manager of the premises concerned, or both. A decision to recommend prosecution is to be based on the nature of the offence, the previous history of the premises or person, and the efforts made by the premises or person to comply with the legislation.

15.4 The period after the legislation came into effect: March 2004 to date

On 29 March 2004, the day the smoke-free initiative was enacted, all three national broadsheet newspapers (*The Irish Times*, *Irish Independent* and *Irish Examiner*) and the three main tabloid newspapers (the *Sun*, *Mirror* and *Star*) carried positive stories on the ban on their front page, and all editorialised in favour of the initiative. A series of media events were organised throughout the day, starting with 'Ireland's first smoke-free breakfast' at 8am in a popular city centre restaurant. High levels of compliance with the ban were apparent immediately to the environmental health officers and the health and safety inspectors charged with enforcing the ban, and were confirmed by the media reporters dispatched far and wide to find bar owners or customers who were prepared to defy the ban. Instances of non-compliance, even in bars in the toughest neighbourhoods and in rural locations, were few. Within a month of the ban, it was reported that a 97% compliance rate had been achieved in all workplaces, including bars.[34]

There were some high profile attempts to defy the ban. In one case a few days after the legislation came into force, a prominent front-bench politician and a member of the opposition shadow cabinet openly defied the ban by smoking three cigarettes in the Dail (Parliament) bar. Although this defiance gained much publicity, the politician involved was fired from his front bench position and the matter died down. In another case in July 2004, the owners of several bars in Galway claimed that they had suffered a 30% fall in sales as a result of the ban, and were now going to allow smoking in their bars. This story was covered extensively in the media. However, the local health authority intervened quickly and the owners were subsequently fined some €10,000. This sent a very clear signal that any open defiance of the ban would be met with the full rigour of the law.

The one-year review of compliance with the legislation demonstrates that implementation has been successful.[4] In particular, the review found that by 2005, 94% of all workplaces inspected under the National Tobacco Control Inspection Programme were smoke-free, 92% of all workplaces inspected by the Health and Safety Authority were smoke-free, and 93% of all hospitality workplaces inspected were smoke-free. The review also found that air quality in bars has improved dramatically since the smoke-free law, with a significant drop in levels of carbon monoxide in non-smoking bar workers.

There is now extensive public support for the legislation among smokers and non-smokers. The public opinion survey conducted for the OTC in advance of the one-year anniversary of the law showed that:[4]

- 93% think the law is a good idea, including 80% of smokers.
- 96% of people feel the law is successful, including 89% of smokers.
- 98% believe that workplaces are now healthier because of the smoke-free law, including 94% of smokers.

Before the introduction of smoke-free legislation, bar owners stated consistently that the smoke-free legislation would have a negative impact on their business.[24] Since its introduction, some bar owners claim that sales are down between 15% and 25% and significant job losses are evident as a result of the legislation.[35] However, in advance of the legislation, market research from the drinks industry showed that the number of regular bar-goers had fallen by at least 20% since 2000.[36] In addition, volume sales of alcohol in Irish bars reached their peak in 2001 and had fallen by 15% before the smoke-free legislation came into force.[36] Many reasons have been postulated for this shift: changing demographics, increasing price of drink in bars, health concerns about alcohol, commuting times and stricter drink-driving legislation. Recent objective data on retail bar sales and volumes in Ireland from the Central Statistics Office show that the overall effect of the smoke-free initiative has been one of a net small loss to bar owners (see Chapter 12 for detail). The claim by the Vintners' Federation of Ireland that sales fell by 25% since the smoking ban was instituted is, therefore, unsubstantiated.[37,38]

Despite all the negative rhetoric from vested interests surrounding the introduction of the smoke-free initiative in Ireland, the impact that it has had on the Irish population was perhaps best captured on a programme broadcast on national television on New Year's Day 2005. Market research carried out for the programme, '2004: How was it for you?' found that from a list of 30 positive events that happened in Ireland in 2004, including many memorable international sporting achievements, the implementation of the smoke-free initiative in all workplaces topped the poll, and by a clear 15% more than the second placed event.

15.5 Commentary

The implementation of the smoke-free legislation was a brave decision for the Minister for Health and Children, and the success of the initiative has surprised many observers. Before the introduction of the legislation, experienced tobacco control advocates from the United States and Canada suggested privately that with a background smoking prevalence of 27% it might be too soon for Ireland to embark on such an initiative, and recommended that it might be best to wait until the prevalence rates fell by at least another 5%. Fortunately, they have been proved wrong.

Several factors are likely to have contributed to this success. It is likely that the comprehensive nature of the legislation was one key factor, since this made it clear to all, be they employers, employees or customers, where they could or could not smoke. This avoidance of ambiguity was especially important within the hospitality sector where exemptions to allow smoking in some bars depending on whether they served food, or if they could provide separate ventilated rooms, would have caused confusion and could have undermined the principle behind the legislation.

Equally important to the success of the smoke-free initiative was the 14-month media debate in advance of the legislation being implemented. It has been estimated that in that time period media coverage of the smoke-free legislation filled in excess of 20 million words, equivalent to some 10,000 pages of newsprint, and 2,000 hours of national and local broadcast time.[39] The media coverage and the consistent messages about protecting the health of workers was crucial in establishing public understanding and support for the legislation.

The fact that the majority of smokers wish they could quit smoking has also probably contributed, since many smokers may have seen the implementation of the smoke-free legislation as an opportunity to reduce their consumption of cigarettes or quit altogether. It has been reported that sales of cigarettes in Ireland fell 8.7% in 2004 when the smoke-free initiative was implemented, after declining 3.4% in 2003, and 1.2% in 2002. Gallaher Tobacco, the market leader in Ireland, has reported Irish sales dropping by 10.7% from January 2004.[40] Preliminary data from the National Smoker's Quitline also show an increasing number of smokers quitting or reducing consumption.[41] However, it will be at least another year before the true effect of the smoke-free workplace initiative on the prevalence and consumption of cigarettes can be properly estimated.

Over the last year, many policymakers with an interest in pursuing similar smoke-free legislation have visited Ireland to understand how success was achieved. For most, actually going out to visit bars and talking to bar owners, staff and customers – both smokers and non-smokers – has provided the best insight and demonstration that unambiguous smoke-free policies in public places are successful, popular, and highly effective.

15.6 Summary

- Smoke-free legislation in Ireland has proved to be highly popular, and has encountered no major compliance problems.
- Public support for smoke-free policies has increased substantially since legislation.
- Smoke-free policies have proved to be an effective means of protecting workers against ETS effects.
- Although not the primary objective of the Irish legislation, it is likely that smoking prevalence and consumption will now fall in Ireland, contributing to a major public health gain.

References

1 *Public Health (Tobacco) Acts 2002* and *2004*. Dublin: Stationery Office, 2004.

2 Howell F. Ireland's workplaces, going smoke-free. *BMJ* 2004; **328**(7444):847–8.

3 Howell F. Smoke-free bars in Ireland: a runaway success. *Tob Control* 2005;**14**(2):73–4.

4 Office of Tobacco Control. *Smoke-free workplaces in Ireland: a one-year review*. Clane, Ireland: Office of Tobacco Control, 2005. www.otc.ie/article.asp?article=271

5 US Department of Health and Human Services. *The health consequences of involuntary smoking. A report of the Surgeon General*. DHHS Publication No. (CDC) 87–8398. Rockville, MD: DHHS, Public Health Service, Centers for Disease Control, Center for Health Promotion and Education, Office on Smoking and Health, 1986.

6 *Tobacco (Health Promotion and Protection) Act, 1988*. Dublin: Stationery Office, 1988.

7 *Tobacco (Health Promotion and Protection) Regulations, 1990*. Dublin: Stationery Office, 1990.

8 Howell F, Doorley P. Employee attitudes to involuntary smoking at the workplace. *Ir Med J* 1991;**84**(3):94–6.

9 Health Promotion Unit, Department of Health. *Clean air at work.* Dublin: Department of Health, 1992.

10 Health Promotion Unit, Department of Health. *Working together for cleaner air.* Dublin: Department of Health, 1994.

11 *Tobacco (Health Promotion and Protection) Regulations, 1995.* Dublin: Stationery Office, 1995.

12 California Environmental Protection Agency. *Health effects of exposure to environmental tobacco smoke.* Sacramento: California Environmental Protection Agency, 1997.

13 Department of Health and Children. *Quality and fairness: a health system for you.* Dublin: Stationery Office, 2001. www.doh.ie/hstrat/index.html

14 Department of Health and Children. *Towards a tobacco-free society: report of the tobacco free policy review group.* Dublin: Stationery Office, 2000. www.doh.ie/publications/tobacco.html

15 Joint Committee on Health and Children. *A national anti-smoking strategy. A report on smoking and health.* Dublin: Houses of the Oireachtas, 1999.

16 Joint Committee on Health and Children. *Second interim report of the subcommittee on health and smoking.* Dublin: Houses of the Oireachtas, 2001.

17 Repace J. Right to life overrides right to smoke. *Irish Times* February 11, 2002.

18 Allwright S, McLoughlin JP, Murphy D, Pratt I *et al. Report on the health effects of environmental tobacco smoke (ETS) in the workplace.* Dublin: Office of Tobacco Control/Health and Safety Authority, 2002. 69.20.28.11/article.asp?article=34

19 Licensed Vintners Association, accessed 3 May 2005. www.lva.ie/page.php?intPageID=3

20 Vintners' Federation of Ireland, accessed 3 May 2005. www.vfi.ie/aboutvfi/news_events.asp?article_type_id=1

21 Dearlove JV, Bialous SA, Glantz SA. Tobacco industry manipulation of the hospitality industry to maintain smoking in public places. *Tob Control* 2002;**11**(2):94–104.

22 Enstrom JE, Kabat GC. Environmental tobacco smoke and tobacco related mortality in a prospective study of Californians, 1960–98. *BMJ* 2003;**326**(7398):1057–66.

23 Vintners' Federation of Ireland. *Publicans propose realistic alternatives to proposed smoking ban – 'Customer choice and common sense'*, 28 August 2003. www.vfi.ie/aboutvfi/article_detail.asp?article_type_id=1&article_id=28

24 Vintners' Federation of Ireland. *Research Shows 10% job loss in New York pub sector since introduction of smoking ban*, 10 October 2003. www.vfi.ie/aboutvfi/article_detail.asp?article_type_id=1&article_id=38

25 Humphreys J. Smoking ban concerns raised after US murder. *Irish Times*, 16 April 2003.

26 O'Brien C. Tobacco firms say no justification for smoking ban. *Irish Times*, 27 August 2003.

27 Office for Tobacco Control. *Smoke-free workplaces.* www.otc.ie/communication_smoke-free.asp

28 Department of Health and Children. *Statement from the office of CMO on smoking in workplace ban*, 21 August 2003. www.dohc.ie/press/releases/2003/20030821.html

29 Department of Health and Children, 2003. www.smokefreeatwork.ie

30 Office of Tobacco Control. *Smoke-free works*, March/April 2004. www.otc.ie/smoke-free_campaigns.asp

31 Office of Tobacco Control. *Guidance for employers and managers. Public Health (Tobacco) Acts 2002 and 2004. Section 47 – Smoking prohibitions*, 2004. www.otc.ie/smoke-free_publications.asp

32 Health and Safety Authority. *Smoke free workplace*, 2004. www.hsa.ie/publisher/index.jsp?aID=305&nID=213&pID=97#employer

33. Office of Tobacco Control. *Smoke-free workplaces lo-call compliance line.* www.otc.ie/smoke-free_locall.asp

34 Office of Tobacco Control. *Smoke-free workplace legislation implementation.* Progress report, May 2004. www.otc.ie/Uploads/Smoke-free%20workplace%20legislation%20progress%20report%20may%2004%20FINAL.pdf

35 Vintners Federation of Ireland. *Smoking ban seriously hurting rural pub businesses – drinks suppliers confirm 15–25% drop in sales*, 21 June 2004. www.vfi.ie/aboutvfi/article_detail.asp?article_type_id=1&article_id=89

36 Paul O'Kane. Calling time on the pub? *Sunday Tribune*, 22 February 2004.

37 Una McCaffrey. Retail sales rise of 2.8% marks turnaround – CSO. *The Irish Times*, 22 January 2005.

38 Richard Curran. Pub sales dip raises doubt on impact of ban. *The Irish Independent*, 25 January 2005.

39 Gilmore N. *Clearing the air: the battle over the smoking ban.* Dublin: Liberties Press, 2005.

40 Carty E. Calls for Britain to follow Ireland's smoke-free lead. *Irish Examiner*, 30 March 2005.

41 Department of Health and Children. *7,000 fewer smokers in Ireland: Quitline and smoking ban attributed to 33% decline in prevalence of smoking*, 26 September 2004. www.smokefreeatwork.ie/news/detail.asp?id=22

16 Key conclusions and recommendations

1. Passive smoking currently kills about 12,000 people in the UK every year. These deaths are entirely preventable.
2. Most of the deaths are caused by passive smoking at home, but about 500 each year are due to exposure at work. Exposure is particularly high for some workers in the hospitality industry, such as bar workers.
3. There is an unanswerable moral case to protect all people from passive smoking at work. All employees have a right to work in a safe environment, and all employers have a duty to ensure that they do.
4. Comprehensive smoke-free legislation, making all public places and workplaces completely smoke-free, without exception, is the only effective means of achieving this.
5. A clear majority of the public supports smoke-free legislation. Where enacted in other countries, smoke-free policies have proved to be extremely popular and attract high levels of compliance.
6. Comprehensive smoke-free policies also improve public health by helping existing smokers to quit, and discouraging young people from starting to smoke. As a consequence, smoke-free legislation will also generate long-term health improvements and reductions in social inequalities in health.
7. Preventing passive smoking at home, particularly for children, is a public health priority. Home exposure is prevented only by encouraging parents and carers to quit smoking completely, and/or by making homes completely smoke-free.
8. By helping smokers to quit smoking, and by changing usual patterns of smoking behaviour, smoke-free policies in public and workplaces increase the number of smoke-free homes. Strong and sustained health promotion campaigns are required to enhance this process. These and other population and individual-level interventions to encourage smoking cessation are the most effective means of reducing ETS exposure at home.
9. Making the UK smoke-free would benefit the economy by about £4 billion each year.
10. We recommend that the UK Government enact comprehensive legislation to make all workplaces and other enclosed public places smoke-free at the earliest possible opportunity.